SITUATION MOMEDY

A First-Time Mom's Guide to
Laughing Your Way through Pregnancy and Year One

JENNA VON OY

MEDALLION
Medallion Press, Inc.
Printed in USA

Published 2015 by Medallion Press, Inc.,
4222 Meridian Pkwy, Suite 110, Aurora, IL 60540

The MEDALLION PRESS LOGO
is a registered trademark of Medallion Press, Inc.

This work reflects the author's present recollections of specific experiences over a period of years. Dialogue and events have been recreated and in some cases compressed to convey the substance of what was said or what occurred. Some identifying details have been changed to protect the privacy of individuals.

Cataloging-in-Publication Data is on file with the Library of Congress

Typeset in Adobe Garamond Pro
Printed in the United States of America
ISBN 978-194254601-6

10 9 8 7 6 5 4 3 2 1
First Edition

DEDICATION

For my enchanting girls, Gray and Marlowe, who are already teaching me that everything I thought I knew about being a mom pales in comparison to the overwhelming joy of actually being one. You made it nearly impossible to find time to write this book, but even your distractions were an inspiration! I love you stars and moon . . .

And also for my mom, who kissed my boo-boos, over-saved all my kindergarten art projects, and read me the bedtime stories that inspired me to write in the first place. Thank you for showing me what kind of mom I wanted to be.

CONTENTS

One-year-old Gray sheds her fancy skirt and bemoans the fact that her parents are amateurs. Some things never change. *Photo courtesy of Mimosa Arts.*

PREFACE

The Only Thing I'm an Expert at Is Being a Novice

Let me begin by saying I'm not a pediatrician, an OB-GYN, or a certified consultant of any kind. I don't hold a PhD in any baby-related field, nor am I an expert in child psychology. I don't even drive a minivan or know where to find the closest Gymboree. (Oh, the shame!) The only thing I'm truly an expert at is being a novice. If you need advice on how to cure cradle cap, I may not be your gal; I'm probably at home over-Googling that information right this very moment. I can't claim to have superior knowledge about raising a child, because I'm still driving slowly around the learning curve.

So why did you write a guide to pregnancy and motherhood, you ask? Is it because you're an actor who used to wear awesomely tacky hats and talk really fast on a TV show, so you must know everything?

Hell no! Being on TV doesn't really qualify me for anything other than owning a Screen Actor's Guild union card. And perhaps some red-carpet access to Hollywood clubs that don't offer babysitting in the VIP lounge.

Rather, the answer is pretty straightforward: as a mom, sometimes it's nice to know you're not alone in the madness.

Misery loves company, especially while cleaning pureed peas off the dining room walls . . . and the television screen . . . and the dog.

This isn't meant to be a how-to book. There are already tons of those out there, and they cover everything I can't, won't, couldn't, and shouldn't. Instead, this is meant to be a best friend's guide to laughing about the realities of motherhood. Because sometimes laughter is a contagious cure-all. You grew up watching me gossip about boys, battle acne, develop breasts, and flirt with Joey Lawrence, so why not let me share pregnancy with you too? I'll even poke fun at myself with some scenic views of my past, so some popcorn might be in order!

In your current quest to absorb everything related to having a baby, you should hear that other women out there have experienced less-than-perfect pregnancies, feared they wouldn't be good enough mothers, and struggled to find balance with the new lifestyle a baby brings. And why not hear it from someone else who's grappled with the same concerns?

I, too, have questioned my own sanity during bouts of colic, suffered through back-to-back episodes of *Barney & Friends*, and worried that my local Mommy and Me classes were a boot camp for cult recruitment. I think it's easier to gain perspective when your digestion of information is aided by some humor, which I hope is what you'll find here . . . despite the fact that my oldest daughter has repeatedly told me I'm "only funny sometimes." There's a sense of security in knowing you can laugh at yourself, and that's what motherhood continues to teach me. Every. Single. Day.

Mayim Bialik and I meeting for the first time, in 1990. The producers got us together to test our chemistry for *Blossom*, which was immediate. Right after this photo was taken, I auditioned in front of the network heads at NBC. They cast me in the role of Six right then and there. *Photo courtesy of Jenna von Oy*.

Truth be told, I spent my entire childhood being really uptight. I craved approval too desperately to see the benefit of benign self-mockery. There's something seriously warped about not having the courage to laugh at oneself while simultaneously getting paid to tell jokes that make others laugh. It was irony at its finest. My years on *Blossom* and even *The Parkers* were spent fretting over everything and nothing. I was a worrywart who was starved for acceptance and unachievable perfection in both Hollywood and my personal life, which makes for some wacky and pitiful—albeit hilarious—tales of woe. I'm happy to divulge them, since God knows it's fun to throw the younger me under the bus. These days, I can thank motherhood for reminding me to take it all in stride and laugh at my own expense. Being a mom constantly teaches me how to let go of shallow insecurities so I have more time to focus on what's truly important: raising my daughters with love and a sense of humor. Laughter really *can* be the best medicine, and your doctor may not be the right person to prescribe your dosage.

Mo'Nique and I celebrating at *The Parkers'* 100th episode party. Talk about laughing your way through experiences . . . That woman made me laugh my way through five years of filming a TV show. *Photo courtesy of Jenna von Oy.*

Before I go any further, I think it's important to get out the message that no mother completely has her act together. Some may try to convince you otherwise, but they have their moments too. Even the soccer moms. And just because the celebrities in magazines make it *look* like a breeze, that doesn't mean they are any less frazzled than everyone else. Right after that paparazzi photo was snapped, that well-composed starlet dropped her Starbucks all over the park sandbox and found a sticky rice puff lodged in her hair.

Not everyone has the benefit of nannies, chefs, and physical trainers. There's no supersecret society handshake or decoder ring, you aren't missing some kind of required "mommy gene," and there's no rule book that gets passed around. Baby 101 is a hands-on class with continuing education, and everyone learns at a different pace. That said, parenting doesn't require formal training. The only true requirements are passion and love, with some natural instinct thrown in. It may surprise you to hear this, but the rest of us are making it up as we go too. Welcome to the wonder and the chaos!

I'm not interested in telling you how to handle your own motherhood trials and tribulations. I'm sure that would go over like a leaky diaper on your favorite silk blouse. (Which, by the way, you should just go ahead and retire for a while.) You have, and will continue to have, your very own brand of anarchy during the course of parenting. I'm just providing some anecdotes that I hope will encourage you to giggle your way through it.

I'm always inspired by the parents who turn lemons into lemonade. Or a lemon meringue pie. Or a lemon drop martini. Okay, *especially* the lemon drop martini. I admire the friends who don't sweat the small stuff, and I'm doing my best to follow in their footsteps. Think of me as your self-deprecating Jiminy Cricket with a baby on her hip. I'm your comedic life coach, if you will, and I'm learning along with you. There are no "perfect" ways to approach motherhood so you don't make your kids crazy; there are only ways to laugh at the thought of motherhood "perfection" so *you* don't go crazy. This book is a tongue-in-cheek take on my personal adventures with pregnancy and parenting. Like a good margarita, I hope it takes the edge off.

Peace, Love & Dirty Diapers,

One of my dear friends captures a sweet moment as I form some early bonding with Gray. Just call me The Womb Whisperer. *Photo courtesy of Brooke Boling.*

CHAPTER 1

Houston, We Have a Pregnancy!

A SCENIC VIEW OF MY PAST

It was season four of *The Parkers*, the black sitcom on UPN on which I'd been costarring since episode one, and I still felt totally out of place. I didn't fit in, and it made me insecure. You know the old *Sesame Street* song that went, "One of these things is not like the other"? I was "one of these things," and I was having trouble letting that roll off my back. They could talk about things I couldn't. They had stories to tell that I couldn't relate to and special inside jokes to share that proved I wasn't "one of them." I wasn't a member of their exclusive club. Every now and then, Countess Vaughn would even make a comment like, "You can't possibly understand. You just haven't been through the same struggles we have." Gee, thanks. Way to make a girl feel like an outcast. Way to make me feel like . . . the *nonparent* I was. What, you thought I was referring to being the only white cast member? Ha! Not a chance. Skin color never made an ounce of difference to any of us. In fact, Mo'Nique often quipped that I wasn't Caucasian, just "light-skinned."

Being the only cast member on *The Parkers* without a kid made me feel like a petulant child in a roomful of working adults. I was the only one who didn't have a family to go home to, who didn't know what it was to be a parent and have that special love in my heart for a tiny human being. And I wanted it desperately.

So desperately, in fact, that I started adopting dogs. Lots of them. Which led me to believe, in all my twentysomething wisdom, that I knew what it meant to be a parent. Why alienate me just because my kids had four legs instead of two? Because they barked instead of crying? Because they left their toys strewn across every room of my house and drooled all over my furniture? (Technically the latter two examples cover both dogs and children, but you get the idea.) I thought parenting puppies should at least grant me a pass for their elite clique, but no one else seemed to take that notion seriously.

Single life was sucking big-time, and my biological clock was spinning out of control. I wanted a family to ground me; I wanted to finally belong . . .

CUT TO . . .

So much for a feeling of belonging. Turns out I had no clue what to expect when I was expecting, dogs or no dogs. After all, my canine kids go to sleep when I tell them to, clean up any food that gets dropped on the floor, and were potty trained by two months old.

And wanting a family to *ground* me? What was I thinking? Impending mommydom made me feel like I'd been sent to orbit the moon for a while, armed with only fuzzy pink slippers and a casserole dish . . .

But hey, at least I was finally in on all the jokes.

MY CRADLE CHRONICLES

"So you're having a baby." In my experience, most instructional pregnancy books start out with this phrase or some equivalent of it. Thank you, faceless authors, for stating the obvious and handing me my sign. After peeing on a stick (or four), racing to the doctor faster than I could say "biological clock," throwing out a refrigerator's worth of soft cheese and deli meat, flagging every baby name site on the Internet, reading all the back issues of *Parenting* magazine, prematurely plotting a nursery design, and indulging my urge to tell every pregnant woman I saw that I was becoming a member of her club, I'm pretty sure I'd already established the fact that I was bringing a child into the world.

Or had I? It's amazing how long it took my head to catch up to my heart.

But still, "So you're having a baby" seemed like such an unceremonious introduction. After waiting for so many years to get knocked up (I was thirty-five when I gave birth to my first daughter, Gray), I wanted a parade in my honor, dammit! But one has to start somewhere, right? Parades take time to plan, and I suppose a float in the shape of a uterus would be a little weird. Also, "So you're about to spend the next eighteen years letting a tiny human be the CEO of your life, huh?" doesn't have quite the same ring to it.

In retrospect, I guess there's really no better conversation starter than the one they've all resorted to. But how about adding a little enthusiasm to the mix so it sinks in? I know it isn't feasible to be showered in confetti or offered a congratulatory neon marquee via book pages, but some amount of excitement is nice. You know, slightly more than one might experience when one's bologna is ready at the supermarket meat counter.

How about trying this version on for size: "So you're having a baby. *Holy hell!*"

Or "So you're having a baby? You did it! You got the little guy to swim upstream! Go kiss your spouse and celebrate with a pint of peanut-butter-and-chocolate ice cream, for heaven's sake. You deserve it! Here's a coupon for a complimentary cream puff!" I swear I'd send you all a bottle of champagne right this minute if it were feasible. On second thought, perhaps I'd send a nonalcoholic beverage such as sparkling apple cider, so the pediatric police don't hunt me down. Either way, consider this my written version of a celebratory rally for you. I'm whistling "Hail to the Chief" as I type this.

Bottom line? You are a rock star, and I'm out here rooting for you. If no one else remembers to tell you this important phrase, soak it up now: You can do it. You have what it takes!

If you're anything like I was, the simple words "I'm having a baby" are taking some getting used to. I had to put that mantra on repeat in my head for a while before I began to absorb it. It takes a while to wake up and smell the breast milk! Whether you've planned to get pregnant or not, there's a sort of fuzzy disassociation that occurs at the start of it all. I promise it isn't just you who's experiencing it, and it doesn't mean you aren't ready for motherhood. I felt it when I finally got pregnant too, and I'd been obsessing over a baby for so long that I'd even considered freezing my eggs as a twenty-fourth birthday gift to myself.

If you want to get technical about it, *none* of us is really ready, no matter how long we've yearned for it. There is no such thing as an instaparent. We don't blossom overnight. (No pun intended, I swear!) We all learn by trial and error, and we try to do the best we possibly can. There's a natural inability to reconcile that a little person is growing inside us or that our lifestyle and mind-set have been altered in the blink of an eye. I think our hormones, aka our horror-mones, start to fire vulgarities at our brains when they realize the pande-monium we're about to put them through for the next nine months. Well, ten months, if you want to get real about it. (Yeah, that math will get you every time.)

The physical imbalance of pregnancy rendered me per-petually disoriented. It perfected my deer-in-the-headlights expression, which may or may not be something to brag about.

To put things into perspective, I'll share my story. Find-ing out I was pregnant for the first time went like this: On Sunday, October 2, 2011, my husband and I were spending a leisurely day around the house with our canine brood. We have an old record player in our living room, and we were listening to Bob Dylan's *Blood on the Tracks* album. I had just finished whipping up some pancakes and bacon, and we'd enjoyed an unhurried breakfast together. With mimosa in hand, I paused to look out at the supremely beautiful day. I closed my eyes and smiled serenely. That's when I had an inkling. The moment was just too rapturous not to think there was something more to it. Something *other* than a mimosa buzz, that is. Since my biological clock had been ticking louder than *The Tell-Tale Heart* for the last two decades or so, I was fairly convinced I was on the road to motherhood. It sounds crazy, but I was filled with a sudden sense of purpose.

Looking at my empty glass, I thought, *If I take a pregnancy test and it's negative, I'm having at least two more of these tasty suckers. If it comes out positive, I'm going to spend the next hour asking Siri whether or not I've doomed my child by enjoying the ones I've already had.*

I ran downstairs and made a beeline for the pregnancy test I'd been saving. (One of my best friends had given it to me as a not-so-subtle suggestion at my bridal shower in 2010, which I thought was pure genius.) I peed on the stick and blinked in confusion as the blue line immediately surfaced.

It's amazing how the movies make it seem like you're going to have to wait an interminable amount of time to get your results, isn't it? I mean, whole plot lines have transpired while someone waits for pregnancy test results.

Not so much. I had my answer in under thirty seconds.

Of course, I opted not to believe it and took a second test to be sure. Also positive.

I happily dismissed the notion of another mimosa as my body buzzed with excitement, adrenaline, and champagne bubbles.

Then, in a not-so-brief moment of insanity, I decided the

tests must be too close to their expiration dates to be correct, so I ran out to buy a brand-new box of life-changing plastic.

Those both came out positive too.

Oh, you thought I was kidding about taking four pregnancy tests? Not a chance, *mon amie.* Two packages later, I called my OB-GYN to schedule a blood test. You know, just in case all those store-bought ones were faulty.

"If you've taken four predictor tests already and they've all come out positive," the nurse told me sardonically, "you really don't need a blood test. You're pregnant." I could envision her shaking her head and writing *rookie* in my patient file.

I scheduled the blood test regardless.

Seriously? Did I still need validation? Enough to get poked with a needle unnecessarily?

I chalk this up to being in my newfound maternity trance. Or, for good measure, I suppose I could continue to implicate the mimosas. For more on the clouding of judgment during pregnancy, see chapter 3, where I discuss baby brain. It's like a really bad, nine-month-long blooper reel.

Pregnancy makes us do wonderfully zany things, because it is overwhelming to know you are bringing a new little person into the world. It's tough to fathom that there's a human being smaller than a blueberry (or whatever edible member of a fruit salad the maternity websites are comparing your fetus to this week) in your belly, wreaking havoc on your emotions, your thoughts, and your body.

And there isn't necessarily a single, sudden moment when

it all registers. In fact, it didn't really register for me until Gray was there, swaddled in her hospital blanket and sporting the obligatory, gender-neutral nursery hat.

You may find the same to be true. Reality may not set in until those sweet little eyes stare back at you and your nights are filled with soft coos . . .

Oh, who am I kidding? Your nights will more than likely be jam-packed with screaming, crying, groggy feedings, and punch-drunk diaper changing. The reality of motherhood will probably hit you with the impact of the Titanic.

You're going to be a mommy! Insert my happy dance here, and try to stop freaking out. While you're at it, laugh a little . . . it does a pregnant body good.

THE MORAL OF MY STORY

Usually I agree with Groucho Marx, who said, "I don't care to belong to any club that will have me as a member." But this is my exception to the rule. I'm proud to say I'm a card-carrying, life-time member of motherhood, and the benefits are unparalleled! Even if it required nine months of hazing before my official induction ceremony.

"Morning" sickness kicks my ass during my pregnancy with Gray. The pugs take this opportunity to offer their services as living, breathing heating pads. (From left to right: Boo, Bruiser, Ruby, me.) *Photo courtesy of Jenna von Oy.*

CHAPTER 2

Wacky Pregnancy Ailments

A SCENIC VIEW OF MY PAST

I watched the fish swimming by my crappy, foggy, rental goggles and tried to concentrate on breathing through my regulator. With an increasing sense of dread, I glanced over at my buddy Jed, who was scuba diving beside me. He raised his eyebrows and questioned if I was okay by giving me a thumbs-up. Being underwater was providing us with a less-than-stellar line of communication. Let's be honest, there's just really no way to appropriately get across via sign language the idea that you're about to blow chunks into the Jamaican waters. Especially when every microscopic movement might lead to heaving and purging. I knew I shouldn't have had that extra drink with the damn rum-soaked pineapple the night before! What was I thinking? Maybe a day of watching my dear friend Dulé Hill get married had stirred my post-breakup need to overindulge on booze and boys. Note to self: attending a wedding at a romantic resort in Jamaica one week after being unexpectedly dumped from a four-year-long relationship is begging for trouble. Tropical islands are a breeding ground for sin; they grow it like coconuts over there.

How did I get in this predicament, you ask? I was originally scheduled to go on the trip with my boyfriend, but he'd abruptly hit the road, leaving me with an empty house, a splintered heart, and two round-trip tickets to Montego Bay.

Timing was never his strong suit.

So there I was, left to sunbathe and hobnob with wedding guests on my own. I was in too much of a state of disrepair for that (read: emotionally unstable and *far* too insecure), so I wound up flying my best friend out to accompany me instead. Basically, I wasn't crazy enough to attend nuptials by myself, but I was nutty enough to go scuba diving off a rocky shore while horribly hungover. Go figure. At least there was some peace and quiet down there in that pristine water; it gave me some much-needed time alone with my thoughts.

I reflected on the beautiful wedding I'd witnessed the day before. It wasn't just your typical lovefest; it was also a showcase of the who's who of Hollywood. This included most of the cast members of *The West Wing*, which happens to be one of my favorite shows of all time. While I was excited to meet the esteemed actors I respect so greatly, thinking back on Joshua Malina and Richard Schiff in their bathing suits wasn't making me feel any better in my underwater hangover hell. And that visual was nothing relative to the knowledge that I would be heading back home to an empty house for the first time in years. I couldn't keep myself together any longer. Turning away from my diving buddy, I promptly fed the fish.

CUT TO . . .

Morning sickness made me feel equally hungover, without

the pretty view of a Jamaican coral reef. Not to mention, I couldn't even resort to overdosing on any alcoholic hair-of-the-dog concoction remedy. *Warning: not abstaining from sex can lead to abstaining from alcohol and strong pain relievers for nine months.* And that's just the beginning of the modifications you'll be making for your baby. Bring on the bodily rebellion.

MY CRADLE CHRONICLES

Not everyone has a flawless pregnancy. I wound up looking like the result of a procreation experiment by Medusa and Beetlejuice, and that was on a good day. At this very moment, your body is probably throwing a temper tantrum that could rival *The Real Housewives of New Jersey.* I could smugly smile and say, "Get used to it; there's more where that came from when the baby arrives," but I'll leave that for another chapter. Suffice It to say that right now your system is screaming obscenities and devising ways to exact its revenge on you for allowing a tiny human to take over its domain. Or at least that's what mine did. Take a deep breath and tell your body, "Get over it!" To be fair, you've got to expect a little protest when your insides are being shoved aside. In fact, I think my intestines picketed with signs that said Hell No, We Won't Go. If it's any consolation, you will more than likely forget about the extent of your suffering by the time you have the next kid anyhow. I did.

I won't lie: there will be good days and bad days. It's not all butterflies and waterfalls. If you're one of the lucky few who aren't plagued by morning sickness, I'm thrilled for you. No, really, I am. Just keep that on the down-low for the rest of us, okay?

I, for one, was not blessed with a retch-free or symptomless pregnancy. I got super sick around week seven, and it lasted through week fifteen. With my second daughter, Marlowe, it started even earlier. Let's just say it was a full-time toilet-worshiping, pickles-and-ice-cream-craving, weird-rash-in-places-you-can't-mention, not-a-chance-in-hell-you-can-sleep kind of experience.

And you know what made me sicker? Friends and family telling me they'd enjoyed a perfect pregnancy and never had any aches, discomfort, or nausea at all. While I can appreciate that some women have completely effortless and trouble-free pregnancies, I suspect that's relatively rare. It's difficult to fathom your body forming an entirely new living and breathing entity without enduring a few side effects! The majority of folks who will try to convince you that carrying a child was a piece of cake must have conveniently forgotten what went into the baking process. They must have locked those memories away in the steel-reinforced maternity memory vault for safekeeping. I've actually heard women make ridiculous statements such as, "Oh, the contractions never hurt at all." Really? That's like suggesting that if I skydive without a parachute, I'll walk away with only a bruised knee. I'm pretty sure they aren't called labor *pains* in an effort to be ironic.

Make no mistake, I'm not judging anyone for manifesting a sunnier version of their journey. In fact, I don't blame them at all. Labor isn't chock-full of the warm, fuzzy feelings you want to bottle up and save for a rainy day; I guess I'm just not a fan of sugarcoating my personal experiences. I empathize with those of you who will spend the next nine months feeling like a seasick Weeble Wobble because I did too, and I believe I would be doing you a disservice to pretend everything was smooth sailing.

With all that said, do you know what the best part is? Despite all the physical melodrama, I wouldn't change my pregnancy experiences for the world. I loved every bit of them . . . Yes, even the crappy phases. Don't worry, I'd be skeptical of me too. To clarify: did I love having my hands go numb for six months or dislocating a rib? Let's not get crazy. But those were small prices to pay in the whole scheme of things.

You may or may not eventually feel the same way; it's not always easy to have perspective while you are in the throes of it. And it's perfectly acceptable if you *never* enjoy being pregnant. Don't let anyone make you feel bad or guilty if you don't! It doesn't mean you love your child any less at the end of it, and it doesn't make you an inferior mother. But I hope it provides you with some measure of comfort to hear that I look back on my pregnancy fondly, regardless of the plethora of ailments that accompanied it.

GETTING THE SHORT END OF THE SICK

Here are a few highlights from my own sordid adventures, in case they make you feel better about yours:

"Morning" sickness can't tell time.

During my first trimester, I felt like I was perpetually recovering from a long night of Jägerbombs and sledding down snow-drifts on a plastic catering tray. And please don't ask me how I know what that feels like.

In case you're still under the impression that morning sickness only transpires in the a.m., I should warn you that it's a misnomer. That term was probably coined by some dowdy little man in wiry glasses and a plaid bow tie, and he's likely still laughing maniacally about bamboozling us for so long.

On average, I barfed six times per day with baby number one. I actually *lost* weight during the first trimester of my first pregnancy. I spent so much time hovering over the toilet that I snoozed on the bathroom floor during intermissions. While my husband was at work, my dogs would often come in and camp out on the rug with me. For a little while, they were pretty excited that I'd created an impromptu dog bed. We were a heap of moaning, gagging, snoring, drooling, furry, inert lazybones. I'll let you decide which of those adjectives applied to me.

Morning sickness or not, the reality is that most of us feel miserable at one stage or another. The truly phenomenal thing is that when you hold your child in your arms for the first time, it obliterates every minute of misery you might have felt. I promise!

As a side note, none of the antinausea medications prescribed by my doc did anything for me. Well, unless you count getting so constipated during my second pregnancy that I almost had to be hospitalized. I'll let you insert your own foul joke here. I'm still having nightmares about it, so it's just too soon for me to find the funny. But let that be a lesson to you. If you are taking anything to combat your morning sickness, I *strongly* urge you to drink lots of water, get enough fiber, and take a stool softener okayed by your OB-GYN. We'll leave it at that.

Eating during the first trimester was equivalent to playing Russian roulette.

For the first two months of my pregnancy with Gray, I virtually subsisted on pretzels and Gatorade. It wasn't the ideal diet, but it's all I could get down. And I am a *serious* foodie, so that was a severe setback! Even water made me gag, and taking my prenatal vitamins left me feeling like I'd swallowed rotten meat.

It worried the heck out of my husband, who volunteered to pick up anything and everything edible within driving distance. I can honestly say I wouldn't have made it through with such aplomb had it not been for his patience and support. I was the luckiest puking, part time couch potato in the state of Tennessee. In his words, "Every night was a parlor game of 'What can Jenna eat tonight without throwing up?'"

I didn't have cravings; I had anticravings. For example, wonton soup sounded good one evening, so Brad raced across town to get some. By the time he got back, the thought of said wonton soup had me turning a lovely shade of chartreuse. And as Kermit the Frog so aptly phrased it, "It's not easy being green." But perhaps you've already discovered that for yourself.

Dislocating a rib isn't as fun as it sounds.
When you're growing a future trapeze artist and contortionist in your belly, it can be a bit debilitating. For me, that came in the form of a dislocated rib during pregnancy number one, which was highly painful. I'm not the tallest human (five feet on a good day), so as my infant Cirque du Soleil entertainer got bigger, she quickly ran out of room to swing.

Apparently, my belly hosted the Baby Olympics.
It truly brings new meaning to the sport of synchronized swimming when there's a wriggling, writhing human in your belly. Though my first daughter didn't have enough amniotic fluid to float around in, there was plenty in there for my second daughter—the Esther Williams wannabe. I was especially fond of her inclination to conduct lengthy aquamusicals on my bladder at 3:00 a.m.

Heartburn wasn't just a pain in the heart; it was a pain in the ass.
Fortunately, we're not talking literally. During the latter part of my first pregnancy, pizza and pasta sounded alluring, but they weren't so great an hour after consumption. Just when my favorite foods stopped triggering nausea, they started inciting riots in my esophagus. The reflux crept in with ninja-like prowess. It soured my appetite, provoked a flare for spontaneous belching (sexy stuff), and forced me to sleep sitting up. You know, because sleeping wasn't difficult enough already.

While scouring the Internet for a list of acid-inducing foods, I discovered there are some odd culprits out there, including peppermint and avocados. Who knew?

Evidently digestion is slower during pregnancy, and the stomach runs out of real estate for your baby, your dinner, and your organs. Good times.

I started resembling a Pillsbury Dough Girl, minus the annoying giggle.

Some folks gain weight gradually and gracefully; others blow up like puffer fish. I was the latter. Of course, my affinity for rabidly cramming confections down my throat probably didn't help.

While pregnant with Marlowe, I just couldn't stay away from the sweets. I wasn't hankering for anything specific, just sugar in general. No pastry within a twenty-mile radius was safe from my evil clutches. It was total dessert domination. I wanted my couch to be made of macaroons, I thought ice cream should be strongly considered as a replacement for one of the five major food groups, and I developed a whole new appreciation for Cookie Monster's focused hyperactivity. God forbid the Girl Scouts came a-knocking with their yearly supply of Samoas and Thin Mints! I was coveting cupcakes and sneaking candy bars like they were porn. I was begging my agent to find Food Network bake-offs I could judge, just so I could contract to be paid in turtle pies and cherry cheesecakes. I was a mess. Consequently, I gained more weight than the online calculators suggested I should have. But to hell with those weight-watching bigots! Since when do computerized calculators understand the intricacies of pregnancy cravings anyway? On a good note, my belly ultimately doubled as a built-in TV tray.

I got hotter than a barbecue pit in hell.
This is mostly self-explanatory. It's amazing how much heat you generate while making a baby! If menopausal hot flashes are anything like those I experienced during pregnancy, kill me now. I'm pretty sure I saw steam rising off my body like it was made of asphalt, and my boobs ran a fever on a daily basis. I could have grilled steak skewers in my cleavage and coined a new dish called "kaboobs."

Sex became less desirable than being tarred and feathered in a windstorm.
This may also be somewhat self-explanatory, depending on where you are in your pregnancy right now. I wanted to fool around about as much as an armadillo wants to meet a Mack Truck on the highway. That is, until the second trimester, when I was virtually humping the air like a dog in heat. Please skip directly to chapter 14 if you're overly curious about my sex life. Oh, go on. I'll never know.

I got winded climbing into our bed.
Seriously. I couldn't have been more out of breath if I'd scaled Mount Everest on a tricycle. Making it up a flight of steps should've earned me a freakin' gold medal. Or at least a pint of frozen yogurt.

My hands and feet swelled more than Charlie Sheen's ego.
Don't be an idiot like I was . . . Take off your rings in the first or second trimester and wear them on a necklace for safekeeping throughout the rest of your pregnancy. Or you can do what I

did during my second pregnancy and set a weekly reminder to check their fit.

During pregnancy number one, I was determined to sport my rings all the way through until delivery, because I'm (understandably) sentimental about their significance. It seemed odd to remove such a meaningful symbol of my marriage while carrying another special symbol of that marriage in my belly.

Also, when you live in the Bible Belt like I do, not wearing a wedding band while pregnant tends to invite savagely nasty looks. I might as well have been soliciting on Sunset Boulevard or dangling a baby out of a five-story window.

When I realized my rings hurt too much to wear for the duration of my pregnancy, it was already too late. I tried everything from slathering my fingers in olive oil and Windex, to icing my hand until it turned nearly hypothermic. Sadly, none of that worked. I thought I'd have to get the rings hacked off. Grisly scenes from the movies *Saw* and *127 Hours* were dancing in my head.

Ultimately, I was able to wind dental floss so tightly around my finger that it cut off all circulation. I then made my poor hubby twist and pull the rings until I almost passed out. It took two hours to remove them, and my finger wound up almost as bruised as my mental state. I'm pretty sure my C-section scar healed before my ring finger did. So . . . don't do that.

My pregnancy acne rivaled the pizza-face I exhibited during the good ol' Blossom days.

Thank God we didn't have HD television in the '90s, so you probably don't know just how zit-covered I was. But take it from me, my face was overcrowded with pimples. The make-up artists had to cake on the foundation like I was Tammy Faye Bakker at a Cover Girl convention.

Pregnancy made me resurrect my jumbo makeup bag. Not that I don't love wearing makeup regardless—I always have—but this took it to another level. I laughed inwardly and thanked the baby every time someone told me, "You have such flawless skin!"

You want to know what really gave me my pregnancy glow? Bronzer.

I am one of the lucky ladies who tends to get pregnancy-induced carpal tunnel.

From approximately three months before giving birth to Gray, to three months after the fact, all ten of my fingers were on pins and needles. And by that I mean they went completely numb. I couldn't feel the difference between hot and cold, so I ended up with several cooking-related burns. And chopping onions became more dangerous than walking a tightrope on stilts.

I had an overzealous, irrational sense of smell.

By week fourteen of my first pregnancy, I thought my shower curtain smelled like a forty-day-old chicken carcass. Need I say more?

Sometimes I had to urinate so badly I prayed I wouldn't sneeze.
You may need to pee anywhere, at any time, for absolutely no reason at all. Beware of spontaneous fits of laughter in public, and don't try to convince yourself you can control your bladder through the entire length of an Oliver Stone film.

One time I got stuck in forty minutes' worth of traffic after I'd just consumed a super-sized lemonade. By the time I got to a toilet, I was doing an interpretive number that might have inspired Bob Fosse. I looked like I was campaigning to get on *Pee Pee Dancing With The Stars.* My recommendation? Don't drink and drive.

Random crazy people wanted to touch my baby bump, with no provocation.
What, that doesn't sound like an ailment to you? Well, believe me, it's a freaking epidemic. When your baby bump starts showing, people will rush your belly like shoppers on Black Friday. Folks approached me and stroked my stomach like they would a llama at the local petting zoo. Geriatric, cane-toting men with halitosis wanted to have a little rub-a-dub, as if it would liberate a genie from my belly button. Starbucks baristas reached out to cop a feel as they handed me my tragically decaffeinated toffee nut latte.

You see, something about a swollen stomach makes people forget all form of manners—assuming they ever had any to begin with. I briefly contemplated wearing a sign saying, It's Not a Baby, It's a Tumor so people would leave me alone. But then I realized just how un-PC and offensive that would be, so I thought better of it.

My point? Don't be afraid to tell people to leggo that preggo belly!

During the second trimester, I thought I'd have more energy than Richard Simmons on speed. Instead, I was the equivalent of Rip Van Winkle on Ambien.

With the knowledge I'd gleaned from friends and the blogs I'd read, I thought I'd have enough stamina to reconstruct the pyramids by week fourteen. They all lied.

For some, that second trimester vim and vigor is as mythical as the Loch Ness monster. I was still so drained by the end of each day that I could barely stuff myself into pajamas. Sometimes I didn't even bother trying.

Leg cramps cramped my style.

Screw Charley *and* the horse he rode in on! I got more nightly muscle spasms in my calves than I can count, and they were more intense than Christopher Walken in . . . well, virtually any movie he's ever done. I found that making sure I was hydrated helped a lot, as did eating a banana each day. The latter was a suggestion I found on *LIVESTRONG.com*, and I went with it. Now, keep in mind that constantly consuming bananas doesn't just make you feel like an orangutan, it can also constipate you. Pregnancy is notorious for causing issues in that department, so I warn you not to overdo it!

I drooled at night.

A lot. More than that mastiff from *Turner & Hooch*. And, as my husband will attest, it was super attractive.

I had strange dreams.

And this is coming from the girl who dreamed she was dating a guy with multicolored armpit hair extensions when she *wasn't* pregnant.

I found myself having dizzy spells.

We're not talking slightly off-kilter, can't-look-down-while-driving-on-the-Bay-Bridge here. We're talking long-night-of-sake-bombs-and-waking-up-in-a-stranger's-house dizzy.

These dizzy spells happened during my second pregnancy. After a quick trip to the doctor, I found out that babies sometimes compress the inferior vena cava, which is the big vein that brings blood to your heart. Basically, every time I lay on my back, Marlowe was giving me the spins.

Pregnancy hormones made me a better person.

True story! They had a bizarre effect on me. Instead of bouncing off the walls, I embraced serenity like it was a fall fashion trend. I traded in my usual type-A, OCD self and became a calm, unflappable, laid-back person. And that's not just me tooting my own horn. I was so tranquil, I'm pretty sure my family and friends are secretly praying I'm barefoot and pregnant for the rest of my life.

IT'S WORTH THE WAIT . . . AND THE EXTRA WEIGHT

While I think it's important (not to mention, hilarious) to spotlight some of the side effects that pregnancy can generate, I feel it's equally essential to confirm just how profoundly it's worth every one of them. I hope you'll look back fondly on your maternity, despite any challenges you might endure. It all leads to a gorgeous little miracle! Complaining about the strange bodily idiosyncrasies associated with pregnancy doesn't mean you hate being pregnant. I think that's a common misconception in the mommy community . . . You are allowed to embrace pregnancy and the beautiful baby it creates, while simultaneously acknowledging you're feeling uncomfortable. Don't feel guilty for admitting that!

The truth is that pregnancy sucks some of the time. Fortunately, that has no bearing on how you will view your child when he or she is born. Try to have realistic expectations of yourself as you grow your tiny human. It's probably a fair assumption that you'll have some discomfort here and there.

Most of us won't experience nine months of peaceful perfection with zero suffering, but that's part of the trade-off. Putting up with a bit of pain and woe makes your new arrival that much more enchanting and wonderful. Technically, pregnancy is prep work for all the selflessness that will be required of you once your child arrives. Mommyhood has officially begun!

THE MORAL OF MY STORY

I'm ready, willing, and able to go through another nine months of praying to the porcelain god, puffing up like a French pastry, breaking out in hives, suffering through endless back pain, and feeling like I've been lifting weights from my tatas, if it means having another child who's as perfect as the two I've already got. Wow. I may have just publicly admitted I'm ready for baby number three.

Pregnant with Gray. "Duh" pretty much sums it up.
Photo courtesy of Brooke Boling.

CHAPTER 3

This Is Your Brain on Baby

A SCENIC VIEW OF MY PAST

When I was eighteen years old, and right after *Blossom* ended, I craved a return to the grand theatre. I'm far from a trained Shakespearean actor (which I imagine is fairly obvious), but I'd performed in quite a few off-Broadway productions as a child and I missed being a triple threat. There's no ego boost quite like singing, dancing, and acting all at the same time, followed by the immediate gratification of rowdy applause. And as one might expect, an ego boost is what every actor lives for. Validation is our life force, our magic bullet, and our substitute for a therapist. It invigorates us like jelly-filled donuts dunked in a quadruple espresso. That's why there are so many damn award shows.

So with that in mind, I asked my agents to be on the look-out for something stage-related. In response, they sent me on an audition for *Rent*, which was, at the time, at the pinnacle of its highly touted success on Broadway in New York City. Ask and you shall receive! I'd requested a play audition, and I'd gotten it . . . in much the same way one orders "some sort of red meat" and winds up getting a Kobe steak. I certainly wasn't complaining.

I spent a week learning Maureen's lengthy monologue and practicing the accompanying song, until I'd rehearsed in front of every wall, dog, and piece of furniture in my house. I was prepared. In fact, one might say I was overly prepared.

I set an early alarm for the morning of my big audition. Wanting to make the best impression possible, I thought a few more hours of studying sheet music couldn't hurt. At 6:00 a.m. when my clock started its incessant beeping—because that was before an iPhone served as judge and jury for everything I do—I stretched and swung my legs over the side of the bed. I padded across my carpet, reached the bathroom, and turned on the light.

"Achoo!" I sprayed snot all over my bathroom mirror and squinted at my reflection. My eyes were practically swollen shut.

"Achoo!" My heart sank. That's when I realized my throat was on fire, and my head felt like I'd been clocked by Muhammad Ali. Okay, I'm exaggerating. It felt like I'd been clocked by his daughter, Laila. But she packs a serious punch too. Regardless, I clearly had a knockdown, drag-out cold.

I immediately tried calling my agent to reschedule, but Hollywood was still asleep. I don't know if you know this, but agents don't get up at the butt crack of dawn. Hell, it's a good day if they roll out of bed at noon, still sporting the suit they wore on the red carpet the night before and drooling on miscellaneous contract pages. Most of them would probably say the same about us actors, so here's hoping I'm granted a mulligan on that comment.

I drummed my fingers nervously on my kitchen counter as I listened to the phone ring and prayed some overworked, glorified gopher of an assistant had passed out on the office couch the night before. I was far from optimistic. After ten minutes of office-stalking my entire agent-manager-publicist trifecta, I gave up. I needed to suck it up and go on the audition regardless, didn't I? I owed it to myself to make that good impression.

It was, of course, extraordinarily depressing when that backfired on me. You see, I also thought I should do everything in my power to combat my sudden onslaught of cold symptoms by taking NyQuil. Eighteen-year-olds don't read directions; otherwise I might have known I was in for an afternoon of drowsiness, slurred speech, and overall incompetence.

When I got to the *Rent* audition, I couldn't recall how I'd gotten there, and I would've been hard-pressed to tell you my own name. Or how old I was. Or whether or not I had ever been on a show called *Blossom*.

It was a disaster. When I began my monologue, I trailed off into outer space like I was channeling Lindsay Lohan or had downed a preparatory bottle of sedatives. Or both. As soon as the piano player started playing my song, I opened my mouth to begin singing and nothing came out. Turns out those cold symptoms had turned into acute laryngitis . . . of the throat *and* the brain.

It was an epic fail, and it rocked me to the core—well, once the thought-paralyzing delirium wore off, which was after I went home and slept for nearly a decade. When the NyQuil haze had dissipated and my major embarrassment began to sink in, I panicked.

After calling my manager, who told me he was sure it

wasn't as bad as I thought, I decided to reach out to family instead. Family is always supportive, right? Technically, it's their job.

I called my brother, Tyler, who sings like an angel despite resembling a lumberjack. He has been on stage more than I have, and I knew he would have some advice for me. I laid out my pitiful tale and awaited his response.

"That sucks," he said.

That's it, *mi hermano*? That's your much-anticipated pep talk?

"I had the same thing happen to me a few weeks ago during a performance," he offered.

Now I was getting somewhere. Thank God for siblings with worse experiences, or we'd never feel good about ourselves.

Tyler went on to tell me how he'd forgotten the most crucial phrase in a reciting of Edgar Allan Poe's "The Raven." I was shocked he'd frozen up like that and, admittedly, I was secretly pleased. I mean, who forgets the phrase "Quoth the Raven 'Nevermore'?" It's the crux of the poem, for Pete's sake! At least my screw-up could be blamed on congestion and pills, rather than a spontaneous brain fart.

Mind you, Tyler was barely crowding eight years old at the time, so I suppose I may have been expecting too much of him.

Oh. Did I fail to mention I was calling my little brother who was still in elementary school? My bad. A girl's gotta take her inspiration where she can get it, even if it's from someone who isn't even close to qualifying for a driver's license yet.

Needless to say, I didn't get the part.

CUT TO . . .

If I thought NyQuil was bad, I was in for a rude awakening when the "baby brain" phenomenon set in. It's amazing how a fetus the size of a poppy seed can make your mind mushier than Cream of Wheat. It's a state not unlike the murky memory fog one might experience after a night of pounding tequila shooters at a dive bar in Tijuana. Not that I would know.

MY CRADLE CHRONICLES

My short-term memorization ability has always been relatively advanced. Case in point, I would often find myself with three pages' worth of continual dialogue in our *Blossom* scripts. Since every line was meant to be said at speeds exceeding Mach 10, one slipup would have sent me off track like a freight train with no brakes. Playing Six certainly helped me hone my skills.

That said, my long-term memorization is for the birds. I can't remember birthdays to save my life, and I seem to selectively forget things involving anything entertainment-related. For example, if we meet, don't bother telling me, "I loved that *Blossom* episode when you made out with Mark-Paul Gosselaar in the backseat of that car . . ." or "Remember when you and Blossom overflowed that hotel Jacuzzi with bubble bath?" I can tell you right now the answer will be "No, I don't." After two series' worth of scenes and story lines, everything has been sent out of my head and into the episode oblivion.

I am also a veritable dumping ground for everything I've ever watched on television or seen in a movie theater. My brain is the equivalent of a back-alley mob disposal, except characters and plots go there to die. It's actually quite the parlor trick.

I've watched *The West Wing* series three times in its entirety, and I never remember how it ends. I'm lucky if I can remember that it's a show about the White House. My husband is simultaneously horrified, amazed, and envious of my talent. Of course, he's equally thrilled that I'm willing to watch *Arrested Development* over and over again. Why not, since I never recall that the money is in the banana stand?

But pregnancy brought about a whole new level of mind-blowing amnesia. During those nine months, my mind and memory pitched a tent in my uterus and camped out there for a while. In fact, they were in there singing "Kumbaya" and roasting marshmallows on the fire.

There's no easy way to avoid making a spectacle of yourself unless you feel like embracing social purgatory, so prepare to be idiotified!

The term *baby brain* wasn't invented to make you feel better. In anticipation of going through the most bizarre series of changes it has seen since puberty, I think the body's logic and reasoning go on lockdown. Or, as my dear friend Brittany likes to say, "My brain just likes to hide things from me now." Welcome to your new state of being—dazed and confused. I perpetually felt as though Harry Potter had waved his magic wand over my head and shouted, "Stupefy!"

Baby brain isn't some farcical malady created for your spouse's amusement. It isn't your fault you drove to the bank in your robe and slippers or left your car keys in the vegetable drawer of the refrigerator. You aren't even to be blamed for forgetting your mother-in-law's name and phone number. Hell, some women do that on purpose, pregnant or not. Nonetheless, baby brain is the real deal.

While it probably won't win you any prizes for intellect, it might win you some memorable looks from your coworkers and, if you're lucky, a few laughs. There's nothing funnier than the preggo chick in the office who manages to walk around all day with her skirt inside out and who accidentally put the boss's business cards through the paper shredder. Just think . . . your entertainment value just went up tenfold! You, my brainless little baby mama, just became the funniest act since *The Three Stooges*.

You think I'm kidding? Go ask your husband*—though if he's smart, he'll avoid answering. Consider your newfound stupidity an opportunity to blame things on the baby. You've come by it honestly, and there's no sense in putting a good excuse to waste!

You're not the only clown in this parade

In an effort to help you feel a bit better about your own baby-brain misadventures, my friends and family and I pooled some of our ditziest maternity moments for your reading pleasure. Consider us your commiseration coalition. Some names have been changed to protect the intelligent.

---

*I use the term "husband" a lot in this book because that's who I eat, sleep, and breathe with on a day-to-day basis. Please substitute "significant other" or "wife" or "partner" or "BFF" as it applies, and let's keep rolling down this mommy learning curve together!

On any given Saturday

No need for substitute names on this first story. It is one from my own treasure trove of stupidity and folly.

While I was pregnant with Marlowe, some fellow mommy acquaintances invited me to brunch. We all had toddlers in the same day care class, so I suppose it was under the pretense of having a mommy's day out. It may also have been with the genius intention to bemoan the terrible twos while under the influence of something fun. My *something fun* was tap water, given that I was pregnant, but at least the other moms got a margarita out of the deal.

Anyway, I didn't know these moms very well, having seen them only while performing my pickup and drop-off duties at Gray's school. However, I asked myself, why not broaden my friendship horizons? Not to mention, everyone can use an ally at day care, which will probably make significantly more sense to you at some point down the road.

The mom organizing our luncheon sent me a confirmation e-mail, and I responded that I'd see everyone there . . . which might have been true had I properly written the details down on my calendar. Lo and behold, I showed up for a Sunday brunch on a Saturday. I even got as far as valet parking my car, racing through the pouring rain, searching for the table where my new friends were expected to be seated, and texting them to say, "I just can't seem to find you guys!"

What's that old adage about first impressions?

Ho-ho-ho-ly baby brain

My good friend Anne has three sons. This makes her a saint in my book (or a complete lunatic, depending on how you look at it). There's a reason God gave me girls (well . . . so far), since I wouldn't know the first thing about what to do with a kid who uses the toilet for target practice or who thinks it's cute to smear boogers on the dining room walls like he's Jackson Pollock. Ergo, I have the utmost respect for women who manage to survive the total chaos of raising a posse of boys.

During Christmastime one year, while Anne was pregnant with her third son, she was headed to the last place anyone wants to drag two rowdy young lads during the holiday hustle and bustle: the mall. But who can skip the tradition of throwing her kids on the lap of a spiked-eggnog-breathing, smoker's-cough-hacking, faux-bearded, senile, skinny guy in a fat suit? She was determined to get that yearly Santa photo.

She braved the horrific holiday traffic to get to the mall before the photo booth closed for the day, and they barely made it in time. In fact, they were last in line, and Santa himself attempted to cut them off at the pass. I mean, where was the Christmas spirit? Where was the ho-ho-ho-spitality? (Sorry, I couldn't resist.)

Given Anne's efforts to haul her kids there in the first place, and perhaps because she also has a penchant for being saucy, my friend fought back. The fraudulent St. Nick, none too happy that he was forced to extend his camera time, got huffy. Nonetheless, he sat down and reluctantly hoisted the boys onto his lap.

Apparently, karma is not only a bitch; it can be messy too. As soon as Anne's youngest son climbed onto the grumpy big guy's lap, he took the opportunity to pee . . . all over the Santa suit. Turns out, in Anne's rush to get to the mall, she'd forgotten to put a diaper on him.

You can lead a horse to water, but you can't make her remember it.

I'm telling on myself yet again. When I was about six months pregnant with Marlowe, I reached the apex of my baby-brain denseness. I was honestly operating at about half of my normal IQ. Therefore, getting Gray to preschool was more laborious than it should have been. I'm surprised I never forgot to change her out of her pajamas, pack her lunch bag, or pick her up before I received a cautionary phone call from one of the teachers. I'm still pretty proud of myself for those accomplishments!

Still, I had my moments of foolishness. Just ask Gray. Because rest assured, a child will *not* let you off the hook for your baby brain. Your husband may be wise enough to ignore it, and your friends may sympathize because they've been there themselves, but your kid will always call you on your shit— even if you think they're too young to successfully pull that off.

One hot summer morning, I was desperately trying to get Gray out the door. Her school isn't terribly close, and traffic slows us down. Consequently, our routine is often a rushed one. I'd set out all the necessary gear the night before, and I was going over my checklist aloud. Each time I mentioned something, Gray nodded in support. Two-year-olds are quite savvy at offering encouragement, even when you're talking to yourself like a nutcase.

Just as I was finishing my tally of the requisite supplies, I thought of one last item I desperately needed for my own well-being during the car ride. I explained why I was running upstairs and asked Gray to wait for me by the back door. Halfway up the steps, I stopped in my tracks.

I'd lost all sense of what I'd been going to retrieve.

After a moment, my daughter's sweet face appeared around the corner. "Mommy," she said, "are you okay?"

"I'm fine. I just forgot why I was going upstairs."

She eyed me like I was a post-Chernobyl, three-headed mutant toad, and then her sarcasm kicked in. "Um . . . you were getting *water* for yourself." She said it like she was already picking out a color for my straitjacket. (Knowing her, it was probably purple and glittery.)

Thankfully, she was too young to look up the number for the psych ward, so I figured I was safe. At least for the time being.

Frosty the Snowmom

My mom had four kids. I begin by telling you this because I feel it's important you start out with an accurate perception of her mental state at any given moment during my upbringing. I mean, having two kids is a serious game changer. When I double that number in my head, the number of dirty diapers and sanity-defying temper tantrums grows exponentially. I'm not entirely convinced I would have enough hands, tolerance, or access to antianxiety meds for four kids. Nonetheless, my mom managed it with a decent measure of poise and balance, so I'm impressed.

One wintry afternoon, my parents made plans to take the three of us kids ice-skating. My littlest brother was still happily residing in the womb (he has always been reluctant to leave the comfort of home), so my pregnant mom was doing her damnedest to outfit all of us in the appropriate seasonal gear. Getting us ready was a production. Tubs of hats and mittens had come down from the attic, various sizes of boots were strewn across the floor, and my other brother and I were engaged in a friendly game of tug-of-war with a knit scarf. It didn't help that every time my mom zipped one of us into a snowsuit, we suddenly felt the urge to pee, and she was stuck undressing and dressing us all over again. Fun was being had by all. My dad was initially supposed to accompany all of us on this outing, but he'd gotten called in to work at the last minute. Now, against all odds, my generous mom—God bless her—was endeavoring to follow through with the plan.

After grabbing a mug of coffee for herself on the way out (with that many kids to wrangle, even decaf can be an urgent necessity), she finally got us herded into the car and buckled in. We were about a mile down the road when that cup of joe flung himself down the front of our van, streaking the windshield with brown liquid and crashing to the gravel in front of us. We ran him over for good measure. That java had gone on a mile-long joyride on the roof of our car before tragically ending his own life on the harsh pavement. I think my mom may have shed a tear or two, and his eulogy was a lengthy and mournful one.

Fortunately, the coffee incident was instantly forgotten when we arrived at the ice-skating rink. Unfortunately, that was because Mom discovered she'd failed to bring her own coat and mittens along for our time in the arctic Connecticut weather.

I guess one could say it was a bitter cold day in hell for her that afternoon.

Show me the money!

My little sister, Alyssa, recently had her first baby. Since I've experienced baby brain ad nauseam, I was downright gleeful to induct her into the Baby Brain Hall of Fame. You *did* know we had our own organization, right? No monthly fees, no boys allowed, and the enrollment sometimes lasts a lifetime!

When my sister first called to tell me she had a bun in the oven, she also revealed this little gem that occurred when she was only seven weeks along. Which goes to show that the idiocy can set in early! At that stage of the game she was barely even registering her pregnancy, much less thinking about the impending stupidity.

Alyssa was out running errands and stopped by the bank to deposit a check or two. Sounds fairly innocuous, doesn't it? At her local branch, which she had been to hundreds of times, my sister stood at the kiosk and filled out her deposit slip. She knew her account number by heart and proceeded to write it into the space provided. After proofreading her paperwork, she approached the teller, handed everything over, and awaited her money.

The teller punched the numbers into her computer, frowned, and executed a few additional keystrokes. "I'm sorry, but you aren't in our system."

Alyssa was thoroughly baffled. "I don't understand. I

come here all the time, and I've never had any trouble."

But she received only a sympathetic smile in return.

"Let me try spelling my last name for you," my sister offered. "It's not the easiest."

Finally, the teller hit the jackpot. "I've got you. The problem was that you wrote down the wrong account number."

My sister was skeptical. Glancing down, she reread the deposit slip. The account number she'd provided definitely consisted of numbers she knew intimately . . . since she'd written her husband's cell phone number instead.

"I wasn't totally off," my sister rationalized to me. "At least they both start with the same digit."

I had a different take on it. "I hope the teller didn't think you were trying to pass off your husband on her."

See? If you aren't careful, baby brain will even attempt to set your spouse up on dates with random women!

It's a wrap!

I'll end with another of my own tales. It was a week or two before Christmas 2011, and I was in my typical preholiday, gift-wrapping frenzy. I'd been decorating and prepping for several hours, and I had only a few items left to package. The caveat? I was trying to accomplish all of it before my husband got home from work, which was only a few minutes away. To compound matters, morning sickness was being a bit of a Scrooge.

I cut and folded as rapidly as my little fingers could go. Suddenly, I realized I'd forgotten a crucial component and raced into my office to retrieve the needed item. I bolted back into the room seconds later, clutching the stapler.

I repeat, the stapler.

I wasn't sure what the heck I was doing holding that stapler, because for the life of me I couldn't recall what I needed it for. Five minutes later, after staring thoughtlessly at my table of ribbons and gift wrap, it finally dawned on me . . . I didn't. I'd gone into my office for the tape dispenser. Which, as it turns out, is a much more practical tool for wrapping packages.

SMART COOKIES DON'T CRUMBLE

I've witnessed or heard about a lot of ridiculous incidents, thanks to that curious culprit called baby brain. You might find yourself ringing your husband up on your cell phone to complain you've lost your cell phone, failing to turn the shower off after washing up, or forgetting to put the car in park after you've pulled into the garage. I have friends who've accidentally left the dogs outside in the rain for two hours, forgotten who they telephoned and had to ask, and driven away from the gas station pump with the hose still attached to their tank.

When Gray was born, a woman walked into my hospital room and asked me how the baby and I were doing. "It's weird," I answered. "You look so familiar. I feel like I've met you before."

"You have," my husband whispered. "That's our pediatrician."

While pregnant with me, my mom once dried the dirty clothes before washing them, and I have a girlfriend who went to the grocery store and completely forgot what she'd gone there for in the first place. She came home with a box of brownie mix instead, so I think that incident is *entirely* forgivable. How can you go wrong with brownies?

But let that be a lesson to you: lists are your new BFF! Just don't forget where you put them. And when you catch yourself doing something silly, laugh about it! Everyone else will.

The moral of my story

During pregnancy, I pondered whether my brain cells had been beamed to a secret location where they were being held for ransom. Yours might be out there hiding with all the socks that have gone missing from your dryer, buried in the odds-and-ends drawer underneath the birthday candles, or stashed in a safety deposit box until you're back to your fully lucid self. Who the hell knows? Will they return to you someday? The jury is still out on that. In fact, I don't even have enough of my own brain cells left to come up with that answer for you. Nonetheless, you are donating them to a worthwhile cause! Expect to have some serious blonde moments from time to time, regardless of your hair color, and be sure to document the really funny ones. You'll thank me later.

BABY BRATCHER

A beautifully packaged gift given to us at Gray's baby shower. The little vintage shoes are still on display in her room because I can't bear to part with them. Those boots were made for walking down memory lane. *Photo courtesy of Jenna von Oy.*

CHAPTER 4
I Dream of Diaper Genies

A SCENIC VIEW OF MY PAST

"I absolutely *must* have this," I sanctioned for what must have been the ten thousandth time in my twenty-one-year-old life.

My coconspirator, the waiflike sales clerk who undoubtedly grew up in the 90210 zip code, nodded enthusiastically and snapped her bubble gum. "That dress looks amazing on you," she cooed. "It fits you like a glove!" (Because no one lies or blows smoke up anyone's ass in Hollywood.)

I stared at my reflection. A Dolce & Gabbana dress was exactly what the doctor had ordered; I was certain of it. It was my choice antidote for boredom and insecurity and, since I was feeling extra self-conscious lately, maybe I needed that full-length coat to match. Then my closet would be complete and I'd never have to shop again.

I'd said that the last time I'd gone out for retail therapy, but this time I really meant it. It would be my new mantra. Then again, there was a pair of to-die-for stilettos at that store down the street that I definitely couldn't pass up either. And if I had those shoes, didn't I need an appropriate purse to match? And a scarf? And . . .

You get the idea.

My heart leapt as I extracted the credit card from my wallet. Cash would mean I was actually watching the money walk away, and I'd be forced to acknowledge my addiction. Who needs that kind of self-awareness or financial prudence? Handing over a credit card was just so effortless. Hell, I could do it in my sleep (and probably had). Since I wouldn't see the bill for another twenty-five days or so, it gave me plenty of time to forget all about my indiscretions and continue with my daily life as if I'd done nothing self-destructive whatsoever.

The girl behind the counter smiled and hummed along to an All-4-One tune as she rang up item after item after item. As the receipt generated, I thought back to the ticket stubs I used to get while playing Skee-Ball at the arcade. I'd been so excited to pick out a stupid little toy like Chinese handcuffs or a Whoopee Cushion back then. Now I'd graduated to the big leagues; that meant I was maturing, right? My adrenaline raced as the register spit out a Santa's list worth of name-brand baubles and apparel. I numbly picked up my bag, which was filled to the brim with designer clothes. Peeking in, I saw my pile of purchases nestled sweetly in their tissue-paper bed of perfection. I inhaled deeply. I was high now, and I felt no pain. It was better than wine and chocolate. Or sex. Or wine and chocolate during sex.

And then, just as suddenly as I'd gotten high, I came crashing down. The shame settled in as soon as I pulled into my driveway. I rushed into the house before my boyfriend could see the telltale signs. I cut off the incriminating tags and buried them in the bottom of the trash can amongst the banana peels and coffee grounds. I even stashed a few in an empty toilet paper roll for safekeeping.

I smiled with satisfaction. The clothes were formally part of my wardrobe now. Since I'd taken the stickers off, nothing could be returned; mission accomplished.

I looked at my dazzling new treasures, suspended from matching velvet hangers in all their trendy, fashion-forward, overpriced glory. (How else could one explain dishing out three hundred dollars for a pair of jeans that already had holes in them?)

What had I even bought? I wasn't entirely sure. The experience had been a blur, and it didn't even involve booze or pharmaceuticals. I'd had another fiscal blackout, which seemed to be happening more and more frequently. I was officially a junkie, but no one sold my drugs on a street corner downtown. They masked them in high-end boutiques with swanky names, good lighting, and dressing-room fun-house mirrors that made me look more like Kate Moss than any five-foot-tall girl ever could or should. I was in deep. I mean, when you spend enough money that stores start sending you Christmas gifts, you know you're in a dark place. Hell, I even got a pair of shearling UGG slippers one year. How much dough did I have to drop in order to receive those?

Marilyn had her sleeping pills, Van Gogh had his absinthe, and I had my American Express card. I was a fanatical disciple of retail therapy, and I was content with self-medicating. It was my catharsis, my sanity, and my salvation. Except, of course, that it was none of those things. It was draining my bank account faster than you could say "Jenna seriously needs to hire a money manager," or "Somebody get that girl a decent calculator."

It wasn't like a long night spent loitering on a bar stool. No one was there to cut me off, take my keys, and call me a cab when I overindulged. As addicts often do, I hid my proclivities from everyone who might have seen my struggle for what it was and called me on my shit. Instead, most folks only knew to say, "I like your blouse. Is that new?"

Those who had an inkling chalked it up to a young girl sowing her wild oats and, take it from me, it's nearly impossible to tell an adolescent who thinks money grows on trees to simmer down. Especially when she makes enough money to support her habit.

Not to mention, most folks don't take a shopping dependence all that seriously; it isn't a glamorous addiction. And I'm using the term *glamorous* very loosely here. Heroin ravages your body and tears families apart. The only thing shopping ravages, especially when you aren't yet married with kids, is your financial stability. That said, it's no less destructive to one's spirit, and mine was in the toilet.

I was in a downward debt spiral. I couldn't go to the grocery store without stockpiling enough salami and cheese to feed a small army. Or enough Kleenex to wipe a trillion boogers. I didn't buy just one or two bottles of wine at the vineyards in Napa Valley; I bought enough cases to start my own cellar. I was young, foolish, and unstoppable.

Cut to . . .

They had me at the words *baby registry*. That old familiar feeling crept back in, and I immediately felt seduced by the scanning gadget I held in my hand. It was drawing me in more hypnotically than Dennis Rodman to piercings and spandex. I was falling (or, perhaps more appropriately, vaulting) off the wagon with every baby bloomer, rubber ducky, and industrial-sized burp cloth I passed by.

My cradle chronicles

Let's be honest, "gearing" up for your new addition is one of the most exciting parts of the prebirth process: the Pack 'n Play aisle basking in the glow of the fluorescent lights, the lull of the cash register's *cha-ching* . . .

Your introduction to the wonderful world of baby supplies can be such an inebriating adrenaline rush that it's open season on every lusted-after, baby-oriented gadget your money can buy. If you didn't know it before, now you do—addiction isn't relegated to Valium and cheap liquor. It can poison your maternity judgment too.

I know you are super excited to have your baby out of the womb, and stocking up on miscellaneous bambino-related junk seems like a solid temporary fix. But before you've bungee jumped off the baby bridge, please heed my warning: avoid the paraphernalia pitfalls.

Though we are fortunate to have more technologically

advanced, luxury accessories for the modern baby, in some ways our parents may have had it easier back in the day. That whole idea of *Keep it simple, stupid* comes into play when you're trying to assemble equipment that comes with a thicker handbook than *Neurosurgery for Dummies*. Before you go getting wistful on me about the olden golden days, may I remind you that our parents also delighted in decades of bellbottoms and shag carpets? I think we're even.

THE SECRET OF MY SIGN-UP SUCCESS

New technology doesn't always equal better, and there's an oversaturated marketplace out there. So don't throw yourself at every gimmick it offers!

Or, in other words, don't do what I did. Because I made enough spontaneous Babies "R" Us checkout line purchases to cover both of us, I assure you. Here are some general rules I wish I'd followed:

1. Baby registries aren't meant to be a free-for-all.
This isn't the buffet line at your local dim sum restaurant, so try not to pile too much on. Don't get me wrong, it's your prerogative to register for whatever you wish. I don't begrudge you shooting for the moon and choosing things you won't buy for yourself; it's your opportunity to dream big. But keep in mind that people purchase items from your registry because you're telling them it's a list of things you truly want or need, not a list of things you think would be hilarious to have. For example, you may not need to register for the kitschy sock monkey lampshade, the Barbie Dreamphitheatre, or the

frame for your baby's future college diploma. I'm just saying.

Registries are best suited for practical items—you know, the things you hate spending money on because they aren't fun, such as a breast pump and its accompanying finery. I don't know about you, but breast pumps aren't exactly what I would consider a party. They don't have a built-in slot for your iPod, and you're not supposed to drink any alcohol while using them. I rest my case.

2. In general, your friends and family want to know you'll think of them every time you use whatever gift they buy you . . . even it it's fancy-schmancy butt paste. (Thanks, Cindy!)
It's worth noting that this can work against you if you aren't careful. If you don't want your creepy neighbor (who strangely resembles Cousin Itt from *The Addams Family* and said he wanted to get you something to remember him by) to envision you breastfeeding, you may want to refrain from touting that awesome organic nipple cream you heard about. No one wants to think about Peeping Tom each time they rub salve on their breasts. Unless, of course, that sort of thing turns you on. My advice? Tell your way-too-friendly, weirdo neighbor you'd love a gift card instead of forking over your registry information.

3. Try not to register for too many articles of newborn clothing.
I know it's tough to avoid the itty-bitty lederhosen or the wee little argyle socks, so if you fall in love with something, far be it for me to stop you. If you're going to lose sleep over not getting a pair of bloomers, I say they're fair game for the registry.

Otherwise, keep in mind you'll probably receive clothing regardless, since you're not the only one who can't resist making your baby look even cuter than he already will be!

4. Don't hesitate to ask for gift cards.
It isn't a cop-out, and you'll be glad you did it. There will be things you forgot to register for (or didn't know to), and already having the money set aside to pay for them will keep your wallet happier in the long run. For instance, one of the best pieces of advice I got was to wait on a long-term stroller purchase, which can be a *serious* investment. Instead of registering for a deluxe baby-bob-jogger-mini-bugaboo from the get-go, we waited to see what would best suit our lifestyle once our daughter was in it. In the meantime, we signed up for a very practical, easy-fold, snap-and-go stroller that Gray's car seat could lock into. That got us through the first eight or nine months, at which point we were better equipped to know what sort of stroller system was most appropriate for us.

5. You don't need two of everything, unless you have twins. Or unless you're purchasing breast pads.
Resist the urge to hoard baby supplies. If you need a therapist before you even *have* the baby, you might be beyond my assistance. And let's be honest, most households can really handle only one gizmo junkie. If your husband is anything like mine, he's probably got that covered in his tool trove of a man cave, otherwise known as the garage.

6. Accept that your archaic aunt Bertha, who refuses to abide by the rules or look at your wish list on "that newfangled nonsense called Amazon" will give you random stuff you don't need and can't return.

My suggestion? Find a local charity to give it to if you can't stand toting it to every family reunion from now until the end of time. There are moms out there who would thoroughly appreciate a nursing cover-up with neon-pink unicorns or a newborn-sized Christmas sweater with a giraffe dancing the Nutcracker ballet, and it's always nice to know you've helped someone out. Even if tweeting photos and caustic comments about the items is a seriously tempting alternative.

7. Reject being wooed by the price gun.

The scanner makes you feel immortal. It offers a sense of empowerment that tantalizes your senses like some sort of perverted merchandise pheromone. Hone your consumer counterattack skills and keep channeling your anti-over-registering mojo. Just say no!

8. Ask friends who have recently had a baby if they'll give you a copy of their registries, including what was already purchased for them.

Online registries are typically still available for quite some time, and friends' lists are the best source for obtaining a general consensus of what you will need. When I began the registry process, both of my amazing sisters-in-law offered to share their checklists with me. Because they'd both recently had kids of their own, they were really on top of what was and wasn't necessary. They'd essentially already done the research for me.

Don't get me wrong, I'm type A, so I still did some of my own. But it was beneficial to have a blueprint to follow. At the very least, viewing someone else's list will give you a starting point.

9. Consider your lifestyle and be realistic about how your registry should reflect it.

I signed up for a plethora of bottle-feeding supplies because that's what I assumed I was supposed to do. If you have an infant, you need bottles, right? And if you have bottles, don't you need the bottle warmer? And the sterilizer? And the specialized brush? And the steam-cleaning bags? Well, *you* may need all those items, but I certainly didn't. I'm a stay-at-home mom who breastfeeds. The only times my daughters used bottles were while bonding with their dad and grandparents or when we hired the occasional sitter. Otherwise, they were attached to my boob like a marine barnacle. I discovered, albeit a bit belatedly, that breastfeeding plus stay-at-home mom equals no need for every bottle-related product on the market. Not to mention, some babies refuse a bottle and never look back. By the time I tried to return the bottle supplies I'd been gifted at my shower, which was many months after having my baby, nothing translated to a full-price exchange for the things I really did need. Lesson learned.

10. Put the Pee Pee Teepees back on the shelf and try to focus on items that won't fall out of trend or be flung into the dark recesses of a drawer in two weeks.

Once you become an expert diaper changer, you won't bother with some of the extras such as a cover for your son's you-know-what. (Also, you'll eventually accept that you'll be peed on a few times here and there; it's in the job description.) It's more practical to stick with products that stand the test of time, which is why I tried to make a habit of staying away from spontaneous add-ons. In other words, I avoided purchases costing only a dollar or two that I was tempted to randomly toss into my cart as an afterthought. Those items are easily attainable later and won't break the bank if you decide you can't live without them. Meanwhile, it's going to be tough (not to mention illegal) to drive home from the hospital without putting your baby in an infant car seat. So don't forget to register for the important items!

IN MY OPINIONATION . . . ESSENTIAL REGISTRY ITEMS

You know the saying "Necessity is the mother of invention"? Well, sometimes invention is the necessity of mother too. Here are a few things I was exceedingly thankful I registered for—things I couldn't have survived without. To clarify, these aren't products I was paid to promote in this book; they just made my life easier, so I thought I'd share.

1. The video monitor

I know some folks think splurging on a video monitor is overzealous. It gives them nightmares of staring into a screen for hours on end, lulled into a hypnotic trance by the mere ebb and flow of their child's breathing. First of all, I'm not recommending investing in a full-time aquarium channel here. I'm suggesting that there are benefits to knowing what your kid is up to. And yes, that sometimes includes breathing. If you can bypass the compulsion to turn the monitor into an all-night reality show starring your favorite new celebrity baby, that's the route to go. A monitor enables you to go upstairs and indulge in a pint of Ben & Jerry's while your kid naps peacefully. It's a win-win.

The one hurdle of a video monitor is the creepy night-vision eyes; your kid *will* look like something out of *Village of the Damned*. This is especially true if your child is anything like mine. Gray used to be very quiet when she woke up. It began at birth—no crying, no talking, just silence. She was also keenly aware of her monitor and had a tendency to gaze stoically into the camera until I retrieved her. While it was unnerving to glance over and see her laser-beam eyes staring me down, I was grateful to have some way to know she was up and ready to start her day. That is, of course, once I'd shaken off the unsettling feeling that her head was going to make a 360-degree spin as she crawled backward up our stairs.

2. The snap-and-go stroller
As I touched upon earlier, this saved us from spending money on an excessive stroller system until Gray was old enough to sit up in one. It has also served as a grocery cart, an airport luggage transporter, and my very own traveling junk drawer. The idea of the snap-and-go is this—it's a lightweight, easily foldable stroller frame into which you can lock an infant car seat. That way, you don't have to wake your kid up every time you go into the market. Or Starbucks. Or to get a mani/pedi. (You know, because we moms have so much time for such luxuries.) Regardless, it saved me a million times, and that's no exaggeration. No mother wants to wake a sleeping baby,

right? This allowed me to take my girls along with me, without lugging the car seat everywhere in my arms. That said, if you're yearning for arm muscles to rival Schwarzenegger's, go ahead and haul around that car seat. It'll be a blast.

3. *The baby swing*

The swing was often my saving grace. When all else failed, this thing put my kid to sleep faster than Dramamine. Well, I've never tried that, so who knows if that's true? But back to the swing . . . It's like a little one-man show. It plays soothing lullabies and nature sounds, has interactive pieces, and rocks the baby. The only thing it doesn't do is make gin and tonics or fold your laundry, but that's what husbands are for.

Oh, but beware of its proclivity for overenthusiastic momentum. Though the photos on the box may indicate a sleeping infant swaying peacefully, the lowest setting can be the equivalent of Space Mountain until your child is big enough to weigh the machine down a bit. Mode one on the model we got was puke-inducing; mode five threatened to launch my child like a human cannonball. Go-Go Gadget Ejector Seat!

Friends of ours wound up putting five-pound weights in the bottom of their swing, just so their son wouldn't get seasick after five minutes. We opted to wait on using the actual motion settings until Gray was a bit heavier, which somewhat defeated the purpose. A swing that doesn't swing is, after all, just a seat. That said, I cannot deny the thing still had the magic touch, and my daughter loved it—with or without the movement.

When I had my second daughter, the mamaRoo made

our first swing seem as outdated as a rotary phone. It's the best thing since the invention of the iPad. It's a practical, space-saving, technologically advanced force to be reckoned with, and it replicates all the motions that keep my daughter happy. Best of all, it never threatened to throw her overboard.

4. The cosleeper

We might agree to disagree on this one, and I'm okay with that. All I ask is that you hear me out. For the first few months of having your baby home, you'll most likely want to keep a close eye on him. There are quite a few options for this, including cradles, bassinets, and cribs. Your cohabitation situation, as well as your bedroom setup, will probably dictate which of these options makes the most sense for you. Who knows, you may have already decided cosleeping isn't an idea you are open to. I initially thought the same.

My husband and I, in all our prebaby wisdom, had decided a bassinet would be the perfect solution for us. As we have a very narrow space on either side of our bed, we (rather foolishly) thought, *We can keep the baby across the room. When she cries in the middle of the night, we'll just get up and get her.* Ha! Night one of having Gray home saw us deliriously shuffling furniture.

We maneuvered the bassinet in between our mattress and the wall just so I could see her sweet face whenever I woke up. Which was every hour on the hour. To clarify, I wasn't waking up hourly because my kid was screaming for the milk dispenser; I woke up hourly because sometimes new mommies do that. In fact, since our daughter didn't cry a whole lot, I had to resort to setting alarms at night so I would wake up for feedings.

Our reality, which may or may not be yours, was that I wanted my baby near me, not across the room. After one week of cramming a cradle next to our bed in such a way that I couldn't even get up to go to the bathroom, we agreed there had to be a better alternative. Cue the cosleeper. It butts up to our bed, with three higher sides and a fourth that's level with our mattress. This allowed for easy access during nighttime feedings and the ability to hear our baby when she woke up, despite her lack of crying (which she more than made up for during her terrible twos). I slept far more comfortably and solidly with both children, thanks to the cosleeper.

It also has storage underneath, where I keep extra blankets and swaddles. And how can a built-in linen closet be a bad thing? The beauty of the cosleeper is its good bedside manner. It is one step removed from having your child sleep directly in bed with you and your spouse, but your baby is still in the near vicinity. The best of both worlds, I say!

5. A temporal artery thermometer
These doodads are fantastic. If you dread using a rectal thermometer, and I can't say I know many people who would enjoy it, this may be your ace in the hole . . . mostly because it doesn't have to go into a hole at all. This product will be slightly more costly than your average dime-store version, but instead of being inserted under the tongue or in the baby's bum, it detects emitted heat from her forehead with an infrared scanner. It's noninvasive, so I'm all for it!

6. The WubbaNub pacifier

It's a pacifier . . . It's a stuffed animal . . . No, wait, it's a pacifier *and* a stuffed animal! It's also a magic sleep-inducer, and infants can grab onto it a lot sooner than they can a normal binky. If you're going the pacifier route at all, this is the one. Can you tell I'm a huge fan? I warn you, however, these little guys are addicting.

We've owned eight animal pacifiers between my two girls (though Giraffe and Monkey both met untimely ends, which was traumatizing for *all* of us), and in our house we've fondly termed them "Wubbies." Unfortunately, the Wubbies have proven to be a difficult habit to break. Convincing Gray to give up her "friends" was met with more resistance than the return of Hammer pants. I had an easier time potty training her. Which, no joke, actually happened first.

As a side note, a company called Uggogg and Inny makes stuffed animals that attach to pacifiers, so you can throw out the old pacifier without torturing your kid by also trashing his beloved toy. Brilliant!

7. A housekeeper

Though I'm generally not one to splurge on something so luxurious, and my husband and I prefer to handle our home affairs on our own, sometimes short-term help is a necessity. Admittedly, this isn't something we could have registered for at any of the major baby outlets, and we probably wouldn't have thought to do it anyway. That said, my mom and aunt hired us a housekeeper for the two months following the birth of both girls, and it was the single biggest help. Talk about the gift that kept on giving! With five dogs, a newborn baby, and the inability to catch up on much-needed sleep, who has time to bleach the shower and mop the floors? Having someone come out to deep clean every couple of weeks was a blessing we accepted with open arms. I can't recommend it more highly!

IN MY OPINIONATION . . . OVERRATED ITEMS

Here's a list of things I wound up deeming overrated. Don't just take my word for it, though, because I could totally be wrong about some of these items . . .

1. Nursing pillows

Though I agree that propping your baby up while breastfeeding is essential, not one nursing pillow I tried did a whole lot to assist me. Perhaps if you are a bit better endowed than I am, you'll find it easier. Basically, if you're Pam Anderson, you might have a better chance of your boobs and your baby meeting in the middle. Since I'm slightly lacking in that department, I was stuck slouching to get milk to my daughter regardless of my snazzy, stylishly printed helper. It was like having a well-dressed assistant who took calls for me but didn't include names and phone numbers on my message slips. It all fell a bit short. I was forced to hold the pillow up, along with my baby, which just made the whole thing more cumbersome and difficult. And learning to nurse a newborn is hard enough as it is! I ultimately resorted to putting a second pillow under the first for additional support. I also had a C-section with both girls, so I couldn't rest a nursing pillow against my stitches for a few weeks after, which rendered having one pointless.

On their own, most of the nursing pillows I found were just too soft to hold my daughters up to my liking. This isn't to say there aren't some out there that provide more support. There probably are, and I'm planning to try every one of them if I have a third child. For now, however, I'm keeping to my assessment: I should have stuck to using our couch pillows. They essentially did the same thing, and I didn't have to spend any extra money on them.

As an aside, if you *do* get a nursing pillow, make sure to get a separate cover for it so you can remove and wash it. It's bound to be covered in spit-up in no time flat.

2. Baby backpacks and frontpacks

I see the day care moms wearing these things like a fashion accessory, and I imagine them in their little cliques squawking, "Baby carriers are the new black—didn't you know?"

Actually, most folks I know swear by them. In fact, I know babies whose feet haven't touched the ground in months! I *really* wanted to love using a carrier too, but I found that I'm just too damn short to be comfortable in any of the ones I tried. Apparently the majority of them aren't designed for munchkins, horse jockeys, or former child stars with semi-stunted growth. Not that it isn't fun to sport a baby while simultaneously carrying groceries, texting my husband, and humming "She Works Hard for the Money," but I just never got on board. They tugged on my lower back and stealthily pushed my pants down until I was exposing things that could have landed me on the cover of the gossip mags. Or at least on one of those Images of Walmart Shoppers websites. I discovered a one-piece fabric wrap that worked better for my needs, as it didn't have any metal bars, plastic buckles, adjustable waist belts, or befuddling crisscross harnesses that made me feel like I was voluntarily stuffing myself into an Edwardian corset. It also didn't require a ten-man team to get it on. By the time I strapped on the bigger badass carriers by myself, my daughter could have been applying for colleges. I just couldn't find a decent method of getting them on without help, and here's a shocker—you can't ask a newborn to adjust a back clasp for you.

My husband, on the other hand, loved wearing the baby carrier. He felt it was perfectly comfy and encouraged his bonding time with our daughters. Of course, he's not knee-high to a grasshopper like I am.

3. Musical crib mobiles

To be fair, this item didn't end up on my registry because I've never been a big fan. Some people love them; I just don't personally get it. For the most part, I find them to be aesthetically unappealing and as overstimulating as watching *Magic Mike*. I mean, how many times can you follow the costume-clad sheep around in a circle without getting dizzy? In my opinion, there's enough spit-up happening without the added incentive. Also, I've found that many mobiles are accompanied by creepy Muzak versions of nursery rhymes. I'd rather not encourage my kids to have nightmares of being trapped in an elevator with Kenny G and a herd of dancing mutton.

Instead of dangling, discordant zoo animals, we hung paper lanterns and tulle pom-poms in our nursery. They offered a quieter, but still colorful, novelty to fixate on while waiting for Mr. Sandman to make his appearance.

4. The Pack 'n Play

I'm not at all confused why this item is beneficial. For your sake, I hope your kid begs to be put in one of these doohickeys so you can free your arms for a rare fifteen minutes. You know, just long enough to vacuum the living room or cram a piece of pizza down your gullet.

I, on the other hand, had a child who took to the Pack 'n Play like cats take to water. I couldn't put Gray in there for fifteen seconds, much less fifteen minutes. By the ceaseless howling and tears, you'd have thought I was sending her to solitary confinement at Rikers Island, equipped with only a pacifier. That contraption was also harder to close than a confessional after spring break, so . . . there was that. After numerous attempts that resulted in meltdowns of mythic proportions, I gave up on any hope of putting the minislammer to good use.

Once Marlowe came along, we were gifted with a wonderful product called the Breeze Playard. The Playard put Mr. Pack 'n Play to shame, so he was banished to our attic like an expatriate. I can't say he has been missed.

Then again, he did make one hell of a laundry hamper.

5. The baby bouncer (the sort that attaches to a door frame)
I recall my little sister jumping in one of these things for hours on end when we were kids. Granted, it was probably closer to ten minutes, but it seemed like forever at the time. I can still picture her beautifully toothless smile and that adorable drool flying every which way as she jumped to her heart's content. She was like a midget kangaroo in Garanimals overalls. Meanwhile, my mom was rewarded with some quality time to herself. Of course, by that I mean she was helping me flip through vocabulary flashcards for school with one hand and changing my brother's diaper with the other. She might even have had enough "time to herself" to simultaneously assemble our sandwiches.

With that in mind, I immediately registered for a similar apparatus. Yet again, I was thwarted by a rig designed for larger children. As with the swing I spoke of earlier, size really does matter. Both of my girls were too petite to fit in the bucket seat. Within minutes, their little bottoms would slide through one of the leg holes, aggressively pushing their diapers aside and causing them to bare more cheek than one might see at a Miley Cyrus concert. If your child is a bit more on the average side of the height-and-weight charts, you might have an easier time with this one than we did. By the time our first daughter was big enough to sit properly in the bouncer, she was old enough to say, "Get me out of this thing!" and "Can you put three olives in my martini today? Make it a double."

6. *Designer baby clothes*

Newborns don't care if they're wearing delicately hand-stitched knickers from Gucci or if their bibs are kept in a Prada diaper bag.

I spent the majority of my sitcom career thinking I had to dress to impress. I was convinced (courtesy of the distorted Los Angeles magnifying glass I was squirming under) that I had to buy costly, name-brand apparel to be accepted by my peers and critics. Who, as luck would have it, were often one and the same. As evidenced earlier by the "Scenic View of My Past," I was ruthlessly caught up in the idea that designer clothes were equivalent to a happier, more confident, more alluring me. Babies don't have the same penchant for throwing credit cards at their discomfort. Thank God. They don't resort to fixating on labels in an effort to nurture their spirits. As far as they're concerned, a lactating boob will do just fine.

I won't pretend I'm not fond of nice things or that I don't encourage self-expression through one's wardrobe, but I recommend refraining from spending your child's college fund on mini Versace wear. I know there will come a day when my girls are begging for the newest jeans or the most stylish shoes, but right now they don't know the difference between something off the Target clearance rack and a pair of toddler-sized Jimmy Choos. Every high-end thread my daughters own was given to them by someone else, and I'd like to keep it that way. I swear you can make outfits look just as cute on a tighter budget. Your kids will grow out of their clothes so quickly it'll

make your head spin, so you may want to keep your inner retail monster from going on a rampage at Barney's New York.
If you're really partial to trendy fashions, I strongly recommend consignment. It's significantly cheaper, so you'll have
a better chance of feeling guilt-free when the credit card bill
comes in. You also won't feel as bad when your kid poops all
over himself five minutes after you've put the outfit on him.
Because poop doesn't care if you blew your whole paycheck to
buy the Burberry baby romper.

Million-dollar baby?

I hope this chapter has helped you contemplate what to register
for and/or what to make sure you have on hand when you
bring baby home from the hospital. There's really no way I
can provide you with a comprehensive list of everything you'll
need, as it differs for each of us; my goal was merely to get the
ball rolling. If you're anything like me, you'll spend the next
nine months overthinking everything and worrying you'll
forget to acquire something important that causes you to epi-
cally fail parenthood on day one. The truth is that no one
is keeping score but you, and a newborn requires less stuff
than one would think. Our parents relied on far fewer material items and technological advances than we do nowadays,
and we turned out just fine, right? Sort of?

So long as you have your infant car seat installed, some
sort of bassinet, crib, or cosleeper of your choice, diapers and
wipes, a few bodysuits that snap, and a breast or bottle full
of milk or formula, you're on the right track. You can send

your frazzled husband out to retrieve the rest while you're attempting to sweet-talk the baby through hour forty of nonstop bawling. Your husband will welcome the interruption, even if it means asking the salesperson to hand over the disposable nursing pads.

THE MORAL OF MY STORY

Whoever coined the phrase *sex, drugs, and rock 'n' roll* never experienced the high of shopping for their own baby registry. I found myself amassing diapers like they were about to be discontinued and hiding a secret Onesie stash in my lingerie drawer. Here's hoping you exercise significantly more willpower than yours truly!

Gray displays her lung capacity as Brad and I discover our need for patience. And earplugs. *Photo courtesy of Mimosa Arts.*

CHAPTER 5

Everyone Needs a Pregame "Prep" Talk

A SCENIC VIEW OF MY PAST

In 2007, I moved to Nashville in search of greener pastures. I was yearning for a little grass under my feet. My heart had just been trampled by an ornery wildebeest (aka my ex-boyfriend), and I wanted to put some distance between myself and the four-year relationship I'd mistakenly thought was going somewhere. Don't you just love those? I was in desperate need of a break from the Los Angeles bubble—the fires, earthquakes, mudslides, smog, never-ending traffic, and rampant narcissism. Nashville promised a humble place to hang my hat. And boy, did I have a lot of hats.

While Nashville would provide a more charming and hospitable atmosphere, it would also put me in the path of Mother Nature's redheaded stepchild, the tornado. Though I'm a lover of thunderstorms and eerie weather, I'm not, I would quickly discover, the biggest fan of violently swirling air funnels that take down everything in their path. The way I see it is this: if thunder is God bowling, then tornadoes are God weed-eating the yard. And it seems God likes to do a whole lot of weed-eating in the South during the spring.

My flabbergasted Los Angeles friends exclaimed, "Oh my God, you're moving to Nashville? Are you crazy?" followed by "Are you going to start wearing cowboy boots and a belt buckle with your name on it?" The next question out of their mouths was inevitably, "Don't you know they have tornadoes there?" This was always asked with the sort of wild-eyed hysteria one might expect if I'd said I was moving to Tokyo to pursue a career in window washing.

After I'd been asked the tornado question one too many times, I began second-guessing my respect for Mother Nature and wondering if I was embarking on the nuttiest kamikaze mission since people started sticking their heads in the mouths of crocodiles for sport. I developed a fierce Wizard of Oz complex, certain that every rainstorm would lead to flying cows and hurtling houses. I had PTSD: Pre-Tornado Stress Disorder. So in anticipation of my move, I did what every normal, logical twentysomething would do . . . I made sure my rental house had a basement and hoarded every emergency item I could get my hands on at Walmart and Target. This included but was not limited to pillows, toilet paper, books (in case I got bored of waiting for the Munchkins to show up and sing their lollipop song), a sleeping bag, water jugs, an extensive first-aid kit, board games (to play with my imaginary shelter-seeking friends), work boots, batteries, granola bars, soup, a can opener, all manner of dog accoutrements (provided I could wrangle my best friends into the cellar before the sky fell), and a case of emergency wine. Which was, of course, the most important component of my gargantuan preparedness package. If I was going to be cata-pulted through the space-time continuum in the middle of a cyclone, I certainly wasn't going to go unprepared. Or sober.

The first time I heard those tornado sirens blare, I franti-cally scrambled to collect my three dogs, my computer, and my cell phone. The priorities. It turned out the basement of my rental house wasn't accessible from the inside of the home (WTF?), so I shoved everything out into the wind and rain, in-cluding my baffled puppies, and raced toward the shelter door.

Unfortunately, I'd failed to consider that I'd have to un-lock the damn door with my arms full, and I managed to drop my new laptop down the cement steps in the process. Thank God I didn't have a baby to carry yet.

Terrifying scenes from *Twister* went pinballing through my head. I nearly started calling out for Auntie Em and Toto. I finally got the door open and corralled the pups, and we collapsed onto the basement floor in a cold, wet, stupefied heap. I remained there for two hours, not realizing a tornado warning is generally over in a matter of minutes. Mind you, I might have known we were in the clear if my cell or my Internet service worked below ground level. Note to self: add a severe weather alert radio to the emergency provisions tub.

CUT TO . . .

Packing a hospital "go" bag and decorating a nursery did nothing to prepare me for my birth experience. But at least I got more out of the deal than just a dented laptop and some wet, smelly dogs.

My cradle chronicles

You can plan a luxurious seaside vacation, an elaborate wedding, a birthday dinner, and a romantic date night with your husband. You can even plan a wild bachelorette party that culminates in streaking down Main Street with tassels on your boobs, singing the theme song from *Saved By the Bell* at the top of your lungs. Though I'd advise against that. But you know what you *can't* plan? Your birth experience.

And that's coming from a self-proclaimed anal-retentive, über-organized, type-A perfectionistic, obsessive-compulsive, Post-it note queen of the neurotic kind. No amount of micromanaging could have groomed me for having complications that led to delivering my first daughter three weeks early, via C-section.

That isn't to say you'll be surprised by a similar experience. No two experiences are the same, and I hope your delivery is smoother than Patrick Stewart's head.

You can pick your doctor, your hospital, your baby daddy, and your nose (my inner child had to add that), but you can't pick exactly when your kid is going to make his show-stopping, Krameresque entrance. For the most part, unless you know early on that you'll be scheduling a C-section, you're stuck playing the waiting game just like the rest of us.

I won't lie: the closer you get to your delivery date, the longer the days seem to drag on. By the time forty weeks rolls around, twenty-four hours will have you sweating it like you're stuck on a deserted island braving continuous stand-up comedy from a scantily clad Carrot Top. Okay, maybe it's not *that* excruciating.

Your baby will be on his own schedule, and it helps to accept that fact sooner rather than later. Who knows? Maybe you'll be the one person in a million who has her baby right on time. I met one woman who said her baby came first thing in the morning on her actual due date, so miracles *do* happen. But generally speaking, you'll need to pay closer attention to your body clock rather than the one hanging on your wall.

Nothing made me realize just how easily my plans and checklists could fall apart quite like having a baby. And you know what surprised me most? It didn't bother me the way I assumed it would. I've discovered I enjoy going with the flow more often. Which is a good thing, since it's unavoidable. To a reasonable extent, as a mom you learn to plan not to have plans. Inevitably, just when you've scheduled a vacation, your child will come down with the flu or chicken pox. You can thank good ol' Murphy and his law for that, the meddling rat bastard. It doesn't mean you can't take a vacation for the next eighteen years; you just do what you can to make sure it's refundable! When you go into labor, I hope you have your suitcase at the ready, you're well rested, and you have to push only twice before little Georgie-Porgie bursts out like a kernel of Jiffy Pop. A girl can dream, right?

Making way for baby

Here are some helpful ways to ease into the process of getting ready.

Take the time out to take some time out.

When people tell you you're going to feel exhausted, they mean you might find it overwhelming to simply lift the TV remote and change the channel. As much as I love staying busy, pregnancy made me crash like I was coming down off of a bulk package of Pixy Stix. I know it's tough to slow down, especially when the nesting instinct is kicking into overdrive, but do yourself a favor and relax. I was notorious for ignoring my own advice on this when I was pregnant with Gray. By the time Marlowe was born, I was chasing after a two-year-old. Sitting down was harder to come by than an honest politician.

When you're expending the kind of energy it requires to grow a human, the rest of you tends to shut down. Why fight it? Close your eyes for a few minutes and refuel. Watch a repeat of *Full House,* flip through a magazine, get a pregnancy massage (my personal favorite), stretch your body, or sit and meditate in silence for a while. Whatever your choice method, the key is to rest while you can. When the baby comes, there will be a lot less time for that sort of leisurely alone time, so get it while the gettin' is good!

Prepare your hospital "go" bag well in advance.

Unless you want to send your husband home to pick out clothes for you (you know, the guy who doesn't mind wearing two different socks to work and thinks wrinkles merely add character to his dress shirts), you're better off getting this task out of the way before he winds up doing it for you.

Starting early also allows you time to ease into your packing process. Because if you're anything like me, it's a more elaborate production than *The Lion King* on Broadway. I actually left my suitcase open in our bedroom over the course of a few weeks and slowly added to it. I thought of new and improved necessities on a daily basis. One day I would tell myself, *Hey! I should bring a loose, comfy outfit to put on when I leave the hospital.* The next day I might think, *Ooh. I should make myself an iPod list and pack my travel speakers.*

I'm lying. I totally had a novel-length Excel sheet of amenities I planned to drag with me because I get off on being an *i*-dotter, *t*-crosser, and list maker. But I still forgot a few things here and there. This gave me a chance to think of them before I was in panic mode.

Packing early will also give you a chance to remove any excess items you may have spontaneously (stupidly) tossed in. Be smart about your decisions; no one needs scented candles and lingerie in the delivery room, as tempting as the inclination may be. You aren't headed to Hawaii here, ladies. Comfort is key, and no one cares if you aren't wearing a matching shade of lipstick. Not to mention, there's no shade of lipstick that complements washed-out hospital-gown white. On a good note, if you forget to pack underwear, no worries; the hospital will be giving you proper granny panties. I only wish I were kidding . . . More on that debacle later. For more ideas on which items you shouldn't forget, see chapter 7, "Anatomy of a Hospital Experience."

Once you've finished packing your overnight bag, keep

that sucker by the door or in your vehicle trunk! Many an overwhelmed, freaked-out father-to-be has forgotten to grab the suitcase while trying to rush his wife to the hospital, and there's no reason to set your hubby up for failure. There's plenty of opportunity for that later on.

Here's the biggest piece of advice I have to offer: don't worry if you end up in the hospital with only the clothes on your back! Despite my insistence on getting yourself packed up in advance, it's not the end of the world if you forget everything. The most important thing is a healthy baby and a healthy *you*! The rest will get sorted out. In my experience, you're off to a good start if you have a car seat to bring your newborn home from the hospital in. Beyond that, everything else will fall into place.

Don't fret if the nursery isn't perfect when you give birth.
Unless you have an HGTV design team coming in to decorate the place for you, don't give yourself a hard time if the nursery isn't 100 percent baby-ready when you go into labor. Be gentle on yourself! It may not be practical to climb ladders and hang mobiles when you're physically imbalanced and waddling more than Donald Duck. Having the baby's room ready is truly a luxury, not a necessity. In the beginning, it's really there for storage of all things baby-related and to give family members something to "ooh" and "ahh" over when they visit. The baby doesn't care if the nursery wallpaper isn't up yet; he won't be seeing past your boobs for a few months. If you're anything like we are, the changing table will be the only reason the nursery gets any love for the first four months.

More than likely, it's destined to be one giant dirty diaper distribution center until your baby is old enough to sleep and play in it. And by then you'll be ready to redecorate.

Don't wait until the eleventh hour to have your baby shower, diaper drop, or other celebratory event.
I know some folks who thought it sounded like a good idea to have their shower two weeks before they were due. Guess who the guest of honor turned out to be? Yep, that's right. Mr. I Arrived a Month Early. Brad and I had our coed shower five weeks before Gray was scheduled to arrive, and I wound up having her two weeks later. You just never know!

The last few weeks of my pregnancies were also when I felt most uncomfortable. It may have had something to do with the unseasonably warm weather we had in both instances, but it was my body's response to getting closer to delivery too. Having a celebration well in advance meant I (mostly) avoided looking like an overbaked puff pastry in front of all my friends and family. It also meant I wasn't knocking every guest down like they were bowling pins as I made a beeline for the hors d'oeuvres table.

Another benefit of an early shower is that it still gives you enough time to use gift certificates and make returns to Babies "R" Us. You will, inevitably, wind up with two copies of *Goodnight Moon* and a few too many wipe warmers. Since you won't feel like running around for a while once the baby arrives, it's nice to get as many errands out of the way as you can.

If you cuss like a sailor, start to curb your enthusiasm.
Let the profanity ship sail *before* the baby is born so you won't

have to endure additional torture down the road (ie, when your kid embarrasses you in front of the day care teacher, who looks at you like you've been force-feeding him George Carlin before tucking him into bed each night).

Vulgarity is a hard habit to break; I know this from experience. I have always found expletives to be a delightful accompaniment for storytelling and, truthfully, I was reluctant to shelve them. Hence, my liberal use of them in this book. However, I knew I needed to cease and desist in front of my baby.

My husband and I turned our obscenity disposal into a fun game of "Who can come up with the most ridiculous curse substitute?" This made our efforts challenging and funny and, consequently, easier to accomplish. My reigning favorites are "Oh, Frappuccino!" "Fluffernutter!" and "Sugarpops!" Lame, yes, but also highly amusing after you've just dropped a Dutch oven on your toe.

Preset your infant car seat.
One of the best suggestions we received was to set up the seat long before there was a baby around to ride in it. We were incredibly grateful for that guidance.

Not only was it one less device to fret over during crunch time, but it was good to get accustomed to driving around with it. After the baby arrives, there can be quite a few "Holy crap, I have a kid back there!" moments.

Another fantastic suggestion was to have the local police or fire department show us how to accurately install our car seat. We tried a few firehouses before figuring out the police department was the route to go. In our experience, the firefighters were wonderfully kind, but clueless about baby equipment. So decided when one of them told us, "We're clueless about baby equipment."

The police department was a different story altogether. Initially, we felt silly for asking, but the cop who assisted us was awesome and understanding. She actually said she wished more people would come in to request help with proper installation. After all, there's precious cargo going in there! The bottom line? Good things come to those who let the cops correctly install their baby car seat. And by good, I mean it's one less point of contention between you and your husband when, although he insists he's got it in correctly, the seat is bouncing around in the backseat like Tigger on uppers.

Prep some food and freeze it.
A lot of women begin to feel that peculiar nesting instinct in the weeks leading up to delivery. Even if you generally shun that Martha Stewart–like need to keep your house more sparkling than Christmas tinsel, you may find yourself dusting and polishing with the best of them. That said, you can fluff the crib bedding or wash the newborn clothes only so many times before you start driving yourself (and your husband) crazy. Want to feel super useful? Pull out a few of your favorite freezer-friendly recipes and make some meals you can defrost once the baby is born. If you're lucky, some of your friends will drop off a casserole or two in the days following your return

from the hospital, but it never hurts to have some premade meals to resort to if need be (especially if you have a spouse like mine, who doesn't cook—Kraft Macaroni & Cheese notwithstanding). Lasagnas and stews are always good choices, as they can generally feed the family for more than one dinner, and they survive in the freezer like a postnuclear cockroach. My personal favorite? My homemade eggplant parmesan. I spent hours prepping two platters of it prior to having my first daughter, and I was incredibly thankful I did.

Though that leads me to a quick warning: prepping food in advance can be somewhat of a balancing act when you're also trying to stay off your feet as much as possible. The heat of the oven mixed with the energy spent cooking isn't a terribly good combo, and you're liable to balloon up like you're starring in the Macy's Thanksgiving Day Parade. My feet swelled like sausages during the construction of that eggplant parmesan. And I'm not referring to the yummy little breakfast wieners; I'm talking about the bulbous kind that make you wonder how anyone with a mouth smaller than Steven Tyler's can eat them. I wound up rolling back and forth across my kitchen on my husband's office chair just so I could finish layering the dish. It was like dinner theater at the roller derby.

Don't be afraid to make a birth plan; just get ready to be flexible with it.

No woman should labor for hours on end without any say in how it all goes down. You have every right to put together a list of things that compose your ideal birth experience. You *should* go into it feeling secure in what you want and being armed with enough knowledge to provide instructions that reflect your personal comfort level, even if that instruction winds up being, "Get that baby out of me yesterday!"

Once you have a general outline, it's significantly easier to adjust accordingly. As long as you go into the birthing process with realistic expectations of yourself, and the wisdom to know you may change your mind in the middle of everything, you are a step ahead. Don't beat yourself up, for example, if you were dead set on having a natural birth but then you suddenly start screaming for an epidural instead. (Who knew you might be begging for someone to shove a needle in your spine, huh?) At the end of the day, it's important to make your birth experience look the way you want it to, while working with the doctors to ensure the choices you make are the most medically sound options for both you and your baby.

There may be vital decisions the doctors need you to consider, and it's better if you've given the important stuff some forethought. Critical decision making while you're in the throes of contraction hysteria isn't terribly productive for anyone. It's good for your husband to be involved in any major decisions as well, such as whether he'll remain with you or with the baby if the baby has to be whisked away to the NICU or transitional nursery. This way, he isn't merely serving as your labor-pain hand holder, verbal punching bag, and purveyor of smuggled nonhospital food. Yes, it's your body, but it's possible he might be able to offer a more balanced, level-headed view while there's a tiny human hurtling out of your body. I'm just saying. If you have a husband who's prone to fainting at the sight of blood, on the other hand, you are exempt from my last comment.

Part of developing your birth plan should involve research. Listen to your pediatrician, your OB-GYN, and other medical professionals you trust. You may also opt to consult your mother-in-law, your sister, and fellow mommies you feel you can count on for honesty and support. I certainly don't think that's a bad idea, but don't let all your knowledge come from them. Or from me, for that matter!

Most of us are guilty of overstudying on this one, and none of us—be it family member, doctor, blogger, author, preacher, soapbox-speech deliverer, or random nosy mommy at the park—can tell you everything you need to know. We can tell you only what we've gleaned for ourselves. You can read books, surf Google, and peruse articles until your head is about to explode like one of those middle school baking soda volcano experiments, but the most important source for knowledge is *you*. At the end of the day, trust your own instincts. No one can tell you what you're comfortable with but you, so feel empowered by it! See chapter 10, "Driving around the Mommy Learning Curve," for more on that.

Engage in some seriously positive thinking.
All joking aside, I feel viewing your child's birth in a positive manner is an important component of delivery. I may be a little saucy, but I'm also a believer in searching for silver linings. I mentally prepared for giving birth to both of my daughters

in much the same way I embark upon other experiences that I'm particularly apprehensive about, such as getting on an airplane. (The difference being that I didn't take a Xanax or down a few Bloody Marys before delivering my girls.) Did I look toward giving birth with sunshiny thoughts and Pollyanna-like optimism? Did I blissfully don my little rose-colored glasses and think it would be fluffy puppies and fairy dust? Not exactly. I had confidence in the love and support of my husband, and I counted on the strength of the medical professionals around me. In my heart of hearts, I had faith that my babies and I were going to come out of it all right, and I left the rest up to God and fate. Granted, I might be able to chalk some of that positive outlook up to the pre-C-section-meds super high, but I still stand by the power of good vibes.

Take solace in the fact that billions of women have done this before you. Babies come into this world every day, so even though it's a new personal experience for each of us, we aren't inventing the wheel!

Skip the stress.

Stress is a serious detriment for both you and the baby during pregnancy, so do your best to breathe through those nine months. Even when your mother-in-law is struck by the meteor of poor judgment and decides to tell you how colossal you look in the only maternity outfit you were feeling slim in. Smile and tell her how awesome she looks in her classy velvet jogging suit and pearls too. If you're lucky, she'll take the hint.

I'm a firm believer that babies can feel some of what we

do—that they get a dose of our emotional output, if you will. I'm not suggesting your kid has ESP, but I'm of the mind-set that your mood has an effect on your unborn child. How could it not? Our babies can develop a taste for certain foods based on what we consume during pregnancy, so why not emotions too? If you spend your entire pregnancy agitated and freaking out, I think some of that seeps through.

Bond with your baby before birth.

Take some time each day to develop your mother-child bond. Recite poetry, make up songs, read books aloud, rub your Buddha belly, and say "I love you" often. Any effort is a posi-tive one as far as I'm concerned, because it establishes a con-nection that will continue to grow as you and your child learn more about one another. It's common knowledge that babies recognize voices when they emerge from the womb, so rein-force that as much as possible!

Take classes at the hospital where you plan to deliver.

Early on, my husband and I agreed we would take some of the childbirth education tutorials offered at our hospital. It was just as much about getting us comfortable with the location and process as it was about learning the how-to. It was benefi-cial to have a meeting of the minds and get on the same page where labor and delivery were concerned. Not to mention, it was priceless to see my husband learn how to change a diaper for the first time. It was even better when he discovered that the real thing squirms a heck of a lot more than the plastic doll.

If it makes it more tolerable, you can think of the classes

as some extra date time and plan them around a fun lunch together. Brad even wound up taking the breastfeeding course with me, and I swear it wasn't so he could salivate over Power-Point presentation slides of boobs.

We actually enjoyed the classes we took, finding them not only informative but fun. Do you want a visual that will last you a lifetime? Convince your husband to try on a faux maternity suit if the instructor has one on hand. It mimics the realistic weight of a woman's belly and breasts during the third trimester, and it is sure to leave your husband feeling a little more busty . . . ahem . . . I mean, sympathetic. Just be sure you have your camera ready. He should never be allowed to live that down.

Don't let your weight gain weigh too heavily upon you.
You may or may not gain more weight than the online maternity sources say you should, but don't let that preoccupy your thoughts or keep you from indulging in a special little treat every now and then. If having a piece of chocolate keeps you sane in the middle of a workday, do it! (Provided you don't have gestational diabetes, that is.) Hopefully you have enough willpower not to overindulge and you're getting some exercise to balance it out—even if that exercise simply involves try-ing to tie your own shoes. In my experience, there is a fair-ly wide range of what's normal when discussing pregnancy weight gain. Even when I put on a few more pounds than the supposed experts online said I should, my doctors didn't seem to be concerned. I think the idea is to avoid using pregnancy as an excuse to devour a lifetime supply of Twinkies; it's not

to count calories like you're training for the next Ironman Triathlon. Watch yourself, but don't ignore the psychological benefits of an occasional splurge!

THE MORAL OF MY STORY

No amount of advice or research completely prepared me for having a baby. Anticipating the what, when, where, and how of labor and delivery is equivalent to waiting for the Yellowstone supervolcano to explode. Been there, done that, nearly lost my shit. But you know what? Plan or no plan, your baby is on his way to see you! Woohoo!

Poor Brad, learning diaper changing the hard way. The nastiness has been blurred to spare Gray from future embarrassment. And to keep you from vomiting. *Photo courtesy of Jenna von Oy.*

CHAPTER 6

Father Knows Best,
but First He Needs to Be Schooled!

A SCENIC VIEW OF MY PAST

My father studied to be a Catholic priest. I know that sounds like the start of a joke, but it's the truth. He attended seminary in his twenties, took his first vows, and then decided it wasn't his calling. He later met my mom, got married, had kids, and the rest is history. That's the *Reader's Digest* version.

My mom has always avidly emphasized that she did not cause my dad to turn away from the priesthood, lest we perceive her to be some sort of man-hunting heathen who stole the innocence of a Bible-toting, cassock-wearing man of God—so I suppose I should do the same. I know, I know, semantics. But if nothing else, I'll do my due diligence to help keep her good name clear. And, of course, to dodge any superfluous drama at our next family Christmas.

In case you're curious, my parents actually met while they were both working at the same hotel chain in Connecticut. My dad has admitted he couldn't help but notice my mother's short skirts, so apparently his mind had already strayed from the priesthood for good by then. Or those were some seriously memorable skirts.

My father always kept close ties with the church, and I grew up learning about (and appreciating) God and religion, while simultaneously knowing I would never be drawn to becoming a nun. I had too much sass in my spirit, liked to push the envelope, was overly animated, didn't know how to keep my mouth shut (obviously that's still an issue), enjoyed randomly bursting into song, and got a kick out of sneaking cuss words in when I thought I could get away with it. I don't think most folks were confused about my career path. I also suspect I would have looked like a pygmy penguin in a nun's habit, which could have been a little weird. But I digress.

Perhaps my mystification over why someone would knowingly choose to forfeit all the fun things in life is why, at the ripe old age of fourteen, I was so fascinated by the idea of accompanying my dad to Belgium to attend a reunion at the American college where he'd studied for the priesthood so many years before. Though for the record, if my daughters ever tell me they want to swear off boys and join a convent, I'm all for it.

And so it was that my dad and I embarked on a journey to Europe for a week's worth of bonding, history lessons, delighting in the marvel that is Euro Disney, and . . . getting me tipsy for the first time while chillin' with the priests. Which every kid should experience at least once.

It goes a little something like this: we were staying at the college itself, having been offered a room in one of the student dorms. Now, don't go picturing the typical university accommodations festooned with lava lamps, beanbag chairs, day-old skivvies littering the floor, and an inconspicuous bong stashed in the corner. These were rooms used strictly for the theology school, so they were minimal and uncorrupted, to say the least. Forget about coed; I had the only set of breasts for as far as the eye could see. And at fourteen, I had damn good eyesight.

My dad and I spent our first day exploring the town, praising the sights, and meeting some of my dad's old school buddies, aka clergymen. It was a bizarre scene for a teenage girl who spent the majority of her time on a sound stage, jacked up on coffee from the craft service table, and making audiences laugh with secular humor.

Anyway, that evening, my dad asked me to join him for dinner. Rather than remain at the college, we set out on a little adventure, choosing a local restaurant where we could dine on something slightly more gourmet than university fare. And since we Catholics so infamously love our wine, my dad ordered himself a glass.

I grew up in a very European family, so it wasn't unheard of to be given a token sip (and I do mean a severely watered-down token sip) of wine at the dinner table every now and then. Still, I was somewhat surprised when my dad asked if I wanted to join him. "There's a lovely little drink I think you'd enjoy called a Kir Royale," he told me. "It's essentially champagne with a little crème de cassis in it."

Not wanting to look a gift horse in the mouth, I pretended to contemplate for a moment, then nodded as nonchalantly as I could. Meanwhile, my insides were screaming, "Holy shit! I get to drink in Europe!"

As if reading my thoughts, my dad informed me that kids overseas are allowed to drink earlier than those in the States. I'm still not sure I made the cutoff, but I went with it.

At this point in my story, I think I should mention that my dad wasn't trying to snub authority, contribute to the delinquency of a minor, or try too hard to get his adolescent daughter to think he was cool by giving her alcohol. None of those ideas would have been on his radar. He grew up the child of German immigrants, so he savored the opportunity to introduce me to his European lifestyle and let me partake in a bit of supervised leniency while on vacation.

Of course, he failed to take into consideration that I was the size of a Keebler Elf. God bless him, my daddy got me slightly sloshed in Belgium. I didn't realize this fact until I got up to use the restroom, whereupon I virtually cascaded down a flight of stairs.

Given the ancient cobblestone streets, my walk back to the college was a bit wobbly. My dad was so busy pointing out the impressive architecture that I don't think he even caught on. We made it back to our holy refuge, and I quickly fell asleep—make that passed out—under the wooden cross that hung over my dorm bed. Ah, there's nothing like having the room spin while sleeping under the watchful eye of Jesus.

CUT TO . . .

My dad isn't the only one whose judgment has been slightly impaired a time or two in the colossal undertaking we call parenthood. My husband and I quickly found we weren't exempt from it either. Having a child is like conducting a giant Rube Goldberg experiment, where one inconsequential tug can set off an inexplicable chain reaction that doesn't stop until they're blaming you for it twenty-five years later in their parenting memoirs. (Speaking of which, thanks for being such a good sport on this one, Daddy!) But changing a diaper incorrectly or putting a Onesie on backwards isn't going to make or break your child's life. Ladies, butter your husband up with a cold brew and hand this chapter over. I'll do my best to educate him for you!

My cradle chronicles

Husbands, we acknowledge that you are trying to speed around the parenting learning curve too. We know you have questions, anxieties, and concerns about becoming a new parent like we mommies do. You just don't have an inflated belly to show for it. We hope.

I imagine your wife just handed you this book and said, "Here, honey, read this." I also respect that you'd probably rather be grabbing a beer with the guys, mowing the lawn, or devising a pulley system to transport storage tubs back and forth across the attic. Wouldn't we all? But for her sake, please take a few minutes to at least skim this chapter. Her hormones are raging right now, and she's more uncomfortable than a whale in a goldfish bowl, so if you can find it in your heart to indulge her for a moment, it will mean a lot to her. As a reward, I'll try not to make this painful for you. My husband, Brad, gave a lot of input on this chapter, so it's chock-full of awesome technojargon and obscure movie references that will tantalize your testosterone. (It's really not, but I thought that might pique your interest.) I just figured, who better to help ease your fears than someone else who has recently been through the crap you're going through?

To be fair, you've put up with the mood swings, the 4:00 a.m. binges, the retching at all hours of the night, the displaced hormones, the sexual hiatus, and the obligatory preparatory talk of infant poop. You deserve some appreciation too, am I right? Go pour yourself a nip of something strong, turn on ESPN for white noise, and let's talk about your exciting-terrifying-wonderful impending fatherhood.

If your current perception of being a daddy comes from watching *Raising Arizona* five thousand and one times, we may have some work to do. That said, most first-time dads aren't instinctually predisposed to don their Mr. Mom aprons, nor does anyone expect you to be. If it's any consolation, my husband had never changed a diaper before we had our first daughter, and he was nervous to hold her for fear he'd break something. Guess what. That's totally normal. Any guy who isn't at all worried about holding a dainty, itty-bitty human for the first time is as emotionless as a Vulcan.

SOME GUY-FRIENDLY GUIDANCE

Not to bludgeon you with stereotypes, but in case you aren't prone to asking for directions, we thought we'd go ahead and provide some unprompted guidance for you. Consider us your baby GPS system.

The prepaternal panic

Just because you aren't carrying the baby doesn't mean you don't have your work cut out for you too! I encourage you to speak with some of your friends who have already been through this stage of their lives. They'll pat you on the back, congratulate you, offer you a cigar, and tell you how upside down your world is about to become . . . in the best possible way.

According to my better half, Brad, it all begins the moment you find out your wife is carrying your future legacy. Something inside of you clicks and you start observing every move she makes with the keen eye of a baseball scout. Or a subway pickpocket. I'm not trying to insinuate that you feel your wife is suddenly chopped liver and you only care about your belly-inhabiting son or daughter, and I'm definitely not implying that you now view your spouse as nothing but a baby messenger. Though if that thought has crossed your mind, you may want to buy her some flowers on your way home from work. But you might perceive your significant other to be more delicate now and want to shield her from everything that could potentially hurt her or the baby. You have probably entered perpetual protector mode and could hold your own in a Tarantino film. I don't blame you, and I hope she doesn't either, but you may need to curb your enthusiasm a little. Your spotlight might be blinding her.

Please refrain from swiping the soft cheese off her fork

during your date night or freaking out because she had a glass of wine ten minutes before she discovered there was a bun in the oven. You might want to keep your comments in check too. Voicing the sentence "Man, that dress is getting a little snug, huh?" may not be an ideal move. No one likes to be scrutinized, and she really just wants your support above all else. If you need to address concerns, calm and patience are key. Since she may not have much of either right now, you might need to conjure up a little extra to compensate.

How to "mommy" your wife

Once the initial shock of my pregnancy wore off, Brad's primary concern was making sure I was comfortable. He held my hair back while I puked and frequently drove across town to retrieve any food we thought I might be able to keep down. "No distance is too far," he informed me.

My hubby isn't some self-sacrificing knight at my every beck and call. He was just a typical, first-time daddy, also known as helpless. Once the insemination transaction is complete, you're pretty much benched until the baby arrives, which can leave you floundering for ways to contribute. You may already be discovering there's an innate need to help in any way possible, since you aren't the one carrying your future poop machine . . . I mean, sleepless, boob-hijacking junior . . . I mean, sweet little squirt.

You may find yourself pushing food on your wife like you're her Jewish mother or reallocating your beer money for diapers (we promise not to tell your golfing buddies).

The fact is, there's only so much you can do to assist during these nine (technically ten) months of maternity mayhem. Try to be as composed as possible and get used to asking the all-important question, "What can I do to help?" This is really an expectant mom's favorite thing to hear. And if your wife is anything like me, she loves giving you her input! If you consistently ask that question of us, we don't feel like we have to ask more of you than you want to give, and that's a beautiful thing.

It's definitely okay to offer us some TLC too. "Please don't ask if you can massage my feet," said no woman ever. (Just be sure you avoid any pressure points that can induce labor. It sounds hokey, but look it up.)

Another key phrase will be *follow-through*. Here's the rule of thumb: if you tell your wife you're going to take care of washing the dishes so she can get off her swollen feet for a while, make sure you do them. Don't let her wake up the following morning to a sink full of dirty plates and utensils, or you've only succeeded in procrastinating her work efforts. On top of that, now she's grumbling (whether internally or externally) about the fact that you've left her high and dry. Or not so dry, as the case may be. While we know your offer was made with good intentions, good intentions don't help us scrub pots and pans.

Depending on the circumstances surrounding your child's birth, you may wind up having to take over your wife's portion of the household duties. Please try not to make her feel bad about it. Being pregnant isn't a walk in the park, and sometimes there are complications beyond our control.

When I wound up on bed rest for the final week of my first pregnancy, my husband immediately had to begin handling all the cooking and cleaning. It drove me nuts to give up my micromanaging impulses and, on top of that, I felt incredibly guilty. Thankfully, Brad was quick to remind me that I was already pulling my weight (forty additional pounds of it, to be exact). He also reminded me that we were both accountable for the well-being of our child. If that meant I needed to spend my days on bed rest with my feet up, drinking a swimming pool's worth of water, then so be it. Or as he phrased it, "Even if a giant sinkhole had opened up underneath us, I would still have made sure your feet were up and you had a glass of water in your hand." He took the doctor's orders as earnestly as I did, and that meant the world to me.

Sometimes we just need to hear that you won't be mad at us for shirking our normal responsibilities, even if we know you know it was ordered by our doctor. Offer your wife a few pillows, turn on an episode of something frivolous, and let her veg out. It's your chance to be an integral part of the birthing experience! Even if cleaning toilets wasn't exactly what you had in mind.

Hot, cold, and downright frigid

During pregnancy (and potentially after it too), some women want to be cuddled constantly and some don't want to be touched at all. We can transition from porn queen to ice queen in seconds. If you aren't sure what mood your wife is in, your best bet is to ask. Of course, she may have no idea what she wants either, so your patience is much appreciated.

I know it's tough to imagine what she is experiencing physically, but maybe this will help: if you went on an all-night distillery crawl, got your ass whooped in an underground fight club, and woke up with raw nipples because you thought it was a good idea to have the word *bromance* tattooed across your chest, it still wouldn't come close to what your wife has going on in her body right now. Every second of every day. Don't be afraid to instigate the romance and physical attention, but try not to hold a grudge if she's just not that into it. You never know, maybe five minutes from now she'll be attacking you like something out of your wildest dreams.

To be or not to be involved

I can answer this question quite simply: be involved. This isn't a repeat of your wedding day, where you can just show up in a tux to walk down the aisle and everyone is happy as long as you're shaved and relatively sober. This is an event that requires your full participation. The good news? You don't have to deal with the outrageous wedding planner, the cake tasting that interferes with the Super Bowl, putting a giant hole in your wallet on stupid emasculating details such as tulle chair bows, dance lessons to impress people who already like you, and having to withstand a week's worth of pre-wedding activities with your wife's family. This is your time to step up to the plate and shine, my friend! It's all about being as good of a sport as you can possibly be. If you can find it in yourself to put on a brave face and paint the nursery so she doesn't have to inhale the fumes, accompany her to as many doctor appointments as your work schedule will allow, and assemble the crib (you are officially a saint), I promise you have your wife's gratitude. If you feel like going above and beyond the call of duty, then help her sign up for baby registries and be the first guy to wear the pregnancy simulation suit at the hospital birthing class. Be sure to send me a photo of it so I can express my gratitude as well . . . you know, right after I finish laughing at your expense and plastering it all over my social media pages.

Pack a hospital "go" bag.
Your wife is already in the middle of packing her necessities (no, she probably doesn't need all that stuff, but it's a bad time to question why she's bringing push-up bras and a copy of *Pretty Woman*), so now it's time for you to do the same. Yes, you'll need a hospital "go" bag too! Hey, at least I didn't call it a man purse (more commonly and scarily referred to as a "murse.") If it makes it sound more manly, feel free to call it your overnight attaché, delivery duffle, or something more spiffy and dignified. If planning and forethought aren't normally in your vocabulary, try them on for size just this once. If you can accomplish this task a few months in advance of your baby's due date and leave your bag to rendezvous with your wife's ginormous suitcase until it's delivery departure time, you're a rock star. This keeps your spouse from having to pack additional toiletries and clothes on your behalf, and it means you won't have to return home seven times while she's in labor just so you can retrieve your contacts and boxer shorts.

As a side note, that's the absolute *worst* time you can choose to leave her alone at the hospital. I recommend avoiding that at all costs unless you're prepared to meet the wrath of the wild-eyed, hyperventilating pregnant juggernaut you call your wife.

PACKING YOUR DELIVERY DUFFLE

Here are the things I recommend you take along.

1. Pajamas and/or sweats

At the very least, you'll be comfortable while your wife is squeezing your hand like an accordion during contractions and while you camp out on that rigid, wretched cot they'll kindly call your bed. For that matter, bring your pillow along too.

2. Underwear

Don't shoot the messenger. The fact is, if you forget to pack an item, it'll more than likely be something important. And underwear is important.

3. Toiletries

Be sure to pack a toothbrush, toothpaste, contacts, shaving kit, and anything else you might need. In a worst-case scenario, you can probably get most of these items at the hospital gift shop, but you might spend more than you bargained for. And you'll need every penny you can get for your kid's education fund.

4. Your cell phone and charger

This will double as a photo and video camera so you can document all of your baby's first moments. You'll also want to contact your family members and friends with the good news, so you'll need a fully charged cell phone. Send a brief text or e-mail that includes the baby's name, height, weight, and time of birth. Those are the key facts that most folks (read: all friends and family members of the female persuasion) are dying to know. Let everyone know mom and baby are fine and that you are thankful for their love and support. Tell them you will be in touch after you've had some family time. Helpful tip: Do not respond when people start texting or e-mailing you back. This isn't time to tell your buddy in Peoria all about how babies are born or to assure your mom that you brought a sweater along in case the maternity ward gets chilly. Go cherish some time with your new expanded family!

5. Reading material or any number of electronic companions (aka stress reducers)

This may be in the form of an iPad, iPod, laptop, Kindle, or whatever other gadget is currently floating your cutting-edge, technogeek boat. You may also opt for a good old-fashioned hardcover book, in which case you have my utmost respect. No matter what you choose, you'll need it during the (often extended) waiting periods. My only advice is to refrain from skimming *Huffington Post* headlines or perusing *Wall Street Journal* articles while your wife is in the height of labor pain. She's likely to clock you with a nearby fetal monitor. If nothing else, it'll earn you dirtier looks than you got when you disclosed your crush on Princess Leia.

6. Refreshments

Protein bars are good, as are crackers or mixed nuts. A snack selection will prevent you from having to leave your wife to run to the hospital commissary when your stomach is growling louder than a monster truck. Your kid isn't wearing a watch in the womb, and Murphy's Law dictates that the second you leave he'll make his illustrious entrance, so you may not want to go on a lengthy quest for a vending machine. As a side note, don't bring any snacks that have to be refrigerated; you aren't going to a five-star resort with fancy accommodations. For that matter, you aren't even going to an ice-fishing shack with crappy accommodations. And make sure your wife is cool with you eating while she's in labor. Because a death stare from a hungry woman in labor can be alarming.

Great expectations

Here are some guidelines to assist you with your hospital experience.

Have a plan in place.

Help your wife make as many medical decisions as possible in advance of labor and delivery. In other words, make sure you have a mutually agreed-upon plan in place. For example, my husband and I had already discussed the fact that he would accompany our daughters if they had to be taken to the NICU or transitional nursery immediately following their births. Because our first daughter had to be delivered three weeks early via C-section, this decision wound up being a highly important one. In the moments before they whisked her away from me, my husband didn't need to feel torn about who to stay with. Making an impromptu decision of that magnitude isn't fair when you've just witnessed your

wife going through major surgery and your baby is simultaneously having trouble breathing. Though part of Brad felt he
should remain rooted to my bedside, he knew he was expected
to stay with our newborn daughter while they got her breathing stabilized. My point? There will be plenty of decisions to
make, so at least have a leg up on it all. Center yourself, find
your instincts, and have a game plan.

Be your wife's ally and advocate.
If your wife has created a birthing plan, make sure the nurses
and doctors are in on it. It will be easier for you to be the
mouthpiece while your wife is concentrating on pushing a
baby out. You aren't just her husband now—you are also her
voice, her support system, her labor coach, her pep-talk giver,
her hospital staff liaison, her hand holder, and her mental
health manager. The latter sounds significantly easier than it
is, by the way. As with a touchdown pass in football, you may
need to run some interference every now and then. I'm not
saying tackle everyone in scrubs and send them careening into
medical equipment. I'm saying keep your eyes and ears open
and don't be afraid to ask what's going on if you aren't sure.

Childbirth ain't pretty.
No, really, it's like something out of *Alien 3*, so don't kid yourself. If you're squeamish, be honest about it and don't let pride
get the better of you. Tell the nurses before they find out the
hard way! They'll help you find a spot in the room that allows
you to be supportive without being quite so hands-on. The

hospital doesn't need to worry about you fainting or throwing up while they're trying to usher your kid into the world.

Your new son or daughter isn't going to arrive all prettied up in a bow, looking ready for the Junior America beauty pageant. Instead, she'll be covered in a viscous white goo that looks like you've just dunked her in a marshmallow fluff bath. She may also be a lovely shade of purple, which can be slightly disconcerting if you were expecting your progeny to come out looking more like you than Grimace, that old McDonald's character. A pointed head is common with babies who are delivered vaginally, but refrain from tweeting out comparisons to Dan Aykroyd in his *SNL* Conehead skit. Tell your little lad he's the most handsome guy you've ever seen, and keep in mind that his skull will eventually round itself out. Either way, hopefully you won't have time to contemplate something as trivial as head shape, when you're too busy welling up with more emotion than Brett Favre did during his retirement announcement. The first one.

Help your wife find some breathing room.
Make sure your counterpart has a little space for the first hour or two after baby is born. Don't invite friends and family in unless you're absolutely certain that's what she wants. If you need to hurt someone's feelings, let it be your brother, not the woman who just delivered your offspring. You will both want some quality time to ogle and adore your little angel, so don't allow the room to become a convention center. It can easily get out of hand when everyone is excited to see the new

arrival! If you're both really gung-ho on having visitors so you can immediately show off your brand-new bundle of joy, try to make the session short and sweet. Your guests will understand everyone needs some rest-and-repair time.

Expect that breastfeeding may be a source of frustration and hard work.

If your wife is planning to go the formula route, you can skip ahead. Otherwise, I hope you will read this passage at least once.

Breastfeeding may not be instantly easy and comfortable for your wife and child. It can be a beautiful bonding experience. Not to mention, it offers important health benefits and advantages for baby. However, it also takes some serious getting used to. This learning curve will involve you as well, because it can drastically affect your wife's disposition, sleep schedule, and daily outlook. It's not always an innate skill, and it can be very challenging, stressful, and isolating when it doesn't go smoothly. The truth is, I've witnessed more friends go through hell and back over breastfeeding than any other aspect of motherhood.

While in his twenties, my husband spent some time working in the cattle industry. During the cattle stint, it was quite common for Brad to be around birthing animals, so according to him, he was fairly familiar with the breastfeeding concept. Did I just say my husband compared my nursing our newborn daughter to a cow having her teats gnawed on by her calf? Yes. Yes, I did. If you think it seems like a bad plan to attempt to juxtapose your wife and a bovine, you're probably correct. This is especially true when pregnancy already has her feeling bloated and heifer-like. However, in my case, I knew my husband was coming from a place of good intentions. My hubby had seen many a calf suckling her mama cow, and he knew there wasn't always an automatic union. Still, he was very surprised by the discipline and training it took to get our daughter and me to see eye to eye. Or boob to mouth, as the case may be. Proper breastfeeding is a technique that sometimes has to be taught and practiced. A baby doesn't always latch on like the suckerfish cleaning algae off your dentist's aquarium tank. There are correct angles to be learned, special holding positions to get accustomed to, and tolerance to build before the act of nursing gets remotely comfortable.

The bottom line? It's tough stuff. The more support and guidance you can offer during the transition, the more your wife will appreciate your efforts. And the more likely she is to let you anywhere near her boobies again at some point. Which brings me to . . .

As my husband once quipped, "I didn't know I wasn't going to be able to touch your breasts for months on end. And they were *finally* big!" Sad but true, you may have to restrain yourself from any breast fondling for a while. And just when they're all plumped up and practically screaming, "Come to Mama!"

Nipples generally toughen up during breastfeeding, which may take some time. Until that happens, your wife may be intensely sore and chafed, and even soft stroking might make her want to crawl out of her own skin. The experts say it should never be painful for your child to nurse, but the reality is often a different story. Any pain likely means your wife and child haven't mastered a proper latch yet, which can ultimately be remedied, but it doesn't make the tenderness and discomfort any less real in the meantime. If your wife is experiencing a lot of pain while breastfeeding, encourage her to seek lactation assistance from a professional. And pretty please don't reach over to grope her in your sleep.

Don't panic if the bonding takes a while.
Your kid kind of emerged onto the scene like a bat out of hell, and now you might be in a sudden state of bewilderment, otherwise known as "your new reality." Try to snag some one-on-one time with baby. Skin-to-skin contact is always a warm and wonderful way to bond, so don't be afraid to take off your shirt and hold baby next to your chest for a little while. Let him get used to your scent and feel your heartbeat. He knows you belong to him, I promise! In time, you'll wonder how you ever questioned the bond in the first place, but don't beat yourself up if it's not instantaneous. Believe it or not, women struggle with this too!

Fatherhood can alter your perception of normalcy.
Just you wait! Take the topic of poop, for example. My husband definitely didn't look forward to the tedium of changing diapers, and now he's genuinely curious what the consistency is when there's a major blowout. (Oh, get over yourself. You've seen and heard nastier things—triple that if you were ever in a college fraternity.)

And if you're a father of daughters, someday you just

might find yourself suckered into teddy bear sleepovers, having your toenails painted pink, or sporting a princess backpack as you drop off your sweet little girl at school. You can groan about it now, but I think we all know how secretly pleased you'll be when the time comes.

Let love rule.
Becoming a father is likely to make you sappier than a Lifetime movie, but don't fork over your man card just yet. As my husband put it, "Any capacity I thought I had to love has been completely dwarfed by the reality of it." Embrace your newfound sentimentality. Don't freak out if you shed a few tears. I wasn't the only one who got more emotional after we had a baby. In fact, and this might be giving too much away, Brad and I both sobbed while watching a documentary special about Echo the elephant. Damn you, PBS! We even caught each other welling up during *Monsters, Inc.,* and you should have seen us during Gordon Ramsay's crowning of the first MasterChef Junior. It was a blubberfest. I wish I were kidding.

Fatherhood tends to bring out the schmaltz. My husband, for instance, is almost afraid to look forward to milestones such as walking our daughters down the aisle or holding their boyfriends hostage until they swear to be respectful (if you have a son, you may want to avoid letting him date one of our daughters), because he feels it translates to wishing away the present moment. Each step forward means he has to leave another phase of their childhood behind, and that's tough to reconcile. He doesn't want to let his mind skip over those brief and beautiful stages, such as having our girls fall asleep on his chest, practicing first steps, reading bedtime stories . . . the list goes on and on.

You may find yourself daydreaming about having tea parties with your daughter or coaching your son's Little League team. You might turn into mush whenever your baby smiles, willingly suffer through endless rounds of Disney's Sing-Along Songs, and start leaving work early so you can have five extra minutes with Mini-Me.

My husband found that he even looked forward to having our daughters steal the pen out of his shirt pocket when he arrived home from work each day, and despite his initial annoyance, he fell in love a little more each time they would rip the reading glasses off his face. Sometimes it's the little things that become the most endearing.

You might even realize how much more you love your wife in the process too. You may find, as my hubby did, that it becomes nearly impossible to kiss your wife and baby goodbye in the mornings, even though going to work is a necessary evil. Your weekends will likely be more treasured than ever, as your home life becomes a magnetic force, constantly pulling you in and tugging at your heartstrings. Home truly *is* where the heart is!

Then again, it's also where you'll find the accumulated baby bottles that need to be washed. And the smelly diaper pails that need to be taken out. And the incessant baby screaming that leads to sleepless nights.

But perhaps that's putting the cart before the horse; let's get back to the pregnancy for a moment.

A DOSE OF DECORUM

As an added bonus, here are some dos and don'ts that should help ease the maternity and birthing experience a bit.

Don't use math and percentages to back up your side of an argument with your pregnant wife.

There are times that call for logic and times that call for hugs. When in doubt, always choose the latter. Communicate; don't calculate! If you are resorting to a scientific analysis of why "everything will turn out fine" after your spouse has just informed you she has medical complications, stop right there. The last thing your wife wants to hear while her body is being occupied (invaded) by a wriggling, hiccupping, bladder-kicking, uterus-expanding, belly-monopolizing baby are phrases like "I've compiled the data, and the success rate of a C-section is . . ." or "Statistically speaking, you haven't been in labor nearly as long as most women . . ." There are just some situations that *Scientific American* and *Consumer Reports* cannot assist you with, and one of them is how to converse with your wife during pregnancy. Let her doctor be the one to get clinical while you hold her hand and remain her bastion of comfort and compassion.

We're not fans of having our bodies and our experiences chalked up to an impersonal equation, so if your wife has to whip out an abacus or a dictionary to figure out what you're driving at, it's probably time to reassess your methods.

Do tell your wife she looks beautiful.

Often. Even if she is starting to resemble a walking, talking, overstuffed goose. Most of us don't look like we belong on the cover of a magazine while we're carrying a baby in our body, but please try to see through the mess to our pregnancy glow. When we hear other women say, "You make such a beautiful pregnant woman," it's flattering. When we hear you say it, it's necessary reinforcement.

Do offer to make a dinner every now and then.

And by that I don't mean you should wait to offer until there's a solar eclipse or Halley's Comet makes another round. Please don't wait for your wife to ask (or even politely suggest) you to handle it. If the effort comes from you, it means a hell of a lot more. And for the record, picking up Chinese take-out isn't exactly what I'm implying here, unless that's what she's craving. I'm suggesting you actually turn on the stove, don an apron (if you leave that part out, I'll never know), and make an attempt to pair a protein with a vegetable. If your wife makes meals for you the majority of the time, please do your best to return the favor, even if it means something prepackaged. It's okay if it's a store-bought roasted chicken; we just appreciate the opportunity to get off our swollen feet without feeling like we're depriving anyone of sustenance.

*Don't let anxiety or taking care of your wife cause you to
ignore your own needs.*

As much as we love feeling wanted, we want to know that you don't need us behind you every step of the way. In other words, we don't want to take care of a grown-up man-child until we push the less self-sufficient one out of our body. We don't want to be the only reason you remember to eat dinner, take a shower, or have clean clothes to wear to work tomorrow.

I know it's overwhelming to think about having another family member to worry about. Now your thoughts are going to be consumed with whether the baby's crying means she's in pain, whether or not your partner is getting enough sleep, and what the cost of college is going to be by the time your little girl attends. (And other important considerations, such as whether she'll get there via car or hovercraft.) You are not alone.

However, taking care of yourself isn't selfish; it's a necessity. Self-imposed martyrdom is not a solution. If we don't have to worry about your well-being on top of everything else we have to deal with, we can breathe a little easier.

Thank you for your efforts to take care of us—you are a force to be reckoned with! Now go shave, make yourself a sandwich, and put deodorant on. Not necessarily in that order.

Don't stop communicating. Your wife is pregnant, not comatose.
My husband constantly worried that something he put in motion would unknowingly get passed on to the baby through my stress levels, so he didn't articulate certain concerns. For instance, he was afraid to discuss anything money-related. He felt regret over any quarrels we had, no matter how minor, and he felt helpless because he couldn't, according to him, "carry any of the burden." I totally sympathize, and I respect how tough it must be to sort out which boundaries have changed.

Still, we don't want pregnancy to alter our marriage dynamic. We know our lives will be drastically modified once there's an additional family member in the picture, but we want to build on the foundation that already exists . . . not dismantle it like a Detroit demolition project. We aren't looking to be coddled; we are looking for the same husband we had before there was a kid to worry about. Even if that husband tends to leave his dirty socks all over the bedroom floor for weeks at a time.

Do get your wife a little gift after she has the baby.
It's called a "push present," and it doesn't have to be anything life-altering. Even a sweet card will do. If you can't come up with the right words, let Hallmark do the talking.

Taking the time to get (or make) your wife something thoughtful will overwhelm her in the best possible way. There will be a tremendous amount of emotion flowing after your wife gives birth, and your token of affection and encouragement, no matter how small, will be worth more than you know.

Don't be afraid to ask questions.
Believe it or not, parenting knowledge isn't built-in for women either! I know it seems like we have an answer for everything that's going on with our bodies, or the vaccinations our kid is scheduled to receive, or what the baby is and isn't allowed to eat before he turns one, but guess what. That's because we asked questions too. Or did the research. Or consulted our inner baby Zen master. (You have one of those too, by the way; he just tends to hole up behind those old Atari scores and your favorite quotes from *The X-Files*.) If you have a question,

ask it! No matter how stupid you think it might be, I promise some brave soul has asked it before you. The truth is out there.

Don't be embarrassed if you've never held a baby or changed a diaper.

Neither my husband nor my dad was familiar with diaper changing before having kids, and they're both experts now. My dad used to rehearse on a teddy bear before I was born, which I'm sure gave him a slightly skewed, less wiggly illustration of the real thing. But hey, at least he was honing his skills. No one expects you to know what you're doing from the get-go. Practice may not make perfect, but it should make for a far less messy first experience! Then again, you may want to refer to the photo at the beginning of this chapter. Diapers aren't always foolproof. Or daddyproof.

Do take the initiative to plan a date night.

Our motherly instincts go into massive overdrive when the baby is born, and sometimes we forget to acknowledge that other people need our attention too. It's the squeaky-wheel-gets-the-grease syndrome. Or, in this particular case, the whining-baby-gets-the-boob. It may take some gentle coaxing to get your wife to leave the baby for an evening, so go easy on her and don't push the issue if she isn't ready. (Though if she still won't go out on a date night when your kid is in high school, we may need to reevaluate the laid-back approach.)

The first time we mommies leave our child with someone else, it feels like we're ripping an appendage off. When Brad and I went on our first, postbaby date night, all we could do was talk about our newborn and look at photos of her. Was the evening romantic? Sure, if the definition of *romantic* is skipping dessert so you can rush home to your kid before mama's breasts begin lactating all over the tiramisu. But at least we made it out of the house to begin with.

Having a babysitter also may not be a consideration until you have someone around whom you both trust implicitly. Both of our families are long-distance, for example, and for a long time we weren't comfortable leaving our daughters with anyone other than one of their grandmas.

If you have a hard time finding a babysitter, be creative. Set up a picnic on your living room floor while baby is napping, or rent a favorite movie and make popcorn. The idea is to let your wife know you still cherish your alone time together.

Don't get jealous if you have to take a backseat for a while.
I can only imagine how tough it is to play second fiddle to someone who gets to see your wife without her shirt on more than you do. Suffice it to say those breasts serve a more crucial purpose at this juncture; the milk dispenser has to come first. I'm sure you can reason through that, but it doesn't make it any less painful when both you and baby want the boob and he always wins the argument. Do your best to take it in stride. Someday you can return the favor by chaperoning his first date and doing some booby blockage of your own.

THE MORAL OF MY STORY

Fatherhood can bring about a plethora of new challenges, so give yourself some time to adjust. You aren't immune to the wonder, the excitement, or the trepidation. (You may not even be immune to empathetic pregnancy symptoms!) When all else fails, keep Brad's advice in your head . . . "Pour a stiff glass of bourbon and zone out to a Wes Anderson marathon."

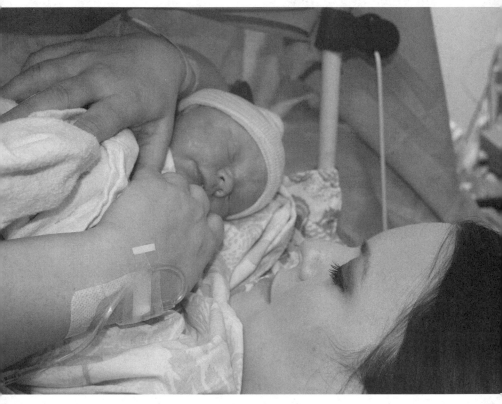

A life-changing moment: the first time I held my sweet baby Gray.
Photo courtesy of Jenna von Oy.

CHAPTER 7

Anatomy of a Hospital Experience

A SCENIC VIEW OF MY PAST

"Take your shirt off," he instructed a bit more tentatively than I would have expected from a guy in his position. I looked at the full sleeve of tattoos on his arm and the spikes through his cheek flesh and shuddered a little. I didn't really want to expose myself to this guy, but what other choice did I have? I removed my T-shirt and bra, then looked back at him uncomfortably. This must be what the casting couch feels like. His hands were trembling, which definitely wasn't a good sign. Was this the first time he'd ever done this? Lord, I hoped not. I didn't want to de-virginize the kid. Was I supposed to lie down in these circumstances? I had no clue. All I knew was that I wanted to be in whichever position would make this experience hurt less. Thankfully, the sake buzz was finally starting to kick in, which calmed my nerves a little. Still, I was starting to wonder if this was a really bad idea. There was no turning back; I'd already paid. I smiled cunningly at the thought that my boyfriend was at work, oblivious to what I was up to right now, and I wondered how long I could keep it a secret. Glancing over at my best friend, I made eye contact. Thank God she was in the room! I wasn't certain I wanted an audience for this, but I needed her for moral support. She knew me better than anyone, so why not share this with her too? I watched as her eyes went wide; she was staring at something I couldn't yet see. And that's when he whipped it out, that eight-inch-long . . .

Piercing needle.

Yep, my idiot twenty-five-year-old self had decided to get her nipples pierced. Why in the hell would I do this, you ask? Not too long before, I'd read a book in which a young woman embraced her own sexuality and rebellion by doing just that. She got off on walking around town with her erotic little secret; it made her feel empowered. I wanted a rebellious secret, I thought. I wanted to feel empowered too. After all, I'd never done blow at any Hollywood parties, assaulted a police officer, or been arrested for shoplifting expensive dresses from Neiman Marcus. I'd never even failed to pay a parking ticket. I mean, how could I deign to be called a child star without having some sort of fuckup to call my own? Not to mention, my relationship at the time was crumbling beneath me, so what better way to celebrate the anarchy of impending heartbreak? For some unknown reason, I was perversely thrilled to have a big-ass needle savagely stuck through my boobs by the nervous nelly, rich kid–turned–tattoo artist, at some shady shop in the San Fernando Valley. But who wouldn't be?

CUT TO . . .

The needle for my presurgical spinal anesthetic was equally long and menacing. Unfortunately, Caesarean sections don't allow for the benefit of a sake buzz. On a more positive note, the anesthesiologist was slightly more practiced (and less sweaty) than the quivering, needle-wielding dude at the tattoo parlor. Thank God for small favors.

MY CRADLE CHRONICLES

Most of us want to spend a few days in the hospital about as much as we want to experience a weeklong hangover, an alien abduction, or a coffee enema. Wouldn't it be reassuring if McDreamy met you at the double doors with his come-hither stare? If he took your hand in his, flashed his wonderfully dimpled smile, and told you how beautiful you look despite your labor pains or C-section apprehension? Well, snap out of it, sister. I'm pretty sure Patrick Dempsey will have better plans that day. You won't be rubbing elbows with Callie or Meredith, the interns won't be fighting over who's going to be your best pal, and you'll be lucky if you spot an orderly who could look like an Abercrombie & Fitch model if you were wearing beer goggles. The closest I came to that experience was a kind surgery technician who laughed at my jokes. (And technically, I suppose my insurance was paying him to do that.) But you know what? You won't care. *Seriously.*

The only thing you'll be thinking about when you head through those hospital doors is *I get to see my baby soon!* In fact, the nearer you get to the birth of your little one, the more you'll realize you have zero inhibitions regarding your body.

For instance, despite any prior apprehensions, every ounce of embarrassment I felt about having my hoohoo on display like the queen's coronation regalia went away once I knew I was so close to seeing my daughter. She was all I could think about.

What's that you say?

My ass is hanging out of my hospital gown? Ass shmass.

You're walking in on me without a stitch of makeup on and my boobs exposed? I hope you like the show, ladies and gentlemen; I'm here all night.

No, it's not pretty to think about flashing your knockers or your furry friend to a roomful of strangers, but those medical folks see more naked chicks than Hugh Hefner. When I say they don't care, I mean they *really* don't care. They aren't secretly thinking, *Wow, this is awkward*. You could be a Victoria's Secret model wearing a diamond-encrusted thong and they wouldn't give a damn (though I could be wrong on that particular example). In fact, I would venture to say it would be more awkward if you *weren't* indecently exposed.

It's their job, so they are trained to maintain their cool. You should try to maintain yours too. The more self-conscious you get about someone catching a glimpse of your private parts, the more stressed out you're going to be by the time your baby enters the picture . . . because it just so happens that his entrance is *through* the aforementioned private part. You knew that going into this mess, so stand proud in all your birthing glory! Let me rephrase that. Lie down in that hospital bed in all your birthing, writhing, sweating, panting, grunting glory!

Let's back up a bit. By the time you get to the delivery

stage, you'll know your OB-GYN so intimately that you'll have his or her number on speed dial, so I hope you really like him. You'll have visited his office so many times that you'll feel like you should know which side of the bed he sleeps on and whether he squeezes the toothpaste tube from the top or bottom. I imagine you'll feel pretty comfy once he arrives on the scene.

But what happens before that? A lot of waiting. You'll wait to check in and be shown to your room, wait for the nurse to assess your vitals, and wait for your baby to poke his head out. Unless, of course, your baby is already making his debut when you arrive at the hospital. In which case, you're likely to see folks scramble faster than eggs.

In my own case, I had to wait five hours until my digestive tract was rid of the huge breakfast I'd eaten. I wasn't anticipating giving birth that day, so I'd gone ahead and gorged myself like a sumo wrestler at an all-you-can-eat Vegas buffet. Apparently they have to make sure your system is clear before performing a C-section, so I was left twiddling my thumbs and biding my time (read: calling my mom every ten minutes to ask another inane question and driving my husband crazy) until it was time to have my surgery. I gladly blame the hold-up on that scheming, conniving, delicious bacon I'd made earlier.

The Zen Commandments

At the end of the day I can't really tell you what your hospital experience will look like, since it's largely based on your location, your doctor, the hospital staff, and whatever crazy ride your baby takes you on. I *can* tell you that it will be an experience like no other and that your emotional approach has an enormous effect on the general mood of it all.

You and your husband will set the stage for the atmosphere in your hospital room, so here's some of my advice.

Do your hospital homework.

The overall quality of your delivery environment will depend on the hospital you're in, since you'll be "vacationing" there for several days. I quickly realized that the doctors, nurses, and other staff were mostly responsible for how smoothly things went for me since they were in control of my general well-being . . . and my postsurgery medicating. Do your research. Ask friends and family whether they had a positive maternity ward experience, and find out where they delivered. Your doc may have a hospital he works through exclusively, so you may not have much of a decision to make in that department. However, logic dictates that if your OB is someone reputable, your hospital probably will be too. At least I'd like to think that's the case!

A good way to get an idea of what you can look forward to is to take a preemptive parenting class or two. (Please refer to chapter 5 for specifics.) When Brad and I took our classes, a tour of the hospital was included. It was incredibly helpful to see the size of the labor and delivery rooms, watch the nurses in action, and get a behind-the-scenes view of the nursery. When the big day arrived and my daughter was whisked away to the transitional nursery immediately following her birth (she was three weeks early due to complications, so they had to monitor her breathing), it calmed my fears to be able to envision where she was. Sometimes knowing is half the battle. Nothing quite equates to the actual experience itself, but a little familiarity isn't a bad thing, so do what you can to educate yourself. In retrospect, spending a few hours getting acquainted with my future jail cell . . . er, I mean, hospital room . . . was well worth it.

Go forth and inspire.
As I mentioned in chapter 5, you have the opportunity to inject positive thinking into your birthing experience. You can choose to be the emotional equivalent of either Yanni or AC/DC. I'm not implying you have to crack jokes while you're in labor; it isn't open mic night at the Comedy Store. And I'm certainly not implying you should be a Blackberry-hurling tyrant. But in the midst of the chaos and tension, it's good to remind yourself to select the path of kindness and quietude. When I'm in pain or nervous, I find it's all too easy to let my fear dictate my responses. But getting into a good headspace really helped everyone else to follow suit! You set the pace, and your approach will affect the outcome of your experience.

Despite my affinity for using sarcasm as a defense mechanism, it was really important to me to remain as serene as possible during my hospital stays. I tried to exercise patience and tranquility, of which (I reluctantly admit) I am master at none. I attempted to embrace my inner Gandhi for my daughters' sakes, because I didn't want them to come into the world sensing frustration or anxiety on my part. Isn't that awesomely hippie-dippie of me? It sounds like I'm channeling peace, love, and Woodstock here, but I'm being as serious as a McDonald's hot coffee lawsuit. It really meant a lot to me to have my kids enter this world in as slow, secure, and carefree of a manner as I could muster. Well . . . as slow as is humanly possible, when we're talking about a girl who made a sitcom character famous for flapping her mouth faster than hummingbird wings.

Have good bedside manners.
You want a simple way to endear yourself to the hospital staff? Learn your nurses' names. Those ladies and gents answer to everyone's beck and call all day long, and it's one way you can thank them for their efforts. I swear it will come back to you tenfold. It creates a more personal connection and lets them know you care.

Memorizing names has always been a big deal for me, as I feel it's one easy way I can offer respect. I can still tell you that when we had Gray, our main maternity nurse was Katie. She took incredibly good care of us, helped us get Gray tucked safely into her new car seat, and waved good-bye as we headed home. She even took some family photos for us before we left our hospital room behind and stopped in for a visit when I returned to give birth to Marlowe! I can also tell you that Toni was the nurse who closely monitored Gray for us that first night when I wasn't allowed to hold my sweet baby yet, due to her breathing troubles. I trusted that woman with my daughter's life, so how could I not learn her name? I'm eternally grateful to the nurses and lactation consultants who assisted us. They supported and encouraged me during my first few days as a mom, which was when I most needed a boost of confidence.

I hope you'll be able to say the same. If your hospital staff is as exceptional as ours was, consider sending them a thank-you note. I imagine they'll appreciate hearing they've done a good job. Don't we all?

Embracing your innermost exhibitionist doesn't mean you can't be tactful.

Here's where I get a bit down and dirty, so to speak, so if you're super conservative or prudish you may want to skip over the next few paragraphs. Then again, if you're super conservative or prudish, I'm surprised you've made it this far into my book.

Someone smart (and clearly more considerate than I am) advised me to get my bush waxed before giving birth. And there you have it, folks; we've officially crossed the too-much-information line. (Well, hang on to your hat, because I'm not even remotely done yet.) I'm not saying it was a jungle down there or anything, but birth requires a certain amount of pubic-hair-shaving—potentially more than normal, depending on your preferences—and you might as well do it on your own terms instead of the nurse's. I'll leave the extent of the waxing or shaving up to you, as that's not really something I feel inclined to have an opinion on. Hell, trim it into the shape of a porcupine wearing a sombrero for all I care. I just find showing up with pretrimmed nether regions to be slightly more diplomatic than showing up au naturel. Less may be more in this particular instance. Do what you will with that information. P.S. If you plan to shave yourself, be prepared to take some creative license in your approach. By month seven of carrying that baby, you won't even be able to *see* your vagina much less prune it.

At the risk of getting too gross, the other subject that bears discussion in regards to hospital tact is passing gas. I'm pretty sure things are different when you give birth vaginally, but if you have a C-section, you're actually required to break wind before you can consume solid foods. I'm not going to get into the medical specifics of why that is, but I can tell you it was the bane of my postsurgery existence. Both times. I'm not lying when I tell you I tend to become a raving lunatic when I don't eat, and lunacy when you're doped up on post C-section meds has its own variety of spunk and pizzazz.

Needless to say, I knew I needed to expel some air pronto so that I could eat the five-star, gourmet hospital fare they kept depriving me of. Now you may have a totally different thing going on with your spouse, and I don't begrudge you if you spend your Friday evenings farting competitively, but my husband and I don't do that in front of one another. It isn't that it would bother or embarrass either of us; it's just a re-spect thing. That said, Brad made me promise that I wouldn't hold anything in that might impede my healing process. In other words, I actually pinky swore that I would flatulate in front of my husband, as often as possible, after giving birth.

And believe me, there's a reason that isn't a standard clause in wedding vows.

Anyway, I missed our normal tact, but I must admit it was a relief not to be worried about sending Brad out of the room every five minutes while I did my due diligence. And without adding salt to your already festering TMI wound, you should be warned that it isn't always an easy feat to let one rip after your insides have been flipped upside down and turned inside out. Your body won't necessarily feel like cooperating.

After thirty-six hours of a strictly liquid fast, I was fiending so badly for a food fix that I was willing to embarrass myself in front of half of the hospital if my body would allow it. Thankfully, I didn't end up drawing a crowd.

With any luck you'll be able to exercise some discretion too, because I promise the staff and your guests would rather not be audience to your symphony. Even if your husband is cordial enough to sit in the front row.

Take snapshots in your head and set them on permanent shuffle mode.

Pause as often as possible to soak it all in. You can't suspend time, but you can memorize some of your feelings of euphoria and store them in your happy place. Brad and I have tried to make a habit of this exercise, especially at whirlwind events such as our wedding ceremony and the birth of each of our girls. It's far too easy to forge ahead on autopilot when you are emotionally charged or taxed. So many of the special birth moments will slip through the memory cracks courtesy of adrenaline, labor meds, and plain old time in general. They will go spinning into the baby brain void, and you'll struggle to make them resurface later. I can't tell you how many of Gray's birth details unexpectedly came flooding back when I gave birth to Marlowe! Every second counts, and the more you can absorb, the happier you'll be down the road. Except, perhaps, for the gruesome parts you'd rather forget, such as pooping on the delivery table. That detail will be forever branded into your head too, and you'll wish you could stuff the image into a box and bury it six feet under. On another planet. In another solar system. Let's just say it brings new meaning to the popular phrase *Shit happens*.

But back to more important things. When the beautiful baby who's been leasing your body for the last nine months is handed to you, grab that visual with both hands and keep it close. Savor the first time you hear your child cry out. He's asking for *you*! Let the thought of his face nuzzling up to your breast linger like a kiss, even when it feels like that kiss is coming from an overzealous, pint-sized piranha. Inhale that nostalgic new-baby scent because, as my friend Beth says, "It smells so good it'll make your uterus glow."

And when your husband looks at you with that extra love and respect because you've just brought his new son or daughter into the world (and because you've managed to defy gravity and several laws of physics while doing so), sear that expression into your brain. Cherish the special glances that pass between the two of you as you exchange smiles through the exhaustion. There will be some trying and thorny times in your future, but these are the mental keepsakes to think back on. They'll help you through the sleepless nights that lie ahead, so embrace them with all you have!

A FEW GOOD MENTIONABLES

Here are a handful of other pointers that might be worth taking into consideration.

Know your birthing rights.
You have the freedom to bring in a doula, listen to an iTunes playlist filled with Tony Robbins motivational speeches, or have a slide show of your childhood photos projected onto the wall if it floats your boat. (I'm actually not so sure about that last one, so you may want to look into that if it speaks to you.) I planned to have a doula present for Gray's birth, though that backfired because of the unavoidable C-section. There are a million options once you get to the hospital, and some of those options are yours to decide on.

For instance, you can exercise the freedom of speech. Speak up if you are uncomfortable or need water. I'm not saying you should hound the nurses every five minutes, because you probably aren't their only patient, but don't be voiceless either. If you're cold, ask for another blanket. If you're in pain, politely ask what they can do to help you. That's what they're there for. It's all in how you inquire.

You also have the right to bear charms. If you want to put out framed photos of SpongeBob SquarePants or New Kids On The Block, you can. I had photos of my family on display in my hospital room following both births, which made a sterile environment feel more like my comfort zone.

When Marlowe was born, the nurses were also kind enough to let me put up a photo of Gray in her bassinet. It was a sweet introduction to her big sister, and it helped Gray to recognize which baby was "hers" when visiting the nursery.

Sometimes a baby blanket from home is a cozy accompaniment as well. That said, there's no telling what sort of goop might get on it, so make sure you've chosen something that's easily washable. I'd also recommend prewashing it with free-and-clear detergent. A baby's skin can be super sensitive!

BYOD (bring your own diapers).
No, not for the baby, because the hospital will provide those. I mean for you. You think I'm joking? Been there, done that, and I'll do it again. You'll need them for postdelivery bleeding, because it takes your body some time to get back to normal. Which is a serious understatement. The hospital will give you maxi pads big enough for a woolly mammoth, but they're not quite as effective. I found adult diapers were easier. I had snazzy peach-colored beauties for Gray's birth and, to spice things up, I drew on a few of them in advance. I wrote goofy things like *Brad's girl* and *Butt-er me up* on the backside. As I shuffled around deliriously, my ass was maintaining the sense of humor I couldn't. I figured it was the least I could do for my husband. In the midst of his concern for my well-being, he looked up to see the words *Hot Mama* on my booty. Yes, it's official, Brad hit the jackpot of crazy when he married me.

Stay as long as your insurance allows.
This is technically what your insurance is there for—to help

you when you need it. There's a lot to learn when you have a newborn, so a few days of assistance from the nurses and lactation consultants, as well as daily visits from your pediatrician, are nothing to scoff at. Take the opportunity to gradually ease out of your new-parent stupor and ask some of the questions that will make things less disorienting when you get home, which brings me to my next point . . .

Don't be afraid to ask questions.
No one expects you to have all the answers, or you wouldn't need the hospital in the first place. There are no dumb questions when you are a new mommy. Embrace being an amateur!

Take as many of the free things they offer as possible.
Notice I specifically said *offer*. This isn't like stealing the monogrammed hotel towels, folks; there are certain items the hospital expects you to take. Kleptomaniacs can find their religion in the maternity ward; it's a pilfering Mecca. But seriously, ask your nurse what they anticipate having you bring home with you, and then don't be afraid to help yourself to it. I know you can drive to Target to get diapers when you run out, for example, but you won't want to leave the house for a few days . . . or weeks . . . or months. Bring a few things that will help you through the initial transition period. It's a gesture of comfort they are offering you, and there's a lot to be said for being comfortable.

THESE ARE A FEW OF MY FAVORITE THINGS
Speaking of being comfortable, your nesting instinct may

encourage you to assemble a suitcase of belongings big enough to join the circus. While I don't advise that you pack your whole house, there are amenities that can definitely make the stay a bit cushier. Some pretty awesome master lists can be found online, but here are some items I was pleased I'd brought with me.

1. An iPod with travel speakers
I even created a soothing playlist of songs I knew wouldn't grate on my nerves when I was worn out and in a state of medicated delirium. Which was all the time.

2. My own hospital gown, with snaps on the shoulders
for breastfeeding
Best. Purchase. Ever. Even though I only wore it for a few days during each hospital stint, this was one of the best things I thought to do for myself. It was more comfortable than the gown they attempted to give me, and the breastfeeding access was far easier.

3. Comfy, loose clothes to wear home from the hospital
Sweats with a drawstring were key for me, since I had no clue how quickly (or by how much) my stomach might deflate when my children were no longer in there. An easily adjustable ensemble is definitely the route to go. Some granny panties aren't a bad idea either, since you'll likely be wearing a diaper home. See? You and the baby have a lot to bond over already!

4. Photos that transport you to your happy place
I, for one, packed pictures of my puppies. I missed those guys,

and I wanted to make them a part of Gray and Marlowe's births in the only way they could be. Since canine family members have no visitation rights at the hospital, framed pictures were as close as I could get. And who doesn't love a gaggle of pugs scowling down at them while they labor away? Whether your happy place revolves around your pets, your mom and dad, or your garden gnomes, bringing along a photo can give you a blissful focal point during the tough moments.

5. My own pillow

I just wanted to feel like I was in my own bed, if even for a moment, before remembering I was trapped in a hospital cot in a perpetually upright position, while my husband camped out on a bench nearby. While we're on the subject, remind your husband to bring his pillow too.

6. My phone charger

This is self-explanatory, since you'll want to call every family member and friend (and hairdresser and random acquaintance you've ever known) with the good news! Plus, after a full day of taking drug-induced selfies in those awesome anti-blood-clot socks they provide (which are provocative as hell, let me tell you), your battery tends to run down. You wouldn't want to miss capturing that exciting video of your baby breathing.

7. An outfit for baby's first pictures

You may or may not opt to put your baby through a pro-fessional, *Vogue*-cover-worthy session on day one, but I can't recommend it highly enough. Assuming your hospital offers this service and does a job that's a step above the glamour shots you can get at the mall, I say go for it. Some folks prefer to hire their own photographer about a week later, and that's certainly an option too. That said, you'll be astounded at how quickly your baby will grow and change, and there's just something about capturing those first few moments. Yes, the baby will look a bit less puffy and waterlogged once he's a bit farther out from being catapulted from your vagina, but you only get those first precious hours for . . . well, a few precious hours.

Admittedly, the hospital photo shoots will run you a pretty penny. If I remember correctly, ours were around $150. But the fact is, hiring a photographer on your own won't be cheap either, if they know what they're doing! My suggestion is to budget ahead of time, if this is something you feel strongly about. If a relative gives you cash or a check to buy something for baby, I recommend setting some aside for this purpose. Could you buy a copy of *Everyone Poops* and a whole slew of unnecessary crib accessories for that money? Sure. Or you could buy a keepsake that your kid can show *her* kid thirty-five years from now, as she says, "Isn't it absurd that tangible photos still existed back then? Thank God we can beam those files into our mind indexes now. We're *so* much more advanced than they were! Now, let's go inject our lunch; I made liquid ham sandwiches."

As a side note, don't forget to pack baby a presentable, weather-appropriate going-home outfit too. Make sure you wash it in that free-and-clear detergent first!

8. A sense of humor

It may not be something you can tuck into your back pocket or hang around your neck on a chain, but be sure to bring your humor with you nonetheless. Yes, giving birth can be a stressful, somewhat scary experience, but there's no reason you shouldn't laugh a little too! I mean, what's not funny about launching something larger than a Butterball turkey out of an opening smaller than a Jujube? That was a hypothetical question.

PREDICTABLY UNPREDICTABLE

At the end of the day, I can't prepare you for the most important part of your hospital experience—delivering your baby. Each birth is so different that it's sort of a Choose Your Own Adventure. You know, "turn to page seven if you want a natural birth"; "turn to page forty-two if you discover you have oligohydramnios (too little amniotic fluid) and your baby is in the breech position, therefore obliterating every hope you had of how your delivery would go down"; "skip to the last page if you birthed your baby while stuck in traffic on your way to the hospital and your husband is now in desperate need of sedatives."

That said, I hope this chapter gave you a few ideas about how to handle your hospital stay, even if they were relatively shallow in nature. I mean, what did you expect from a former child star without a doctorate in pediatrics or gynecology?

THE MORAL OF MY STORY

Arming myself with some knowledge, a few comfort-ensuring necessities, a little decorum, and a sense of humor made my hospital stay go a lot smoother. It wasn't a vacation in the south of France, but it wasn't the bottomless pit of hell I was expecting either.

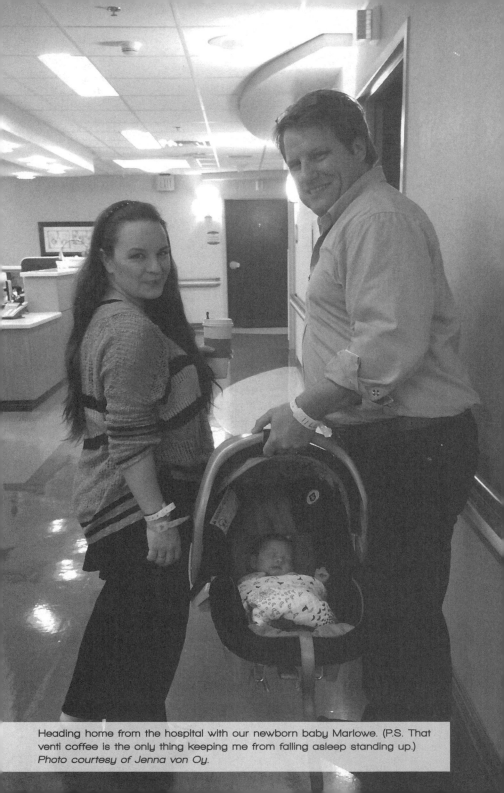

Heading home from the hospital with our newborn baby Marlowe. (P.S. That venti coffee is the only thing keeping me from falling asleep standing up.) *Photo courtesy of Jenna von Oy.*

CHAPTER 8

Bungling Your Way Back to the Bungalow

A SCENIC VIEW OF MY PAST

It was my twenty-third birthday and I'd just been out to celebrate someone else's birthday instead of my own. Said event had taken place at a local club, where I'd been mingling with throngs of young Hollywood elite. It was a gossip-and-schmooze fest, and it wore me out more than listening to a duet between Michael Bolton and Mariah Carey on endless repeat. I'd dabbled in the scene during my teenage years, but now it just made me feel underdressed, underpaid, and underwhelmed. I knew I would never fit the expected mold or say the right things, and I was sick of listening to conversations about agents and upcoming film projects, from lips that hadn't been on this planet long enough to warrant being injected with such prodigious amounts of collagen.

After seeing more boob jobs than I could bear, I ducked out early (if two o'clock in the morning can be considered early) and headed home alone . . . exhausted and ready to get out of my four-inch heels. Given that I normally hit the hay around 10:00 p.m., this was overextending my bedtime by more than my body could handle. I was already starting to feel the effects of my fatigue, but I was only a few miles from my house. I figured I could manage it without passing out. I was twenty-three, for God's sake, not eighty. Shouldn't I have been able to handle one night out on the town without becoming comatose?

I rolled my windows down to let some of the cool air in. Maybe it would be enough to keep me awake. Suddenly, I heard sirens wail behind me. Shit. I couldn't have run a red light, since I was on the freeway. Did I have expired tags? I thought back . . . Nope, I'd renewed everything a few months before. What the hell?

I pulled off at the next exit, as the cops started yelling at me over their loudspeaker (which isn't panic-inducing or anything, causing one to drive even more erratically than one already has). "Pull over on the next side street."

The only street I could see was a dark one to my right, littered with construction equipment. The road was all torn up, and loose gravel bounced off my tires as I rolled to a stop. I wasn't at all comfortable stopping for the cops on such a messed-up street at this ungodly hour, but I wasn't really in a position to argue. The last thing I needed was for them to jump to the conclusion that I was on an OJ Simpson-ish tear through the San Fernando Valley. *News flash: police are in hot pursuit of former* Blossom *star Jenna von Oy this morning. She unexpectedly fled a routine traffic stop, following her first night out of the house in nearly a decade.* Happy birthday to me.

I rolled down my window as the cop shined a flashlight in my face. "License and registration, please." At least he was polite.

I fetched the paperwork out of my glove compartment and handed it over.

After a quick glance, the cop said, "Ma'am, have you been drinking?"

I was honest. "I had one glass of wine about four hours ago, but I can't fathom it's still in my system." Yes, I used the word *fathom*. No, drunk people can't generally get that word to fall off of their tongues so easily. I hoped this fact was obvious.

"Please step out of the vehicle." Again with the niceties. Because that's definitely what this situation called for. Here I was being told to step out of my car in stilettos on a rocky road at two in the morning, and with far less streetlight than I was okay with, but golly that sweet talk just made it all better! My internal monologue was pretty feisty, but I wasn't about to argue with a cop.

"Mind if I remove my heels first?" I requested. "I'm a little nervous about the condition of the pavement."

The cop looked at me like I was cuckoo for Cocoa Puffs, but agreed.

I stepped out of my car in bare feet.

"Follow the flashlight," he instructed as he beamed a high-powered Maglite in my face that could have stunned a deer.

I did what he asked and expected to be told to return to my car.

No such luck. He then proceeded to ask me to perform every DUI test just shy of simultaneously rubbing my belly and patting my head. I suddenly knew what it felt like to be the dancing monkey at the boardwalk, only I clearly wasn't getting any sympathy money thrown my way.

Once I'd recited my alphabet backwards, and faster than any human should be capable of, I thought I was in the clear. But the big guy kept pushing for another few minutes. What was he after? Did he think I was suddenly going to start wheezing whiskey or toppling over like a Jenga tower?

He finally let me leave when he realized I could still pronounce the word *attorney*. Okay, I'm lying. Empty threats aren't really my style. I was turned loose when the younger cop, who could clearly see I hadn't been drinking and they weren't going to make their quota, politely tapped the older cop on the shoulder and said, "I think we need to let her go."

As I was climbing into my car, I overheard the younger cop say, "That girl is on a TV show. It wasn't a good idea to hold her up any longer."

Now, I have the utmost respect for the good men and women in the police force, but I'm still not exactly sure what that implied.

There's nothing like getting pulled over for a DUI when you're stone-cold sober to scramble your emotions and turn your night upside down. It'll set you on edge like getting stuck in an elevator with Glenn Beck.

CUT TO . . .

Getting stuck in an elevator with Glenn Beck, Tom Cruise (circa his couch-hopping *Oprah* appearance), and an amped-up, overcaffeinated Kanye West might have caused me less mental upheaval and anxiety than adjusting to life at home with a newborn. But I was determined to fight the good fight. I donned my fancy ruby slippers, clicked my heels three times, and repeated Dorothy's famous mantra: "There's no place like home. There's no place like home. There's no place like . . . uh-oh."

My cradle chronicles

Take it from me, your hospital room is a pea-sized, flower-and-balloon-filled security blanket. It is a place where you can get uninterrupted sleep, be attended to 24/7 by nurses, and order food via room service. If you need clean sheets, someone else washes them for you. It's like being in a hotel without the pillow chocolates or the keepsake shower cap. It's also your very own sterile comfort zone, because as scared as you were to get there in the first place, it's twice as scary to leave. Suddenly the world seems like one mammoth boxing ring. You begin noticing just how much road rage exists on the highway, how ignorant people are of your personal space, and how much bacteria lurks on every doorknob. Installing babyproof outlet covers can quickly lead to a house that's padded more than an insane asylum. You'll start having nightmares with slow-motion montages of spine-chilling, salivating dust bunnies and seas of grubby, unwashed hands reaching out to wipe their funk on your innocent, as yet germ-free neophyte. (Of course, your kid will be trafficking viruses like a Columbian gunrunner once he's attending day care or elementary school, but I realize you have some stake in keeping him healthy for as long as possible.) Have you initiated your full-time career as a worrywart? Force yourself to breathe, and know that babies are far less fragile than they appear.

Since I experienced enough sleepless nights for all of us, the least I can do is spare you some of the undue fretting. And the hives. And the desire to drink excessively.

SANITY SAVERS

Here are a few things to avoid so you can rest a bit easier during those first few weeks at the abode.

Don't cram everything but the kitchen sink into your diaper bag.
You may worry about your child having a poop explosion bigger than Hiroshima or a puke event more vile than the bratwurst-eating contest at your local Biergarten. This can be especially harrowing when you're in the middle of a church service or you bravely take your child into a friend's swimming pool for the first time. (A handy tip: The swim diapers don't go over the regular diaper. They go on just *like* a diaper, underneath the baby bathing suit. Also, they are waterproof. Ergo, they do *not* hold copious amounts of pee. So wait until you are ready to get in the water before putting them on! You'll thank me later.) Despite those jitters, resist the urge to pack the entire nursery for a quick trip to the dry cleaner. Here's what I have in my diaper bag at any given time, and I generally leave it in the car so it isn't forgotten: (1) three diapers, (2) a package of wipes, (3) sanitizing hand lotion, (4) an extra Onesie in case of an extreme blowout, and (5) a thin muslin swaddling

wrap. The last item can also serve as a blanket, a breastfeeding cover-up, and a changing pad if the restroom surfaces look like they haven't been cleaned since Noah built the ark.

Those are really the essentials. You may find one or two other items that you deem imperative, but I think you'll find you can do without dragging most things along. As the months go by, you'll find yourself ditching the diaper bag altogether and simply throwing a few diapers and wipes into the car on the off chance those pureed prunes hit while you're in the pediatrician's waiting room.

Don't drive like Danica Patrick, but don't drive like a ninety-year-old in bifocals either.

When we headed home from the hospital with both girls, my husband suddenly became more conservative than a tax accountant. I don't think he pushed the accelerator past twenty-five miles per hour, and that included the highway. There were people swerving around us left and right. Don't get me wrong, I thoroughly appreciated his cautious vigilance in both cases, but it bordered on geriatric.

If I'm being totally honest, traveling with a child never stops being scary. Since most of us aren't navigating an armored tank with bulletproof windows, a simple drive around the block can dredge up some serious paranoia. As a friend of ours once said, "I feel like I'm driving home with a bomb in the backseat!"

My husband was pretty adamant about not letting our daughters get into a car with anyone else behind the wheel, unless we were visiting family elsewhere and had no choice. This has extended well beyond the infant phase and into toddlerhood. In fact, the first time Gray traveled alone with anyone other than Brad or me was when her little sister was born. My mom took care of her during our hospital stay and had to shuttle her back and forth to see us that week. I thought my husband was going to have a heart attack about it. Thankfully, he had more pressing things to worry about, such as whether or not I was going to squeeze his hand clean off while the nurse pulled my catheter out.

Generally speaking, it's the other drivers on the road you'll worry about most. When I was seven months pregnant with Marlowe, we were in a car accident. I was on my way home from picking Gray up at school, and it was a busy Friday afternoon. Nashville doesn't have notoriously bad traffic like Los Angeles does, but this was one of those days. We'd slowed to a complete stop on the highway when a woman slammed into us from behind. Evidently she'd been paying closer attention to an accident that had already pulled off onto the shoulder and failed to notice what the cars in front of her were doing. She was unquestionably at fault, but I felt bad for her. The last thing anyone wants to see after they've accidentally rear-ended someone is a pregnant woman climbing out of the driver's side and a two-year-old in the backseat. She was horrified and profusely apologetic. For that matter, so was her insurance company. We were incredibly fortunate that day, as no one was hurt. I went to the doctor for some fetal monitoring (better safe than sorry), and Gray had no side effects aside from a few nights of fitful sleep. We certainly fared better than the woman who'd caused the accident, as my car had barely a dent and her front end had crumpled like tissue paper. I knew there was a good reason for having that tow hitch installed years ago!

My point? Be careful out there.

Stop reading every medical site on the Internet when your baby sneezes.

Sometimes a sneeze is just a sneeze and the remedy is a Kleenex. When baby first arrives home, you'll probably question every sound and movement, and that's normal. Sometimes simply going to the grocery store will be enough to make you a twitching, fidgeting basket case. Everything is new to both you and baby, so you're bound to need some adjustment time.

Try not to let yourself get carried away. *Does that cough mean she's choking? Does that bump on her mouth mean she's allergic to my breast milk? Is that cradle cap or hives?* You'll have a lot of questions, and it might be tough to assess the situation objectively, but try to pause before it's mental Mutiny on the *Bounty.* In other words, don't consult WebMD at 3:00 a.m., when you haven't slept in four days and you can't recall the last time you showered. The Internet can fuel the fire like a can of gasoline.

If you truly feel something isn't right, trust your motherly instincts and call baby's pediatrician. Though many issues can wait until the next business day when your doc is in, don't be afraid to act immediately if you believe the matter is more urgent. For extremely serious issues, I assume you'll know to bypass everything else and go straight to dialing 911.

Don't spend your entire night monitoring your baby's breathing.
Let's face it: you're probably going to stand over baby's crib in the wee hours like some sort of stealthy respiratory sentinel and wave your hand over his face to make sure he's still breathing. We've all done it, all the while cursing ourselves for being a tad overprotective. The good news? It doesn't mean you're a lunatic; it just means you love your kid. My neurosis in this department didn't end with my first daughter. I pestered Marlowe equally often and sometimes spent way too long staring at the rise and fall of her chest. I won't be able to completely abolish your angst on this one, but perhaps it will comfort you to know you aren't alone in it.

I can only hope those fears don't keep you awake all night. It's hard enough to get rest as it is, and Lord knows you'll need it! At some point you're going to have to allow yourself to catch a few Zs, and it's best if you aren't so tired that you wind up hibernating for the winter. Oh, and do yourself a favor— if you know you're predisposed to being paranoid, do *not* get one of those monitors that actively displays vital signs such as oxygen levels and heart rate, for God's sake. You'll make yourself crazier than a kitten in a catnip field.

Install a backseat baby mirror.
It sounds simple, but it's incredibly effective. Mount the mirror in front of your newborn's car seat so you can see him reflected in your own rearview mirror as you drive. Because

I'm not sure which is more alarming—listening to your child
scream while you're trying to navigate a five-lane highway and
being helpless to do anything about it, or not hearing a peep
out of him and worrying he might not be breathing. At least
this way you can see the face you're panicking over.

Don't assault the store clerk just because she's uncouth.
People can be dumb and tactless. We all know that, so just
expect it, and you'll be a heck of a lot better off. I know
that sounds cynical, but babies affect people in bizarre and
bewitching ways. People will let curiosity get the better of
them, and they will want to take a peek at your child at any cost.
Apparently, seeing a newborn baby is as riveting as witnessing the
aurora borealis.

When Gray was only a few weeks old, I took her on an
outing to the local supermarket. I had a case of cabin fever
that might have made an agoraphobe blush, so I was far more
excited to peruse the produce aisle than I should have been.
The cheese case had me downright giddy, and I nearly danced
a jig over a bin of fresh peaches. Let's just say I hadn't been
getting out of the house much. Or at all.

Anyway, as I made my way up and down every aisle, I was
thanking my lucky stars that my child was resting so peacefully
in her car seat, which I'd carried in with me. I'd made it all
the way to the checkout line and assumed my biggest hurdle
was locating my car in the parking lot. (Who said anything
about baby brain going away once the pregnancy is over?)

As the cashier rang me up, the lady bagging my groceries
eyed Gray's car seat like a fox zeroing in on a field mouse. I

had a blanket covering the entire apparatus so I could keep people from messing with my sleeping, not-yet-vaccinated kid, so she was well-hidden and still out cold. "Aw, is there a baby in there?" the woman asked.

No, I like to carry an infant seat around for sympathy and exercise.

"Yes," I answered with a smile, because why take my acerbic tendencies out on this poor lady?

"How old is he?"

Yep, pink car seat plus pink blanket equals boy. Definitely a boy.

"Just over a month old. She hasn't had her immunizations yet, so the doctor asked that I keep her covered up when we're out." I hoped this was a kind way of explaining why I wasn't rushing to rip the blanket off and hold my child up like I was selling her off at a livestock auction.

The woman smiled with what I took to be understanding.

Satisfied, I turned to the cashier, who was patiently waiting for me to dig money out of my purse. As I was handing over the cash for my groceries, I glanced over to see that the bagging lady had taken it upon herself to lift the blanket off my child. She was now in the process of stroking my child's cheek and cooing, "Hi, baby. Hi, little sleeping baby."

Well, previously sleeping baby.

Really? Who the hell *does* that? Would you like to have a little peek under my skirt too? I carefully moved the car seat out of her reach and tried my damnedest not to release my wrath.

Beware of that mama-bear instinct; it can be brutal and

savage! I had *Ally McBeal*–like fantasy sequences running through my head that involved pelting the woman with some of the frozen peas I'd just purchased. Did having my kid under a blanket cocoon not shout *Leave her the fuck alone* loudly enough?

After that incident, I hung a little laminated note from the carriage: *please wash your hands before touching mine*! My single friends thought I'd lost my marbles; my friends with kids went home to hang one from their own child's car seat handle.

Just when you think people won't cross the line, they will. And just so there's no confusion, they will then proceed to stomp all over that line until it's nonexistent. I hope you only run into folks with common sense and consideration from now on, but good luck with that.

Despite my grumblings, I'm actually not terribly paranoid about germs. I just like to joke about them. For the most part, I think they build character and immunity. (Within reason, of course. If your kid has hand, foot, and mouth disease, pretty please don't invite us over for a play date.) More than likely, you'll mellow out after a few months of carting baby wipes in your cleavage and buying stock in hand sanitizer. The pacifier fell on the kitchen floor? Briefly rinse it off and give it right back. A cracker dropped? That's what the five-second rule was made for, unless you have five dogs like we do. Ultimately, you can't protect your child from everything, and only you know what your level of comfort is. You may find you're fairly nonchalant about it all, or you may find that you hit DEFCON 5 every time your kid puts a toy in his mouth.

If you're the latter, prepare yourself for a full-time battle, because babies enjoy toy licking almost as much as they enjoy pooping. Which is a lot.

Don't fear the crying.
Waking up to a baby wailing in the middle of the night can take some getting used to. But then, what did you expect? After a few decades of an alarm clock that awakens you with the smooth sounds of jazz, nature, or Britney Spears (hey, no judgment here), a baby cry can be more jarring than a rooster on dawn patrol. Don't be afraid of it or let it throw you off your game. (Though I'm not sure how much game anyone has at four in the morning.)

I know some mothers who jump at every whimper and moan, then frantically launch into a series of procedures to decipher what that particular crying pattern means. Eventually, you'll probably recognize that a certain cry is representative of a specific issue, but it won't be immediate.

Generally speaking, a baby gets upset when he's hungry, tired, or in need of a diaper change. There are other contributing factors, of course, but in my opinion those are the three to consider before all else.

I've noticed that a large number of parents are quick to blame crying on colic, but not every scream indicates a severe problem. Sometimes it's just a little gas.

Since infants have no way of communicating that to us, and since a tiny gas bubble is probably the worst pain your child has felt so far in his young life, expect some major vocal protests. Sometimes it'll sound like a quiet college sit-in; other times it'll be the Million Man March. With any luck, you'll soon hear the familiar sound of machine-gun fire in your baby's diaper, and all will be well.

Hell, my daughters both burped like they had a mountain lion drinking Pabst Blue Ribbon in their bellies. Ladylike? Nope. Music to a mama's ears? Yep.

Try not to feel undue pain on behalf of your child.
The bane of my mommy existence was cutting fingernails. By baby number two, I thought it would be old hat, but I forgot just how darned minuscule their fingers are when they come out of the womb! When Marlowe was two days old, I made the idiotic decision to attempt clipping her nails. Right there in that hospital room, I made my first bad move on her behalf and managed to draw blood. She'd been scratching her own face at night, so I thought I was doing a good thing. But good intentions don't always lead to a good outcome. At the end of the day, I think it hurt me more than it did Marlowe, since her tears lasted for approximately ten seconds and mine wouldn't stop for a solid ten minutes. Either way, I should have left well enough alone. You know what else I should have done? Let myself off the hook a little. Sure, it wasn't the smartest decision I've ever made, but I didn't need to be so hard on myself either! When you do decide to cut your baby's nails for the first time, try not to let it get the better of you. This would be one of those do-as-I-say-not-as-I-do moments.

Similarly, try not to freak out over the umbilical cord

stump. (The name alone is a little nauseating.) I know it looks like a dried-up grape is attached to your child's belly button, and it's a little gross and creepy, but it'll fall off soon enough. You may wince every time you catch a glimpse of it, but according to our hospital nurses, it doesn't cause pain for baby at all. The waiting is the hardest part. (Well, that and trying to fasten a diaper around said stump without knocking into it.) Just continue to keep it clean and dry—you should get care instructions at the hospital—and don't try to pull it off even if it's dangling precariously.

Heed the warnings, but use common sense.
If there's a recurring theme in my book, other than laughing through all the parenting trials and tribulations, it's this one: trust your gut. No one can give you all the right answers. Hell, we can't even give you all the right questions! Have faith that the motherly instinct is somewhere inside you, even when it seems about as real as the Tooth Fairy.

Don't suffer privately.
Getting baby settled at home will be arduous at first, and you may feel a bit helpless from time to time. Especially when you're lacking the necessary amount of sleep! But please know that every mother has experienced feelings of irritation, exasperation, and even mild defeat. Mood swings and bouts of tears that require more Kleenex than an episode of *Downton Abbey* aren't unheard of. Hear me when I say you are not a failure! This is the most comprehensive and abrupt education

you'll ever receive: your baby isn't the only one who's in training! I'm tired of people hiding their anxieties and then publicly touting how effortless and elementary parenting is. Let's shed a little light on the reality of it, instead of pretending it's all easy breezy until we're behind closed doors, shall we?

To be clear, I'm in no way saying you are suffering by being a mom. Far from it, or I wouldn't have done it myself. Twice over. I am, however, saying you might experience some powerful emotional repercussions from the sudden overhaul of your life. And there's *nothing* wrong with that. Parenting isn't uncomplicated, nor is it meant to be. It's a constant work in progress that requires all your energy and devotion. But you know what? It's also the best and most rewarding thing you'll ever do. And I can't emphasize that enough!

On a more serious note, I want to mention the following: If your feelings extend to hopelessness, insomnia, withdrawal from your loved ones, resentment or unrelenting anger toward your little one, the inability to bond with your new baby, and/ or being overwhelmed to the point of despair, please contact a medical professional to assist you in managing those emotions. Postpartum depression is no joke, and there's help out there. It doesn't mean you suck as a mom, have character defects, or have something to be ashamed of. Postpartum depression isn't uncommon following the birth of a baby, and it is treatable. The most important step toward coping with it is to seek professional help. You have my utmost respect and encouragement.

THE MORAL OF MY STORY

Putting the hospital in our rearview mirror was nearly as jolting as downing a six-pack of Red Bull. It wasn't without its strains and struggles, but we came, we saw, we conquered, and we got the T-shirt. Complete with baby vomit down the front! A few months of trial-by-fire schooling and developing a routine restored a sense of balance. Well, as balanced as one can be with a baby on her boob 24/7.

Two-week-old Gray and I spending some quality time with our pups, in a photo I fondly refer to as "We need a bigger couch." Too bad *that* item couldn't go on our baby registry. (From left to right: Bailey, Mia, Boo, Bruiser, Ruby, Gray, me.) *Photo courtesy of Jenna von Oy.*

CHAPTER 9
Welcome to the Doghouse

A SCENIC VIEW OF MY PAST

It was the Fourth of July, and I was still in my partying-as-a-professional-pastime phase. I jest. As I mentioned, I was never big into club-hopping or the typical Hollywood "scene." That isn't to say, however, that I wasn't interested in indulging in a little let-loose, blow-off-steam, raise-the-roof sort of holiday festivities from time to time. And by that I mean I was up for a night of drinking wine until my tongue turned purple and I slurred my words more than Mike Tyson. Thankfully, that night I was leaving the designated driving up to my ex-boyfriend. We'd been invited to a friend's beach house to watch the fireworks extravaganza, and the night was well under way. We had blankets laid out on the sand, music blaring in the background, and oxymoronic red Solo cups of pricey wine in our hands. But hey, life is too short to drink cheap wine, right? It was the perfect evening.

Cue the adorable pit bull puppy, tugging on his owner's leash and bounding toward my dog-loving, slightly reckless, super-tipsy self. I tossed my beverage aside and immediately headed over to them, calling out, "Can I pet your puppy?" (In certain circles, that phrase could have gotten me arrested.)

"Sure," responded the cute guy who was doing everything he could to manage the dog (who, it turns out, he'd randomly rescued in the park that day, so God knows where that puppy had been).

I opened my arms wide and leaned down toward the creature, who was about as calm as Alec Baldwin during a paparazzi smackdown. That said, he was clearly a friendly pup and as eager to see me as I was to see him. Regrettably, I didn't account for our meeting of the minds. Or rather, our meeting of the craniums. And geez, are pit bulls hardheaded! The next thing I knew, there was a razor-like incisor wedged in my eyebrow.

Stumbling back a bit, I laughed a little (we'll chalk that up to the wine buzz) and put my hand over my wound, where I could already feel the blood trickling out. Not wanting to alert the guy that I was hurt (I wasn't so drunk that I didn't recognize the whole ordeal was my fault, and I wasn't about to let some poor dog go down for my stupidity), I had a brief conversation with him and staggered back to the beach house to locate the nearest bathroom.

As always, there was a line for the ladies' room. By now, the blood was oozing down over my eye and onto my clothes, and there was really no covering it up. In a situation such as this, one would assume I was concerned for my welfare, or at least for the state of my face. If nothing else, vanity should have prevailed, right? After all, I am an actor and my face is supposed to be my moneymaker. Not the case. I was more embarrassed than anything, and I really just wanted to stop the bleeding before anyone noticed what an idiot I'd been.

Which is why I was a bit bummed when one of my best friends walked up, saw the blood, and nearly had a heart attack. I was even more bummed when she informed me that the gash would need stitches and I was hospital-bound whether I liked it or not. So much for the fireworks. And the fun night out. And the wine buzz.

Three hours and two packages of gauze later, I was given a tetanus shot and a few stitches on my face and was sent home to wallow in my own self-pity and post-inebriated misery. And that's how a fun night of wine turned into a miserable night of whine.

CUT TO . . .

A new baby turned *everyone's* life upside down in our house, including the canine kids. To be fair, I shouldn't have expected folks who chase their own tails and eat feces when I'm not looking to have built-in boundaries. Thank God there have been no associated hospital visits. Yet.

MY CRADLE CHRONICLES

Franklin Delano Roosevelt almost had it right when he quipped, "The only thing we have to fear is fear itself." But he clearly didn't have to introduce his precious newborn baby to his gaggle of wily pets.

The play-by-play goes a little something like this: You've just arrived home after days in the hospital. You are sleep-deprived, still in need of physical and emotional repair, and ready for a little tranquility. Your new infant fell asleep in the car, so you might actually get to close your eyes for a few minutes once you get settled inside—oh, miracle of miracles! Suddenly, the doggie door flies open and your pup bounds out of the house at warp speed, leash trailing him like a downed power line. So much for an attentive dog-sitter. He heads straight for the fragile little angel swaddled in your arms as if he has spotted an unattended turkey leg on Thanksgiving. There's a giant blur as the hairy, panting, overzealous mass of fur launches toward you. With his tongue unfurled like a slimy red carpet, he nearly bowls you over as he plants a big wet kiss on the baby's face. There was no time to stop him and you no longer have a hand free for that sort of thing anyway. You're left with a trail of slobber and grime, a screaming baby, and an expression that would make contestants on *Fear Factor* look nonplussed. Are you picturing the scene like some horrific slow-motion montage from *Cujo*? Try not to panic. Having a strategy in place will allow everyone a relatively calm introduction that will keep your pups out of the proverbial doghouse.

The trick to dealing with children and animals is the same: patience, patience, and more patience. I promise you don't have to be the Dog Whisperer to get your kids and pets acquainted, though if Cesar Milan agreed to be my personal pet nanny I'd snatch him up faster than I can eat a box of Girl Scout cookies. And believe me, that's fast. Remember that this is an equally drastic change for all parties, whether they have feet or paws. Please also keep in mind that not everyone involved has the brains to process the sudden change. And that's not my way of making a joke at your husband's expense; I'm referring to your canine. You think baby brain is bad? Try being a dog.

If you're anything like me, you refer to your fur babies as family members and assign them charismatic personality traits. On several occasions I've had to remind myself that my dogs aren't human, despite my tendency to compare one of my pugs' neuroses to Woody Allen's or to pretend that I'm having a heated political debate with my basset hound. As amusing as it is to dye your Chihuahua pink and dress it in a tutu (though I might possibly have lost a little respect for you if you've actually done that), don't confuse your dog's penchant for being fashion-forward with an aptitude for high-level thinking. Animals speak the language of instinct, not English. They don't understand what we mean when we say, "If you bark at the UPS guy one more time, I'll take away your couch privileges," or "Stop sucking on the baby's toes like they're slathered in peanut butter." I know these tactics are failures because I've tried them. Several times over. Unfortunately, neither of those warnings accomplished anything other than inspiring my dog to lick his own balls. Which can be an awkward conversation ender.

A "TAIL" OF TWO INTRODUCTIONS

When you bring a child into the picture, it's important to remember your dogs were a part of your family first and their pack order is about to come unhinged. And by *unhinged*,

I'm saying you're about to fuck up their world like you're the canine Colonel Gaddafi. I'm clearly not proposing that you make pets a priority over your baby; I hope that goes without saying. But they are going to need some time to adjust to the new addition, and it's only fair to give them the opportunity and space to do just that.

Here are a few ideas to help your introduction along, as suggested to me by folks who love their mutts as much as I do.

Put a baby blanket in the dog bed.
We didn't ultimately opt for this tactic, but we were told it can be very helpful. Since dogs are driven by their snouts, the blanket gets them acquainted with your baby's individual fragrance prior to their first meeting. The idea is to take a piece of the birthing wrap, the one they immediately swaddle your baby in after delivery, and let the dogs nose it to their heart's content. Ideally, the cloth should still be marked with the afterbirth blood and goo. The more funk, the better. I realize this concept freaks some folks out, so take it for what it's worth. I'm just the messenger here. In theory, I suppose this technique would work with any fabric that has been against your newborn's skin for a few hours, even without the gunk. The baby's scent just won't be quite as concentrated—kind of like the intensity difference between expensive French perfume and eau de toilette.

Now, I can't speak to the effectiveness of the method either way, so it may be a bit of trial and error on your part. Assuming that you have someone pet-sitting for you, I would recommend having them put the blanket in your dog's crate for the day or two prior to your return home from the hospital. A dog's bed is his den and is generally where he feels safest. Introducing the baby's smell to that comfort zone gives him a sense of ownership (in a non-creepy, good way), and familiarizes him with the idea that baby will now be an integral element of life as he knows it. Be sure not to let your dog chew the blanket or thrash it around, however. The goal is to let him gently grow accustomed to his new family member in a safe and loving way via his sense of smell. If he's whipping the thing around like he's playing carnival Whac-A-Mole, this may not be a tailor-made approach.

If you have a whole litter, introduce one dog at a time.
This was a no-brainer at our house. We absolutely *had* to follow this philosophy, or chaos would have ensued. The kind of chaos reserved for a three-ring circus when the elephants break loose. With five dogs running around, the majority of whom are rescues with various idiosyncrasies, it was crucial to provide an opportunity for each one to individually assess the situation. I strongly believe in allowing the alpha dog to extend his greeting first, since he often sets the stage for everyone else's reception. After that, try going in pack succession, or as close to it as you can get.

In our house that meant our oldest pug, Bruiser, led the way. He's the gang leader; the army colonel, if you will. Thankfully, pugs are a very gentle, family-oriented breed by nature, so I wasn't nervous about his reaction whatsoever. He has spent time around other children in the past and proven he adores them wholeheartedly. In fact, he generally plays a funny little pug version of peekaboo until the child indulges him with some laughter. (Apparently it runs in the family: even my dog is addicted to audience approval.) Once Bruiser had given his own snort of consent, the rest of the pack easily followed suit.

Carefully gauge reactions.
An animal trainer friend once told me the best response to a new pack member (aka a potential threat) is a neutral one. You want your dog to sniff for a bit and move on, without exhibiting too much attention or excitement. In this case, nonchalance is preferred. It doesn't mean your dog secretly has it out for the baby and is hatching a plan to clobber her over the head with a monstrous ham bone; it means he's accepting the situation.

Let your dog come over to your child. Don't force the baby in his face, which could stir his aggressive impulses. Pets need to say hello on their own terms. As a side note, it's always best to put them on a leash and let them first sniff baby's feet, instead of her face, just to err on the side of caution. It also helps to keep the dog at a safe distance until you know he's handling the situation well.

Always be sure to hold the baby in your arms while pets are getting acquainted, and don't leave anyone unsupervised.
Even if your dog is better behaved than Lassie, it isn't fair to allow him the room to screw up. Start setting boundaries immediately, and make sure you don't lay your child down on the floor while the dogs get accustomed to her scent. In fact, it's typically best not to lay your baby down on the floor at

all while pets roam free, even once she can hold her head up and roll over. Though you may feel perfectly comfortable with everyone's disposition and interactions, accidents happen. Even if your response time is lightning quick, there's no guarantee you'd be able to keep a paw from coming down on your child's fingers. Or worse. It's best not to set anyone up for failure.

It will take a while before you can tell if your dog is truly respecting the baby boundaries you've set, so don't underestimate his enthusiasm or overestimate his understanding. I encourage you to be honest with yourself about the expectations you place on your pet. In the long run, it will protect both your child and your dog. Be a good parent to your human *and* your canine.

Give the puppies daily attention.
Don't ask me how, but your dog knows you're taking way more photos of the baby than of him these days. Unless you have a dog that's more clueless than Homer Simpson, he probably knows what's up. Dogs are far too intuitive for their own good. This suddenly diverted attention may cause him to act out a bit, so make sure he has his time with Mommy and Daddy too. Some heavy petting and good old-fashioned ear rubbing is a beautiful thing! (That goes for you and your hubby too. See chapter 14 for more on that.)

If you can take five minutes to play with your dog in the yard while baby naps, or take him for a walk in the afternoon while pushing baby in the stroller, he will be putty in your hands. Remind him he's loved and cherished—animals respond positively to touch just like we do!

It's imperative to give your dog some attention while the baby is around as well, so he sees that you can share your affections. Try giving your pup a treat if he's quietly lying next to you while you're feeding the baby. It gives him positive reinforcement for good behavior around the little one and makes him feel included. You're golden as long as he doesn't have a Pavlovian response every time you whip out a breast. Which, I suppose, could get tricky in certain circumstances.

Continue reminding your dog he is still an important part of your family, whether that's by throwing a tennis ball, earnestly telling him he's your best friend, or fawning over him like a One Direction groupie.

Keep to the routine as closely as possible.
I'm not a huge fan of change, so I sympathize with all my canine compatriots out there. Dogs live and die by their routine. For example, our herd starts getting restless an hour before they know they're supposed to be fed; it's like clockwork. When the time changes in the fall and we gain an extra hour, they go crazier than foxes in a henhouse. Patience is not their forte.

I imagine your pets are also creatures of habit. Let's be honest, they don't have much to worry about beside eating, pooping, and chewing sticks in the yard, so lifestyle changes are a pretty big deal for them. Consequently, anxiety tends to come out in strange ways we may not comprehend. Or want to.

For instance, our littlest pug, Ruby (who is blind), begins humping Bruiser whenever she gets nervous. On the surface, it doesn't seem to make sense that a ten-pound female dog is humping a twenty-pound male dog, until you consider the fact that he's the alpha in the pack. When little Ruby starts freaking out, she demonstrates her jitters by making moves on the big boss.

Mia, our basset hound, fights with Bruiser over food when she is distressed. She actually challenges him to a major duel from time to time, which can get aggressive and scary.

Our corgi/shar-pei mix, Bailey, expresses her anxiety by hiding under tables. This often occurs during thunderstorms and when guests come over. When provoked, she barks ferociously and bares her teeth, but she backs away instead of biting.

Our other male pug, Boo, runs for the hills when he feels the least bit intimidated. You know, like when the vacuum is brought out, someone uses an electric toothbrush before bed, or we let the attic stairs down.

Lastly, when Bruiser frets (or simply when he's overly bored), he mounts and humps Boo. This is a clear display of dominance, since Boo is his submissive. It's starting to sound like something out of *Fifty Shades of Grey*, but dogs often exhibit their tensions via sexual advances toward another dog. Or your favorite couch pillows. Or the stuffed bear you got when you were ten. Or your father-in-law's leg.

All of it is a struggle for their place in the pack, which now has a new and very special member. A member that keeps getting bigger every day, gets Mom and Dad's undivided attention, and has very interesting smells coming from the plastic nappy around its bum.

All dogs have their own eccentricities that surface when change occurs. Don't be alarmed if your lab, who hasn't chewed anything in a decade, starts furiously gnawing the coffee table corners or nosing through your underwear drawer. Some dogs start marking the house even though they have been potty trained for years.

You just never know how the adjustment will affect everyone, so be as understanding as possible. Any discipline should be done lovingly and with the knowledge that it won't last forever. Pretty soon your pup will be following your baby around like . . . well, a puppy dog.

The best way to cut down on maladjustment is early intervention. If there are any aspects of your routine that you know will be altered once baby comes home, go ahead and begin the change ahead of time. For example, we originally had Ruby's dog bowl in our spare bedroom, so she was accustomed to eating her dinner in there. (We spread our dogs out during feedings to avoid conflict.) However, that spare bedroom became the nursery, so we knew we would have to move Ruby's grub station. It took some time for her to adapt, especially when you consider the blind factor, but it was far better to introduce the change before a newborn was around.

Get your dogs used to the idea of a crying baby.
This is where the Internet really doesn't disappoint. You can find damn near anything on the worldwide web, including penis warmers, wolf urine, supposed UFO detectors, and . . . yep, you guessed it, crying baby CDs for pets. What a wonderful generation we live in! Brad and I weren't ready to make the high-end fifteen-dollar investment for baby cries that we would be able to supply on our own a few months later, so we opted

for downloading one "song" from iTunes. Honestly, we just wanted to see how our dogs would react to the mayhem. But I guess that's the point, isn't it? You want to know that your dog isn't going to whine and yap every time your kid has a round of colic or decides to have a conniption over bath time. You'll already have enough to deal with.

Playing the crying track once or twice was plenty for us. I repeat—*plenty* for us. A full CD would have put us over the edge, if the edge is a Grand Canyon–sized cliff that cannot be scaled by mere mortals. Thankfully, our dogs were surprisingly calm about it. Even better, their nonchalance never really went away once they were faced with the real thing. And that's saying something, because there's nothing like up-close-and-personal, bloodcurdling infant wailing. Mind you, neither of our girls were major boo-hooers, but still . . . babies scream from time to time, and it's far from pacifying.

Ruby was the only one who barked a bit at the beginning, and that's because the poor gal couldn't see where the crying sounds were coming from. It was like watching Mr. Magoo trying to take in a football game. Who knows *what* she thought was going on? By the time Marlowe was born, our dogs had more agitating things to fret about, such as why Gray was trying to polish their nails and ride them like ponies.

Buy a doll.

Get your mind out of the gutter. I'm not insinuating that you should make a visit to Hustler for some scary plastic blow-up deal that allows you to drive in the carpool lane on the freeway. (And as far as I know, that's a myth.) Go to the mall and buy a simple kid's doll. If it makes you feel better, order something from Amazon so you can maintain your anonymity. Make sure it's the approximate size of an infant and start toting that thing around the house, especially during doggie feeding time. Use it to teach your pups not to climb into your lap or jump up on you and to get them used to the idea of a breast-sucking appendage.

Set rules for your baby too.
Obviously, it will be a while before your baby is old enough to reach out and pet your pups. But that day will come sooner than you think, and you need to give baby some rules too. My dogs have almost always proven their awesomeness when challenged, but why make them choose between the angel and the devil on their shoulders? (I'm not entirely certain dogs have shoulders, per se, but you get the picture.) It's key to teach baby early. Encouraging gentle playtime and loving exchanges will help you set a solid foundation for your child's behavior toward others. If you are planning to have other kids, for instance, you'll have already set the precedent for not pulling hair or grabbing ears. Baby and puppy need a sense of understanding and unity. Baby learns to pet gently, while puppy learns to put up with it.

But I warn you to take heed when someone growls. Your dog *will* give you signs that baby is committing a misdemeanor— whether you understand what the violation is or not. Your dog can't say, "Hey, woman, get that kid outta my face," so don't put him in a position where he's forced to make his actions speak instead.

Another good rule of thumb is to avoid putting your dogs in a position to guard their territory. As I mentioned before, we spread everyone out at feeding time in our house. When the chuck wagon rolls in, all five dogs have their own space and generally respect it. It helps them to know their kibble isn't being stalked, which makes them significantly less territorial. A baby crawling toward a food bowl at warp speed is definitely going to raise some hackles. Children plus puppies plus dinnertime equals disaster. As a precautionary measure, don't let your kids anywhere near your dogs while they are eating. Just to be on the safe side.

Don't give up on man's best friend, because he might eventually be baby's best friend too.

I'm going to get on my soapbox for a moment here, because I strongly believe pets are family members and no dog should be left behind. If things aren't going precisely the way you hoped, please consult a dog behavioralist before making any rash decisions such as giving your dog away. There are often ways to solve the problem without having to lose your beloved canine family member.

Rescues and shelters seem to be inundated with pets that people give up once they have children. In many of those cases it is because the situation was allowed to get out of hand, leading to a loss of trust between the owner and his pet. I believe this is usually avoidable if you intervene early enough, but it's crucial to find the right people to help you handle it.

If your child were biting kids on the playground at school, you'd have the teachers and guidance counselors to consult with, so don't feel funny about needing some help during this transition. Make the commitment to be a strong parent for your pets too, and know that it will require a lot of love and work on your part . . . which I imagine you already knew when you became a pet owner in the first place.

My husband and I recently read an article about how children migrate toward animals. A study was done by putting kids in a roomful of various toys and then putting an animal somewhere in the room with them. The kids ignored the toys and went for the animal every time, even when it was a snake or a tarantula. There's something inordinately fascinating about another living creature who shares our space with us, so expect your child to be curious—and to do some crazy stuff too!

As an infant, Gray had an affinity for throwing things into the dogs' water dispenser, then splashing around in it until she was soaked. She then boot-scooted trails of water throughout the kitchen and living room. Joy.

She also felt drawn to lying in the dog bed. This was fine with all the pugs but not with Mia or Bailey, whose responses proved to be more unpredictable. The first time this happened, Bailey growled when Gray got within five feet of the cushion. I had to consciously stop myself from punishing Bailey for the sign of aggression, because I realized it was her prerogative not to want an intruder in her bed. I mean, Robert Downey Jr. was arrested when he tried that at a neighbor's house back in 1996. Did I want my child to get bitten? Of course not. But the growl wasn't unjust. It was a warning sign, and it was my job to heed that warning—for Gray's sake as well as for Bailey's.

Even now, the onus is on Brad and me to be sure our girls don't overstep boundaries. Since children watch and emulate everything we do, be sure you're treating your pets the way you want your kids to treat them too.

Maintain calm and always put your baby first.
This is the rule to live by. Dogs can tell when we're nervous or stressed out, so try to keep your cool. When in doubt, remove your child from the vicinity of your pet so as not to provoke unwanted reactions.

HOUSEBROKEN DOGS ARE GOOD; A BROKEN HOUSE IS BAD
Here are a few additional tips we found to be useful where household training is concerned. And by that I mean *your* training, not the dog's.

Heed the indoor leash law.
No, there's no law that mandates you have to keep your dog on a leash *inside* your own home, but doesn't it make more sense at the beginning? It helps with control and obedience. At the very least, you won't be tripping over your precious Sir Beauregard Flufferkins while carrying an infant in your arms.

Install baby gates.
Baby gates aren't just for the safety of the kids; they're the Grand Poobah of altercation thwarters. This has been our saving grace, as it keeps kid and canine from driving each other bonkers. Everybody gets their own play zone, so everybody wins. Not to mention, I don't have to listen to a constant refrain of, "Mommy, Bruiser is trying to steal my yogurt again!"

or "Ahhh, Mia *drooled* on me, Mommy!" or "Mommy, Ruby just ate my crayons!" That last one is, of course, my personal favorite, since it indicates that my dog will likely be pooping rainbows for the next twelve hours.

Crate-train your dogs, not your kids.
Obviously, I don't actually think you'll try to crate-train your child; I'm giving you the benefit of the doubt. I do, however, stand by going this route with your dogs. You might feel bad for a few nights, but you'll get over it and so will they. Our dogs have been crate-trained since puppyhood, and it comes in handy every single time we walk in the door with our kids. No one gets pounced on or licked to death, and the dogs get let out once we are appropriately situated. Having said that, please make sure your kids do not attempt to climb into the aforementioned dog crate. Aside from a few glaring sanitary concerns, it will also have the side effect of stressing your dog out.

Though I will concede that it can make for a funny, one-time photo op.

Get a diaper pail that seals tightly.
Honestly, a diaper pail can be like a savory smorgasbord for dogs. Vile and beastly but true. And the fouler the diapers, the more enticing they seem to be, so just don't go there—especially if you have a hound like we do. Do yourself a gargantuan favor, and don't leave stinky, smelly diapers anywhere within reach of a snout or paw. Tightly bundle baby's waste, and make sure you dispose of it before it attracts more attention than David Beckham visiting an all-girls boarding school.

THE CAST OF CHARACTERS

Kids and pets can bring out the best in each other. They can also bring out the worst. Much like a sibling, a furry family member tends to push a child's buttons in a way that can be both comical and exasperating. The way I see it, there are five different classifications of dogs . . .

1. The puppy pickpocket

Who needs cat burglars when you have dogs? These guys are plotting a hostile takeover of every baby item they can get their paws on. They've gone rogue, and their hunting skills result in the clever acquisition of various infant paraphernalia. Is that the missing pacifier in the dog bed? Is a baby bottle buried in the backyard? Rest assured, they aren't going to drag the baby off next. This is their way of politely asking for attention. Not to mention, what hound in their right mind can ignore a rattling Beanie Baby on the floor? That's like asking an adrenaline junkie not to paraglide off the Eiffel Tower.

2. The menace to society (or to your house, at the very least)

Is that Fido sifting through the empty baby-food jars? These guys are your run-of-the-mill, garden-variety rapscallions. They mean no harm with their rabble-rousing. They aren't trying to piss you off, and they aren't mad the baby has taken over their domain. They just don't think in those terms. Dogs are creatures of habit, and this is a massive change in their lifestyle. You used to pet them while you watched Animal Planet, chase them around the yard with that magic tree branch in your hand, and make them homemade doggie biscuits. Now you're preoccupied by a smelly, loud human who gets fed more often than they do and won't share its squeaky toys. Talk about a bone of contention!

3. The babysitter

This is a pup who's found his new career path . . . as life-long sentry. This dog will race into the nursery when the baby is crying and park himself between the sleeping infant and new visitors. He may even baby block *you*. He is invested in his new sibling's well-being, sometimes to a fault, and wants nothing more than to solidify his position as protector. My dog Bailey spent the first few months making sure the baby and I got up and down the stairs safely and paced in front of the swing while Gray slept. All of this from the dog I worried most about with a child around. Do not underestimate the power of your dog's own maternal instincts!

4. The artful dodger

This dog doesn't want anything to do with the screaming, cooing, whimpering, moving thing that hasn't detached itself from Mommy's boob since everyone got home from the hospital. He is most likely to hide in his crate for hours on end, neurotically peer around corners before entering a room, and reluctantly sniff the baby's feet before hightailing it out of there. Not to worry, this behavior almost always changes. Just give it time.

5. The canine cartel

It is pack mentality taken to a whole new, hair-raising level.

Since there are multiple dogs, there are multiple culprits . . . for *everything.* Yep, it's a bone-a fide mongrel mafia. This is the case in our house, where somebody is always wreaking havoc or creating a mess. For example, as Marlowe spits up on my shoulder, Bailey might simultaneously be dry heaving all over the sofa, and Mia might be sifting through the contents of the bathroom trash can. Someone is always passing gas or pooping. It's like a chronic, gnarly, über-disgusting tournament of bodily functions. There are few moments where one of my kids (canine or human) isn't begging to be held, pleading to be played with, or crying for food. And that's the way I like it. If you haven't already figured it out, I'm a glutton for punishment!

It isn't always easy to have five dogs, because it means five times as much mess to clean up. But it also means there's five times as much love going around, so we wouldn't trade it for anything. Also, we don't have to vacuum food from under the kids' high chairs nearly as often with them nearby, and I'll take any help I can get with the housework.

THE MORAL OF MY STORY

Move over, Rover, there's a less hairy (but equally slobbery) new sheriff in town. Bringing a baby into our pack was easier than I expected, thanks to some good advice and careful planning. I'm just glad I don't have cats.*

---

*If you have cats, I'm definitely *not* the master mentor you're looking for. I'm highly allergic to them, so I don't have a ton of experience in handling them. Also, some of them creep me out more than Chia Pets, the Teletubbies, or carnival clowns. Or Chia Pets of Teletubbies dressed like carnival clowns. Consequently, I avoid cats more than discussions about religion and politics.

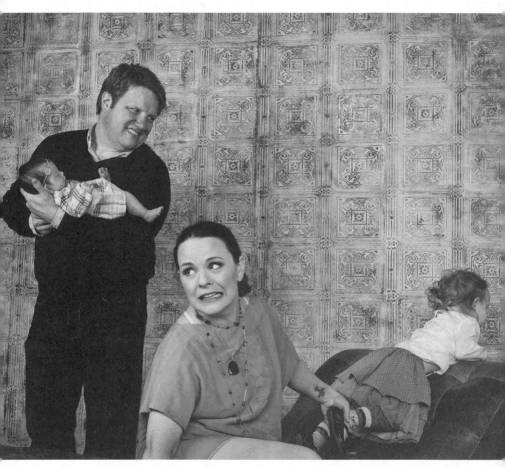

Brad and I perfecting our kid wrangling. Sort of. Not really.
Photo courtesy of Mimosa Arts.

CHAPTER 10
Driving around the Mommy Learning Curve

A SCENIC VIEW OF MY PAST

In 1994, I performed in the TV special *Circus of the Stars Goes to Disneyland*. It wound up being the final season of the popular celebrity-based reality show (back before watching stars publicly fall on their asses was something we couldn't live without in every time slot on every channel), and per usual, it was chock-full of corny jokes and hokey antics. Scott Baio was the ringmaster, so that should speak volumes. Nevertheless, I was seventeen at the time and pretty darn excited to be participating in something I'd never dreamed I'd get to do . . . soar through the air on a flying trapeze. I'll admit it's one of the cooler things I've gotten paid for.

You can sign up to swing on a trapeze rig at some of the all-inclusive tropical resorts out there, but this was a different beast to tackle. I spent months honing my skills for the big debut, and the rehearsals lasted several hours each day, including weekends. It took a lot of hard work to toughen up my hands, incessantly face-plant into a giant net, and persuade my poor seventeen-year-old back that it had a rubber band for a spinal column. And I loved every freaking minute of it. I was proud of my calloused palms, the black-and-blue marks on 90 percent of my body, and the six-pack that rivaled Joey Lawrence's. Which was seriously saying something! I wore my battle scars like a badge of honor, and I couldn't wait to leave the *Blossom* set behind each day so I could go and add to my collection. Also, I had a fairly substantial crush on Shemar Moore, the handsome actor who was learning to walk the tightrope nearby, so that lured me in like an ant to a company picnic. Did I have a chance with the guy? Hell no, but that didn't keep my imagination from convincing me otherwise.

For the record, Shemar was such a good sport about my infatuation that he graciously agreed to be my date to the *Blossom* one hundredth–episode party. He was quite the gentleman to a starry-eyed, pimple-faced, romantic of a teen-ager. Thank you, you sweet man!

But back to my *Circus of the Stars* appearance. After months of demanding training, it was showtime. All of my family and friends had gathered in the audience to witness me go spinning through the air like a yo-yo being dropped off a ten-story balcony because, as with a car wreck, it's hard not to look and think, *Better you than me.*

I was exceptionally amped up, likely on adrenaline and caffeine, a scary combo that made me yammer even faster than I normally did. If that was possible. I was also dolled up in my spiffy sequined leotard, a costume that looked significantly better on my co-flyers, A.J. Langer (*My So-Called Life*) and Debbe Dunning (*Home Improvement*). Still, I was all smiles as I took my place on the platform and prepared to launch myself into the circus-tent oblivion. Did I mention it was the first time they were letting us fly without our ropes and harnesses? Talk about pressure.

The first half of our routine went off without a hitch. All of our tricks landed perfectly, thanks to some superb coaching and catching from guys who had made the rounds in real circuses such as Ringling Bros. We were in excellent hands.

But there was one trick on the agenda that had me apprehensive, and it was quickly approaching. From what my trainers had told me, I'd been hired for the trapeze because I was compact and easy to throw. This translated to "Let's give Jenna all the hard stuff that requires tossing her around like a cobb salad." The mother of them all was called a seat roll, and it consisted of my climbing into a seated position on the trapeze bar itself. I would then fling myself backward, underneath the bar, and get caught by the dude with beefy muscles who was dangling upside down on the other end of the rig. Sounds simple, right?

Wrong. This thing had been the bane of my existence, and there had been talk of not letting me do the stunt at all on show night. But I can be a determined little rascal when I want to be, and I was adamant about proving I could manage it. Which, of course, backfired on me big-time. When I went for the trick, the audience gasped as I narrowly missed the catcher's hands and plummeted to the net below.

Strike one.

I ascended the ladder like an angry elf being stung by a nest of hornets and told my trainer I needed to try it again. I'll be damned if I was going out that way! Scott Baio made some sort of comment regarding being on the edge of his seat (yes, Scott, I'm sure I had you simply reeling), and I jumped off the platform. Yet again, I missed the catcher by inches and fell to the net below.

Sure that there were rumors of my acrobatic incompetence spreading through the audience like pink eye, I gathered up my dignity (what was left of it) and ascended the ladder like an even angrier elf being stung by an even bigger nest of hornets.

As I stomped my way up the rungs, my trainer called up to me, "Do you have another one in you?"

I looked him squarely in the eye. "Martine, I've got a hundred more in me." I'm not entirely sure that didn't pass for more of a threat than a promise, but Martine went with it. I'm nothing if not stubborn. This time, when I launched myself off of the trapeze bar, my hands hit my catcher's wrists with a loud thwack. It was one of the most beautiful sounds I'd ever heard. Take *that*, you doubting sons of bitches! (Which, I suspect, referred to me alone.)

CUT TO . . .

If mastering the art of trapeze entails swinging from a horizontal bar and trusting someone to catch you on the other end, then mastering motherhood is equivalent to flinging yourself off of the Seattle Space Needle without a bungee cord.

MY CRADLE CHRONICLES

Having a baby doesn't mean the secrets of the universe are instantly at your fingertips, so get ready for Mr. Toad's Wild Ride! Getting educated about babies, and all the new adventures they bring along with them, can be more unnerving than learning to drive stick in New York City traffic. I'm sure you've already been enlightened about some of what you have to look forward to in the first twelve months of being a mommy, but what's the truth and what's a myth? Let's see if we can clear a few things up.

FACT VS. FICTION: THE ULTIMATE SHOWDOWN

I've compiled some of the comical impressions and expectations I've heard other first-time moms confess. And yeah . . . a few of these came out of my mouth too. Sometimes more than once.

Love will make your world go 'round.
Myth: You'll feel an immediate bond with your child the second he comes out of the womb.

Truth: You may or may not feel an instantaneous and deep connection with the little guy that's taken over your breasts and your ability to get some shut-eye. You will, however, love him! An immediate emotional attachment doesn't necessarily equate to immediate bonding, and you may spend a few hours (or days or weeks) working toward that relationship. But think about it: did you instantly bond with every single important person in your life? Some of the individuals I'm closest to, including the man I married, weren't even on my radar when we initially met. Most women think they're supposed to feel overcome with profound intimacy from the moment they lay eyes on their child. This isn't always the case, courtesy of sleep deprivation, the intensity of the birth experience, and the process of adapting to life with a baby in general. Give yourself and the little guy time. It will happen, I promise!

The poop scoop
Myth: Kids want to have their diaper changed because it doesn't feel good when it's dirty.

Truth: Kids may not want a messy diaper, but that doesn't mean they'll let you put on a clean one. Changing a baby's diaper is like trying to fit a monkey for a tuxedo. (Minus, I hope, the wild jumping while throwing feces.) Kids squirm, wiggle, writhe, twist, and contort, and every mother should have a full-time baby wrangler as her sidekick. But unless you have a nanny or live-in help—you lucky bastard—you probably don't have someone to hold your child down while you prevent poop from working its way into every crevice imaginable. You know what luxury moms should have? A baby bidet installed at every changing station.

Upchuck upheaval
Myth: Spit-up means your child is sick, and a lot of spit-up means your baby must not be getting enough food.

Truth: I mention puking a lot in this book, but the fact is that vomit and spit-up are two totally different beasts. Spitting up is completely normal, even in healthy infants, and doesn't necessarily indicate a problem. Your baby doesn't have colic just because she spits up. (This was a big question of

mine, and it seems to be a pretty common misconception.)
I've learned there can be copious amounts of spit-up and, like
the Energizer Bunny, sometimes it just keeps going and going
and going. Is it fun to clean up? Meh, not so much. Is it dangerous for your baby? Apparently not if she's still her smiling and happy self. My understanding is that anything that's
forceful enough to look like your kid just finished a beer bong
tournament is something to call the doctor about.

Rub-a-dub-dub, pissed-off baby in the tub
Myth: Babies love bath time because it reminds them of being
in the womb.

Truth: The initiation bath can be slightly traumatic for some
infants, so expect some screaming. A bath takes baby out of
the comfort of your embrace and into very waterlogged foreign
territory. And since your baby can't sit up by himself yet, the
tub is slippery, awkward, and spacious. Even a little infant tub
looks like a football stadium to a newborn!

As a side note, pay attention to the last time your baby
had a notable poop before endeavoring to bathe him. Warm
water tends to loosen the bowels. This is a wonderful help if
your baby is gassy or constipated, but not such a great help
when you decide to hold him in your arms to apply the newborn shampoo. I have video, if you're interested.

You're getting sleepy . . .
Myth: You'll get so used to sleepless nights that you'll start

looking forward to those 2:00 a.m. infomercials from the twin dwarf real estate tycoons.

Truth: That's wishful thinking. There's nothing easy about waking up at all hours, and it doesn't get easier just because you're willing it to. Being kept up all night long by a hungry baby is always challenging, and even Dunkin' Donuts isn't capable of brewing enough coffee to fix it. The most important lesson I learned? Nap when your baby naps, regardless of what you have on your daily to-do list. The laundry can wait. Do I actually think you'll do this? Not a chance. I despised the people who gave me the same advice when my daughters were little, because I knew it was such a pipe dream. That's the only time you'll have to complete your work, mail out thank-you notes, wash your hair, or watch the season finale of *Castle*. And if you want to read another book before the year 3027, you'll be lucky to close your eyes for five minutes without twitching and buzzing like the neon sign at a roadside diner. In theory, it's a lovely idea. In reality, it's guilt-inducing. And yet I go back to . . . scrap the guilt and nap when your baby naps. Even if you hate me for saying it.

The crying game

Myth: You'll get used to hearing your child cry, and at some point it will no longer faze you.

Truth: Hearing your child cry is more agonizing than listening to someone scrape fork tines across a dinner plate with their left hand, as the fingernails of their right hand scratch a chalkboard, while Fran Drescher sings a lullaby into a cheap karaoke mic. It isn't that it's annoying, as my ridiculous analogy might suggest, but rather it stirs something emotional inside you that's tough to ignore. When my daughters cry, it hurts my heart like nothing else, even if those tears stem from an overly dramatic demand for attention or frustration over an unreasonable request I've had to turn down, such as cupcakes for breakfast. There's just nothing comfortable about seeing those sad little eyes well up. The nose scrunches, the lip quivers, and suddenly your instinct is to wrestle the stars down from the sky, if need be.

Basic instincts

Myth: Birth will automatically make your maternal instincts surface.

Truth: I believe every woman has maternal instincts. That said, for some individuals that instinct is gathering dust on a shelf in a long-forgotten storage unit somewhere. I talk a lot about instincts in this book, and I feel it's important not to confuse maternal instincts with your basic instincts or your new-mom anxieties. For instance, your basic instinct might be to panic at the sight of blood, while your maternal instinct is to remain calm for the sake of your child. Maternal instincts don't always kick in immediately; they can take time to gain solid ground . . . you know, like once you finally get more than two hours of sleep in a row. You may spend some time being clueless about how to hold your newborn, how to change diapers, what to do if your child gets hurt, or how to balance life in general. And that's perfectly okay; even moms with kick-ass maternal instincts feel that way sometimes. Instincts aren't errorless, and they aren't always easy to spot beneath the fatigue and tension.

The single most important lesson I've learned is to trust my own instincts. It sounds painfully obvious, but in a world plagued by social media frenemies and an excess of Internet information to sift through, it's easy to look everywhere else but inside of yourself for information. Even if you don't feel you were destined to be a mom, or born with a built-in mommy gene, have a little faith in yourself. Some of the best moms I know initially thought they weren't cut out for it.

Outlaw the input?
Myth: You should listen to every piece of advice you're given and file it away for future use.

Truth: Everybody will want to give you an opinion, but you're the only person who knows how to raise your child. You have to filter through the guidance and do your own soul-searching. Do you really think your bank teller is the best individual to help you decide whether to try an external cephalic version procedure for your breech baby? Is the clerk at JCPenney the most experienced person to explain why you should or shouldn't vaccinate your children? For that matter, is an actress from a popular '90s TV show the gal you should rely on for all of your parenting education? Listen with a kind ear and an open mind, then go follow your gut and the advice of the medical professionals you trust.

A damsel in stress
Myth: You won't have any anxiety after you've gotten used to having a baby around.

Truth: Ha! Good luck with that. The stress doesn't end; it just changes course. Worrying over whether or not your son is ever going to take to breastfeeding gets replaced by concerns over him crawling into sharp corners. Next thing you know, you'll be worrying that he's failing geometry and hooking up with girls in the school supply closet. It's all relative.

Motherhood vs. martyrhood
Myth: You can do it all on your own.

Truth: Excuse me while I fish out my Martyr-of-the-Year Award for you. I know it's in a box here somewhere . . . No, wait. I just remembered I had to forfeit that distinction when I finally admitted I couldn't take care of a newborn, shuttle a two-year-old back and forth to extracurricular activities, make all the family meals, clean the house, wrangle five dogs, and write two blogs and a book simultaneously. Sometimes the strength is in admitting you need a little help from those who offer.

Frustration station

Myth: Moms aren't allowed to get frustrated or feel over-whelmed, so you should suck it up.

Truth: We're only human; it happens. If you feel so engulfed in frustration that you can't see straight, it's okay to walk away. Please don't misunderstand—I'm not saying leave your kid on the floor unsupervised and head to the nearest pub. In fact, I'm not in any way suggesting you should leave the house. Make sure your child is in a safe place such as his crib or playpen, then walk into the next room, take a few deep breaths, and allow yourself a moment to regroup.

I've spoken to the parents of babies that had such bad colic they screamed for sixteen hours straight. As much as the parents felt for their child, they couldn't deny that it took its toll on them too. Sometimes the situation gets so heartbreaking and distressing that you'll need a few minutes of peace and quiet to refocus your energy and spirit.

There will also be challenging moments during which your child will refuse to listen, and it will take every ounce of strength to keep your anger in check (wait until year three!). Again, it's okay to leave the room and compose yourself. I promise this is better than any alternative that might involve taking things out on your child. Even moms need a time-out every now and again, so don't let anyone make you feel like it's abnormal. Just because you get fed up with your child's behavior during an exceptionally trying circumstance doesn't mean that you have abusive tendencies, your kid is bad, or you're an awful parent. We all get frazzled . . . How you handle yourself and your child is the true test.

Errant errands
Myth: Once you've healed from giving birth, running errands will be a breeze again.

Truth: Healing may be the least of your worries. On average, it takes longer to pack your kid and her accessories into the car than it does to run the errand itself. Triple that if you have twins or two kids under the age of four.

À la carte
Myth: You can easily stow an infant car seat in the seat of a shopping cart.

Truth: If you precariously balance the baby seat in the front basket of your shopping cart, you run the risk of it toppling over with baby inside. If you put it in the main portion of the cart, you can fit nary a string bean alongside it. If you push the cart with your left hand and a stroller with your right, you'll feel like you're in a Penn & Teller juggling act. The solution? Wear baby in a sling or carrier, or put the car seat in the main portion of the cart and refrain from buying more items than will fit around it. Or simply send your husband on the errand and skip the drama altogether. I tend to fancy the latter.

You can't save time in a baby bottle.
Myth: Time flies when you have kids.

Truth: Time doesn't just fly; it hurtles through space at a speed that mocks you and puts you on the express train to shuffleboard and prune juice at the senior home.

The art of distraction
Myth: Distraction is a magic trick parents exploit when they don't want to deal with answering their kid's fiftieth "But why?" or "Are we there yet?"

Truth: Yeah, that pretty much sums it up. Make distraction your friend and ally for as long as you can possibly get away with it! There will come a time when your child is ready to start exploring the world beyond his changing table, and he'll begin testing fun things like electrical sockets. Hopefully you've already installed outlet covers on those; it's never too early. Distractions can eventually keep your daughter from watching *The Little Mermaid* for the ninetieth time in a row (if you're lucky) or your son from smearing peanut butter on the toilet seat. At least you *hope* it's peanut butter.

Kid pro quo
Myth: Kids will do what you tell them to.

Truth: Are you high? No, really. Are you?

Cock of the walk and talk
Myth: Early walking and/or talking means your kid is smarter than the average bear.

Truth: Your kid may be gifted and smarter than the average bear, but it doesn't mean he's smarter than all his peers. There's no way to gauge it based on when he hits those milestones, so you may not want to enroll him in Mensa just yet.

Heigh-ho, heigh-ho, it's off to work you go.
Myth: You'll eventually find it's easy to leave your kid behind when you go to work.

Truth: Leaving for work may get easi*er*, but it certainly won't be easy. Our children are part of us, and it sucks to leave them in someone else's hands, no matter how trusted they are. Unless you are an emotionless robot, chances are you will always find it tough to bid farewell to your baby. Even if it's a necessity, and even if she gives you that gap-toothed grin, waving her chubby fingers, and saying, "I love you, Mommy!" Okay, *especially* if she's saying, "I love you, Mommy!" Those little guys sure know how to tug on our sappy heartstrings.

Dawdling mama = day care drama
Myth: When your child is old enough to attend day care, you can start thinking about enrolling him.

Truth: Who knew you had to register for preschool while your child was still in the womb? This may depend on location, but I found it was harder to get on the list for day care than the list for an LA red-carpet event. I didn't want to believe this when friends first told me, and I figured I was going to be a stay-at-home mom anyway, so why stress? When my work schedule picked up and I started realizing my daughter was in desperate need of some independence and social time as well, I was up a creek without child care.

One good learn deserves another.
Myth: You'll teach your child everything.

Truth: You'll teach your kids a lot, but they'll teach you more.

TALES FROM THE DARK SIDE

As much as I joke around, there are definitely aspects of motherhood that aren't quite as lighthearted and cheery. I think it's important to recognize some of the less glamorous sides of parenting . . . because weren't you already feeling so elegant while wiping baby bottoms and being handed boogers? Let's blow the doors open on this one, shall we?

Reach out and touch someone.
Myth: Motherhood is challenging only until you get the hang of it.

Truth: I'm broaching a bit of a sensitive subject here, but I think it's important to debunk the myth that the threat of feeling overwhelmed is over once you're no longer considered a new mom. There's a lot of talk out there about mothers who get severely depressed in their first few months of bringing baby home. The term *postpartum depression* has become a common topic of discussion in the mommy community. Many women who felt completely isolated before finally feel comfortable speaking up and getting help, thanks to the demystification and attention the issue has gotten. I think that's an incredible breakthrough! But we still have a long way to go; our battle isn't won.

While more new mommies are feeling like they can seek assistance and openly talk about it, what about the women who aren't hit with depression until later in their motherhood journey? Feeling overwhelmed and defeated can happen at any time. I think we should be honest about the fact that parenting can be difficult and stressful no matter what stage of it you are tackling.

Maybe you'll find the early years easy but the teenage years will make you question every prior decision you've ever made. Maybe you'll hit a rough patch when your kids are in middle school and you'll secretly cry every night because you're worried you're failing them.

The fact is, at some point we all feel a little daunted by parenthood. It doesn't necessarily mean we're clinically depressed or in need of medication, though I encourage you to seek help if you feel you can't handle it on your own. Parenting is rife with trials and tribulations; there will be phases that seem effortless and phases that make you want to find the nearest blunt object so you can bang your head against it.

You may never be afflicted with clinical depression, but I'd rather see us all maintain an open line of communication when the going gets tough. New moms aren't the only ones who need love, support, encouragement, reassurance, and close friends to confide in. If you experience periods that are emotionally grueling, don't go through them alone.

Little Mister & Miss Perfect?
Myth: You will feel your kids are perfection every minute of every day, simply because they are yours.

Truth: You won't always like your kids. You'll love them no matter what—even if they practice their alphabet on your bedroom wall with permanent markers or spill soda all over your laptop. Loving them despite their mistakes, whether those mistakes are accidental or not, is the easy part. But you may have moments where you don't like your children very much, and that's okay; there's a vast difference between the two. You can love your child every minute of every day and wholeheartedly know they are a blessing from God, while still acknowledging that sometimes you wish you could be beamed to a sandy dune in Bali where you can freely sip mai tais until your kid's temper tantrum subsides. Or until your husband comes home from work and provides some parenting reinforcement so you don't have to be the bad guy all the time.

Fake it 'til you make it.
Myth: All of the other moms you know are doing fine; you're the only one who is struggling.

Truth: Everyone has to adjust to parenting, and everyone has moments of sheer, tear-your-hair-out insanity over it. Anyone who says different is lying either to you or to themselves! Just keep taking those baby steps, and tell yourself you're doing fine. One of these days you might just believe it!

The blessing of "sacrifice"

Myth: You can have it all, without making concessions.

Truth: Kids are more than worth it, but adjustments to your lifestyle will have to be made. Constantly. Having children can turn your world upside down, and not everyone goes into parenthood with realistic expectations of that. Babies don't simply slide into your way of life and grow accustomed to your schedule. A new baby brings new priorities, and I can only hope that's a challenge you are eagerly anticipating.

I'm the last person to suggest you can't maintain being a parent and a career woman simultaneously, because I'd like to think I'm managing to do that right at this very moment. And I'm enjoying the hell out of it! But it requires a careful weighing of priorities. My husband and I have found our own sense of equilibrium with what feels appropriate to us and to our children. You will too, and sometimes that might mean an unconventional game plan. Every now and then you'll miss a ball game or a ballet lesson. Other times, you might forfeit a work luncheon, a meeting, or a conference in Boca Raton. I can't tell you not to feel guilty, because I still have no idea how to let myself off the hook. It's one of those parenting secrets I just haven't mastered yet.

I once read a quote by Chris Rock that said, "When I hear people talk about juggling, or the sacrifices they make for their children, I look at them like they're crazy, because 'sacrifice' implies that there was something better to do than being with your children." In some ways I agree with his statement, because I believe having children is an honor, pleasure, privilege, and reward. I would always rather be with my kids too! But that doesn't mean the choices that have to be made are always easy ones.

Learning to find balance can, in fact, be a juggling act; I don't think that term should automatically be seen as a derogatory one! That's just the reality of it: sometimes you have to find a way to devote quality time to both your kids and your other responsibilities in order to give everything and everyone the attention they deserve. You will surrender certain aspects of your current lifestyle. You will have to be less selfish. You will have to make tough decisions that make you feel like you're between a rock and a hard place. But I hope you will also love every minute of the exciting adventure!

The moral of my story

Sometimes nine months of preparation for parenthood leads to one giant belly flop after another. I've learned it's all in how we forge ahead. There's no way to "conquer" parenting, and the knowledge isn't going to be magically absorbed into our systems through osmosis. The education will continue no matter how old our kids are, because every age brings unique experiences along with it. Expect to make mistakes, and then expect your children to tattle on you to anyone who will listen. Because kids are generous and forgiving like that.

Have snack, will travel. Breastfeeding Marlowe in a parking lot, in between errands. *Photo courtesy of Jenna von Oy.*

CHAPTER 11

The "Breastaurant" Is Open for Business

A SCENIC VIEW OF MY PAST

It was the series finale of *Blossom*, and we were in the process of filming the Blossom and Six epic good-bye scene. I'd even dredged up a few tears for the occasion, though I suspect that had less to do with my acting chops and more to do with the three pots of coffee I'd consumed by midafternoon. I was jitterier than an alcoholic with a bad case of the DTs. Anyway, after five seasons and over one hundred episodes, everyone and their mother had shown up to witness our show take its final bow. The studio audience was full, and family and friends were abundant.

Which is, of course, why I was just thrilled to be stuck in pajamas for my last hurrah. What seventeen-year-old sex symbol wannabe longs to be remembered in a baggy, *Golden Girls*-esque nightie? And, go figure, that damned nightgown is where things went awry. In the middle of our teary farewell, I realized my pajama top had come untied and my nipple was about to make its television debut. You might question how that would even be possible, given that I should have been wearing a bra. Well . . . I wasn't wearing a bra. Suffice it to say

Mama didn't have much of a prize inside that Cracker Jack box, so I'd skipped the undergarment altogether. In a desperate effort to keep from being mortified, I clasped my hands in front of my chest as if it were part of my reaction to Blossom's speech. I pretended to be freaked out about the Russo family's impending move. Of course, in reality I was freaking out about my imminent nip slip.

As soon as the scene ended I frantically flagged down Ted Wass, who was directing the episode as well as costarring in it. "You can't use that take!" I squealed. "My shirt came undone, and I think everyone saw my boob!" I scanned the backstage area for a paper bag I could hyperventilate into.

"Nobody saw anything," Ted calmly replied. "The take was perfect." He turned to the crew and called out, "Moving on!"

I watched him casually walk away, while my addled adolescent brain went into panic mode. How could he do this to me? How could he let my wardrobe malfunction be the last joke I left our TV audience with? (Wasn't I fantastically melodramatic?)

As teenagers are wont to do, I obsessed about it . . . for weeks. In fact, I was absorbed with it until the episode aired several Mondays later. That evening, rather than finishing my homework, I sat in my living room nervously cramming a bowl of Skittles down my gullet. As soon as I heard the show's theme song kick in, I prepared to answer calls from everyone I'd ever known about my fledgling career as a porn star.

Needless to say, there was no boobage. How terribly anticlimactic. In fact, they didn't wind up using that take after all. Think about it—if Janet Jackson couldn't show her rack during the Super

Bowl in 2004, NBC sure as hell wasn't going to allow an under-age child star to be exposed on a family sitcom in 1995, right?

Catastrophe averted. Sort of. Because that's when I started obsessing that the film might be sitting in an edit bay some-where, to be resurrected years later when I least expect it. Cue the *Jaws* music . . .

CUT TO . . .

I'm booby-trapped, and I like it. These days, I'd be happy to advertise my breasts in the middle of a televised three-ring circus if it meant my kids were happy and well fed.

MY CRADLE CHRONICLES

People often ask me if I've kept in touch with Mayim Bialik, who played the always awesome Blossom. I'm pretty sure they'd be surprised to find out that we not only talk fairly consistently, but our conversations most often revolve around boobs. More specifically, *my* boobs. We are truly bosom bud-dies, if you will. Now, before your brain goes off on some twisted tangent about former child stars–turned–lesbians, let me bring you back to reality here. Despite it sounding like a really fun and provocative subject that the media can spin into some titillating press (you like what I did there?), we really spend our time discussing something quite normal: breastfeed-ing. That is, of course, if you think it's normal to offer a full-time dining experience from the nipples formerly known as fun.

The fact is that Mayim has become my go-to guru on all things lactation, since she happens to be a very knowledgeable Lactation Education Counselor. Things that make you go "Hmm," right? Whose flowered hat was floppiest and whether or not our fictional counterparts slept with the same guy in season four of our '90s TV show have become slightly less compelling to us than whether or not my milk dispensers are chafed and why.

Mayim has been my saving grace on multiple occasions, doling out guidance such as how to get my child to latch on without feeling like my tit is in a medieval torture device (practice makes perfect and trying different positions helps) and answering all manner of inane questions: "Why does my child ignore my right breast but have a preoccupation with my left?" (Most likely force of habit.) "Does it taste better over there?" (It's anyone's guess. Maybe that side puts out strawberry milkshakes or truffle-infused fondue.) To be fair, Mayim didn't actually say that; it's just my oddball sense of humor talking. Either way, she is clearly a very patient human being!

For some background, I've always known I wanted to breastfeed. I respect that it isn't for everyone, but I was pretty gung ho on the whole thing. My mom breastfed all four of us kids, so I grew up feeling attached to the idea of feeling attached. I've actually had a multitude of vivid dreams in my life, even at the ripe old age of fourteen, during which I nursed my future spawn. I loved it, even when it only existed in my surreal and warped nighttime abyss. It may just be that I've had a lifelong obsession with my lack of voluptuous double

Ds, and that bitter pill decided to manifest itself in my sleep, or maybe my insanity just runs that deep. However, I'd like to think it was my maternal instinct telling me not to fear it. And to stop watching *Rosemary's Baby* at four in the morning.

PUBLIC DISPLAYS OF BREAST AFFECTION

As the years have gone by, I've noticed strange trends emerge where breastfeeding is concerned. On the one hand, it has become less and less hush-hush from a societal standpoint, which is wonderful. Want to whip it out in the middle of a crowded subway? More power to you. I promise you'll have your staunch supporters, and you can probably assemble a million-mom march for the cause if someone kicks you out for doing it. That passion (which I *fully* respect) has also pushed breastfeeding to the focal point of the media such that there's really no way to be discreet anymore, even if you want to be. To feed your child out in the open, even if you employ a cloak-and-dagger routine, often means you can't escape fiery glances from fellow store patrons or airplane passengers, because everyone is on high alert about it. It means you are unwittingly caught in the throes of a heated public debate that exists whether you buy into it or not, just because you are fulfilling your child's basic need.

Breastfeeding is such a natural and centuries-old part of bringing a baby into this world, so why all the fuss? I have my own theory as to how the focus of a nation turned to boobs . . . oh, wait. That's right, it has *always* been fixated on them. Does anyone seriously think we're just kicking up dust on this matter now?

Our headlights have been in the spotlight since Adam and Eve. There are Hooters restaurants in every major city across America, which might suggest we're just looking for new and improved ways to stare at women's knockers without feeling guilty about it while simultaneously drinking beer and eating spicy chicken wings. Why do you think that ancient *National Geographic*, the one with the cover of a tribal woman offering a breast to her brood, is still on display in your doctor's office decades after it was published? Putting thought-provoking photos on the cover of *TIME* is just an attempt to class the attention up a little and make the argument a cerebral one. We've been not-so-civilly enthralled by the topic of breasts for a while now. Don't kid yourself.

With the invasion . . . er, I mean . . . super success of reality television, and our addiction to normal people acting like absolute train wrecks, public breastfeeding seems to offer folks another excuse to pretend they're shocked by something. It's like an up-close and personal version of *The Jerry Springer Show* for some of the wackos out there.

That said—and here's the crucial significance of this chapter—I do it anyway. When my kid needs to eat, I feed her, dammit! It's not like I'm streaking naked across a football field during halftime, participating in a *Girls Gone Wild* video, or exposing myself in an effort to obtain extra Mardi Gras beads; I'm providing nourishment for my child.

I encourage you to decide what your own comfort level is and go with it. To hell with the naysayers, because there will always be some! There will forever be people telling you it's tactless and ostentatious to breastfeed in public. Alternately, there will be people telling you to let it all hang out, regardless of who's around, because it's your right. I, for one, prefer to exercise slightly more discretion when the situation calls for it. The thought of openly breastfeeding in front of my father-in-law, for instance, makes me about as comfy as the pope watching Andrew Dice Clay perform his stand-up shtick. It would make my father-in-law uncomfortable; ergo, I'd like to respect that. I imagine you'll find a happy medium, as I have, but promise me you'll do what you feel is right for you.

I didn't start out being relaxed with the idea of public breastfeeding. When I first started nursing Gray, I felt like I needed to hide *everything*. (Insert absurd visuals of me in a trench coat and dark glasses here.) My inner cynic, who can be quite lively, was sure everyone in a ten-mile radius was waiting for a glimpse of side-boob. (As if there's much to see.) *Gasp! Is that a cell phone camera they're whipping out? Is this going to wind up splashed all over the Twittersphere this afternoon? Oh my God, are these darkened SUV windows magnifying my chest into a billboard-sized ad for La Leche League?* Yeah. I was a little theatrical about it, to say the least.

Here's the thing. No one gave a flying crap about whether or not I was feeding my daughter in the backseat of my own car in the middle of the dry cleaner's parking lot. Unless I'd carried around my very own neon sign that read Peep Show in Progress, nobody was remotely paying attention. People tend to have better things to do than seek out and embarrass a mom who's trying to feed her infant. You know, pressing things like talking really loudly on their smartphones while drinking their lattes and putting on mascara. Your northern exposure is the least of their concerns.

I admit that a little discretion can go a long way, if your kid will allow it . . . Naturally, mine did not. Apparently neither Gray nor Marlowe are really behind-the-scenes kind of gals (I can't fathom who they inherited that from), so they refused to be shielded by any sort of hide-a-hooter thingy.

In the early days of my motherhood, when I was still super concerned about it, I tried rigging Gray's favorite blanket into a makeshift body sling or car curtain, to no avail. I was stuck playing full-time peekaboob instead, which made for some precarious experiences.

I got over it. As Gray and I grew a bit more comfortable in our breastfeeding routine, and I stopped being ridiculously uptight, I discovered it's all about owning it. Sometimes you have no choice but to park a nipple in your baby's mouth and pretend you're so preoccupied with your kid that you don't notice people gawking. By the time you have the second child, you won't care if you breastfeed in front of the president of the United States.

Painful vs. practical

Some people will tell you breastfeeding hurts like a bitch; others will tell you it shouldn't hurt at all. Both can be accurate.

It's much like squeezing into those jeans that are two sizes too small, just so you can impress your fellow PTA moms. You know you'll have to hold your breath all night to keep them zipped up, but it's worth it when you hear one of them whisper, "Man, I can't believe she just had a baby!" Of course, in this particular instance, instead of your ego, your child reaps the benefits, so that seems like more than a fair trade.

The fact is that breastfeeding may not be comfortable or easy at first. As with any new endeavor you embark upon, it isn't without its quirks . . . if *quirks* really means pain and suffering. It usually takes about two to three weeks for your nipples to toughen up, and that time period isn't always fun-filled.

If I could purposely embrace the torment of nipple piercings in my twenties, I thought breastfeeding should be a breeze. In retrospect, I was blissfully ignorant, and I wish someone had been open with me about what I had to look forward to. It certainly wouldn't have changed my mind about breastfeeding in general, but it would have made me feel less panicky when things didn't go the way I expected. I've had my share of breastfeeding hurdles to overcome since then, and I've probably fretted more than I needed to in the midst of them.

Thankfully, at some point I enlisted Mayim's guidance and got on the right track. I encourage you not to get scared off by the prospect of things like mastitis and plugged milk ducts (though I can tell you from experience, the latter is more painful than the name implies); those maladies are out there, and you may do battle with them every now and then. I won't sugarcoat it and tell you that it'll be easy to get your baby latched on properly or that there are no miserable side effects in your future. But no pain, no gain, right? I've lived through both of those examples I mentioned, and they were merely bumps in the road . . . albeit sore bumps. I promise the benefits have far outweighed the sacrifices. And that's a serious understatement.

Despite my love and enthusiasm for it, the first few weeks of breastfeeding took some getting used to. And by that I mean I complained almost as much as a proud Irishman being forced to wear a leprechaun costume and stand on a street corner handing out samples of Lucky Charms. Your boobs will get raw and sensitive, and they'll have to get used to being sucked on constantly. Unless your hubby has a *serious* fetish for that sort of thing, your body needs some time to adjust to the constant attention. For some of us, it's similar to building finger calluses while learning to play guitar. (Which is, I'm sure, an example that's making you yearn to breastfeed!) My troubles didn't end with building up my tolerance. I also had an issue with flat nipples, which kept Gray from being able to latch on securely enough to nurse. I had to use nipple shields to sweet-talk them into coming out. And it's all fun and games until your nipples are being pulled out like a cavity.

Once my second daughter came along, my breasts were accustomed to the process and didn't rebel at all. Gray really paved the way for Marlowe, who latched on without a second thought!

I certainly respect your decision to stop breastfeeding if it just isn't for you. That said, if you feel strongly about continuing it but feel dispirited by the discomfort and pain, I encourage you to speak with a lactation specialist before giving up on the process. Consulting a professional might help you push through to the healing stage. Hopefully they can help you find that light at the end of the tunnel!

My go-to guru would tell me you shouldn't feel any pain

at all if your baby is nursing properly, but my boobs had a mind of their own on that one. Or maybe the fact that my daughter fed like a barracuda had something to do with it. Either way, once you hit your pain threshold you're most likely nearing the end of the gauntlet. Huzzah! Eureka! Now, if you're lucky like I was, you can move on to being a 24/7 breastaurant. Check, please?

MILKING THE LONGEVITY OF YOUR MILK

There are a lot of things to learn about breastfeeding, but the one thing I wish I'd known more about in advance were the general rules of preserving the milk properly. Believe me when I say it is liquid gold, and it physically hurts to watch it go down the drain if you're forced to ditch it. This means one needs to take suitable precautionary measures when pumping and stocking up. Here's what I've learned.

Don't expect babysitters to understand the concept of how precious your breast milk is, because they won't.
First things first, a visible bottle of breast milk in your freezer is a loaded gun. Put another way, you view your milk as a lobster dinner; they view it as a hamburger at a McDonald's drive-through. You'll come home from a much-needed Friday night date with the hubs, only to find that your sitter took it upon herself to thaw the largest packet of milk you have stored in your freezer—you know, the one that took the whole week to pump, since you can't get Mini-Me to take a break from feasting long enough to squeeze out more than a few drops at a time. But "Don't worry, Mrs. Bratcher"—that's my married name—"two minutes after I thawed it I realized the

baby wasn't hungry; she just needed a diaper change. Isn't that great?" Well, no, it's not great. Because guess what. Lesson numero uno, you can't refreeze breast milk.

Tuck that guy into the back of your freezer if you don't want it to be needlessly defrosted while you're away. And I mean the *way* back of the freezer, behind the frostbitten Lean Pockets that sounded like a good idea when you bought them four years ago but haven't been touched since.

Because telling your twenty-year-old sitter to use the breast milk "only as a last resort, once you've made sure the baby isn't just overheated or gassy," is code for "go ahead and use it if my kid whines or makes any sound that prevents you from texting your musician boyfriend."

Unfortunately, the aforementioned scenario means only one thing in our house—that the newly thawed milk probably won't be in any condition to be consumed by the time we get around to using it. I don't know about you, but my kid won't touch a bottle of milk if my boobs are within spitting distance.

Plus, there's nothing worse than having that big container of perishable breast milk looming over you every time you open the fridge to get yourself a snack. And by snack, I mean glass of wine . . . which brings me to the only solid reason to use that baby bottle: Go out and have a few cocktails with your girlfriends while your husband stays home with the baby. You get tipsy, the baby gets the bottle with untainted (non-alcoholic) milk, your husband gets to feel like you actually think he can handle being alone with your kid for more than five minutes, and everyone's happy!

*The general rules that apply to refrigerating breast milk aren't
an exact science.*

How long your milk will keep before souring depends on your
body, your fridge, and some scientific variables I know nothing
about. What I *do* know is that even if I store a bottle in the
very back of my extremely cold fridge, I often find the milk
goes bad after about forty-eight hours, which is significantly
less than I've been told is the norm. Many online sources quote
that you can refrigerate the milk up to eight days before using
or freezing it, but apparently the milk gods have conspired
against me.

For argument's sake, we'll use the current CDC guidelines.[*]

You can leave pumped milk out on a countertop or table
for six to eight hours at room temperature. This gives you
enough time to watch a few reruns of *Desperate Housewives*
before remembering you got too distracted to refrigerate it
like you should have in the first place.

You can store the milk in your fridge (preferably in the
back, where it's coldest) for five days. Unless, of course, your
milk has the life expectancy of a housefly like mine does.

You can keep your milk in the freezer (a normal freezer
that has a separate door from your refrigerator, not a compartment inside of the refrigerator) for three to six months. You
can supposedly keep it even longer, but the lipids in the milk
deteriorate, leaving you with inferior quality. Either way, this
essentially gives you enough time to stock up for the next Y2K
or Mayan apocalypse.

---

[*]"Proper Handling and Storage of Human Milk," *Centers for Disease Control and Prevention*, last modified
March 4, 2010, accessed April 27, 2015, http://www.cdc.gov/breastfeeding/recommendations/handling_
breastmilk.htm.

If you think the milk smells sour, it probably is.
Smelling the milk before giving it to your child is key. If you really aren't convinced, suck it up and taste it. There's nothing wrong with trying your own brand of booze in order to be sure you aren't giving your child something that will potentially make him ill. And for those of you freaking out that I've admitted to doing this, I'm not asking you to consume urine, for God's sake. Somehow, folks have no trouble drinking the milk supply from farmer John's heifer, who's out chewing her cud in the field, but they pale at the thought of tasting their own. You do what you've gotta do. I guarantee that ain't the crudest thing you'll have to do as a parent.

Mommy mammary maintenance
The market is saturated with various items to make breast-feeding easier and more comfortable, and a few of them even work. In case you're curious, my favorites are as follows:

1. *Lansinoh Soothies Gel Pads.* (Other companies make them as well; I just happened to like this brand.) These things saved me. I stored them in the fridge until they were ice-cold, then placed them on my nipples when I was sore. It sounds like some freaky sadomasochism ploy, but it's an incredible relief. They remove the heat from your breasts and give your nipples some well-deserved TLC. If you're more of a home-remedy kind of girl, cucumber slices or chamomile tea bags would probably work too.

2. *Nursing pads.* These guys slip in between your breast

and your bra to form a catchall, kind of like a maxi pad for your boob. I purchased fun, washable ones on Etsy and supplemented with disposable ones when need be. The beauty of the disposables is that they have adhesive, so they don't slide around as easily. This may not save you from embarrassment when your child decides to pull one out and wave it around at your fellow farmer's market patrons, but it will save you from the shame of accidental milk seepage through your matron-of-honor gown at your little sister's wedding. In case you haven't figured it out, I'm drawing from personal experience on those.

3. The Medela breast pump. These guys have it down pat. They not only make amazing hands-free pumps, but they also have a recycling program to use once you're done. Then they turn around and donate new, multi-use pumps to Ronald McDonald House in return. Instead of letting your pump wind up in a landfill somewhere, why not properly recycle it and simultaneously support a fellow breastfeeding mom in need?

4. Lansinoh HPA Lanolin for Breastfeeding or Medela Advanced Nipple Therapy. Lanolin is a salve that's so thick it could catch flies, but it's awesome. A doula friend suggested I liberally apply it to my nipples before showering, to prevent them from getting dry and damaged, because there ain't nothin' funny about cracked and bleeding nipples. It's the equivalent of having a million tiny paper cuts on your tongue. Even mild cleansers tend to dehydrate your skin, so some protection is imperative. The point of the Lanolin is to coat your nipples as thoroughly as possible so the soap and water repel off of it. I greased

---

It sounds as if I'm peddling Lansinoh and Medela merchandise like a high-strung Mary Kay consultant here, but I have no ulterior motive. Although Medela hired me on as their ambassador for the Medela Recycles campaign I mentioned in number 3, no one paid me to put any of this in my book. I honestly believe in these products!

my puppies like I was a meathead prepping for a bodybuilding competition. My nipples had their very own suit of armor.

5. *Motherlove Nipple Cream.* If you're just looking for a soothing salve, Motherlove makes a significantly lighter nipple cream that is also organic and all-natural. It's safe for baby's digestion (the main ingredient is olive oil, if that helps), and it makes for a nice bedtime balm. It's important to use baby-friendly products, since you have so much skin-to-skin contact with your child. Perfumed lotions and oils are likely to transfer to your newborn or, even worse, get into his mouth while he suckles. If you're anything like I was, a five-minute shower can be a luxury; I was lucky to have two minutes to towel off before I had to jump back in the breastfeeding game. With that in mind, I really had to pay attention to everything that went into washing or hydrating my body so it wouldn't cause allergic reactions for, or be ingested by, my daughters.

As a side note, towels and bathrobes can seriously activate your baby's gluttony. Seeing you in any attire that allows for easy access to the booby buffet is a baby's cornucopia. God forbid you walk around naked; it's game on! So if you need a brief recess from serving meals, do yourself a favor and cover up. Or invent a childproof chastity bra.

The curse of colic

You may be asking what colic has to do with breastfeeding. For me, the answer was *everything*, because Gray's trouble with colic was directly related to what I was eating.

To put it succinctly, colic is about as enjoyable as a double root canal. If you're the parent of a colicky baby, you'll be treading the treacherous terrain of sleepless nights and incessant screaming (sometimes both yours and the baby's), with a side of guilt thrown in over being powerless to fix the problem. In a nutshell, it'll make you want to tear out your hair and break out the good vodka.

I wish I had an easy remedy to throw your way here, but the one that worked for me was somewhat of a culinary debacle . . . I had to give up dairy. This notion was only slightly more pleasant for me than discovering a toenail in my coleslaw, but more on going dairy-free in a minute.

Colic seems to be a term that's rather loosely defined by Wikipedia as "A condition in which your otherwise healthy child cries or displays symptoms of distress (cramping, moaning, etc.), frequently and for extended periods of time, without any discernible reason."* Which, ironically, also happens to sound an awful lot like what your kid will go through during puberty. Colic gets a bad reputation for being the bully on the block, but I think he might get blamed for a few things he isn't responsible for too. For example, I have a sneaking suspicion gas or an underdeveloped digestive system are sometimes the quiet criminals. Even allergies can inflict mayhem on a tiny tummy. Regardless of which of those is the true culprit, it sucks when your kid is screaming and you can't determine the cause. There's nothing more anxiety-inducing than not being able to soothe the little person who depends entirely on you. And then, of course, there's the nonstop bawling. It's a laugh a minute.

*"Baby Colic," *Wikipedia*, accessed June 12, 2014, http://en.wikipedia.org/wiki/Baby_colic.

My own experience with colic went a little something like this: When Gray was born, we were informed that her stomach and lungs were still in the process of developing. We were also warned that the need for an early delivery might wreak havoc on her tummy, which was the understatement of the year. My poor baby was a hiccupping, belching, farting mess for the first eight months of her life. (I'm sure she'll be thrilled to read this in twenty years.) Her stomach gurgled so loudly that I thought someone was leading an uprising in there. As if that weren't intense enough, she was spewing projectile vomit like Linda Blair in *The Exorcist*. My little girl was an unbelievable trooper; she rarely cried for any reason other than the bouts of colic. When her abdomen seized up, however, her screams could have raised Elvis from his grave. The toughest part wasn't the amount of time we spent pacing with her during the wee hours of the morning, or the decibel level of her shrieking; it was the fact that there wasn't much we could do about it. Or *was* there?

Haunted by my inability to take my daughter's pain away, I started looking into possible solutions. The technical term for this might be *shooting in the dark*. I experimented with every burping angle, sleeping position, and natural colic aid on the market. I know a lot of folks use Zantac or other over-the-counter acid reflux reducers, but my husband and I really wanted to avoid giving our newborn medication, if at all possible. We were desperate to find a more holistic route, but nothing was working.

Finally, when I was about one gripe water attempt from a

nervous breakdown, a close friend suggested I give up dairy. She swore it had worked like a charm for her son, who'd had similar troubles. What's this you say? Forego all my beloved cheesy goodness for an indefinite amount of time? No butter, sour cream, or (and here's where I got really testy) iced venti, nonfat, two-pump toffee nut latte from Starbucks? That's just crazy talk!

I tried convincing myself the universe couldn't possibly be so diabolical as to conspire against my cheese consumption. I *love* cheese. Eating a triple-cream brie is equivalent to an orgasm for me. I mean there are sacrifices, and there are sacrifices!

But, alas, I was at my wits' end and willing to try anything. I started kicking around the dairy-free idea by researching it and asking around. The first stop was my daughter's pediatrician. She was mostly skeptical. I'm pretty confident she chalked it up to a passing fad and didn't really believe it would do much other than deprive me of my sanity. I didn't disagree, but I was open to throwing a Hail Mary pass. Go big or go home (to a screaming baby), right?

I'd given up wine during my pregnancy, which clearly proved I had more willpower than I'd previously given myself credit for, but no dairy? Was I really ready to take such a drastic step? The answer was a wholehearted and resounding yes, whether Gray's pediatrician thought I was loopy or not. Anything to help my baby get rid of her stomachaches and acid reflux, even if it was a toss of the dice. So it was farewell, yummy Greek yogurt, and hello, soy cheese, for me. Oh, the sacrilege!

The theory that giving up dairy can ease infantile colic

seems to be more and more common these days. In some circles, it's almost considered trendy. Mind you, I don't put much stock in what's *en vogue*. The idea of jumping on the bandwagon and conforming to the masses generally makes me run for the hills. In fact, unknowingly starting a world-wide hat craze at the age of twelve was my one and only trend-setting stint in this lifetime, if I have anything to say about it. But as I mentioned earlier, I was desperate and ready to jump on the dairy-free bandwagon if it would help Gray.

The week after I quit dairy cold turkey (sadly, they don't make medicated patches or gum for that), I brought the plan up to my OB-GYN.

"I'm all for it, and I fully believe it works," my doc told me.

For some background, she has several children and had given birth to a little boy a month or two before I had Gray. I really respect her input as both a mommy and a doctor, so I was interested to hear her take on it.

"I've been dairy-free for two months now," she continued. "I'm telling you, I've noticed a huge difference. My son is finally a happy baby. It takes two to three weeks to completely rid your system of the dairy, but I began noticing a difference about eight to ten days in. As an experiment, I tried reintroducing a little bit of milk last week, and my son started pooping crazy stuff."

Strangely, those words were music to my ears. My mind raced with the possibilities. You mean, like, he expelled the whole Monopoly menagerie out his butt? Or just Park Place and Boardwalk? Now I was intrigued. "Crazy stuff?" I asked, even though I knew not to.

She went on to tell me about the rainbow of fruit flavors

she'd discovered in her son's diaper; I'll spare you the details.

Nonetheless, she had me at "happy baby." It was enough incentive to keep my new diet going . . . especially if it meant avoiding erratic and volatile diaper contents.

As I started wrapping my mind around the dairy-free scenario, I realized a trip to the grocery store was in order. I packed up my little bundle of joy and drove to the nearest market. I drooled my way past the wonderfully stinky French cheeses and salivated over a pastry stuffed with mascarpone that I wouldn't normally hazard a glance at. Because, naturally, the more I told myself I couldn't have dairy, the more I wanted it. Isn't that always the case?

I finally arrived at the dairy-free section and began to peruse the shelves. Okay, I'm lying. I perused *the shelf.* As in, one shelf. A lone shelf with half a dozen items on it, some which looked more like they belonged in test tubes. But I suppose I was lucky to have even that many options, so I threw one of each into my cart.

After I'd shed a mournful tear for all the yummy lactose-filled things I had to leave behind, I arrived home with coconut butter, almond milk, faux yogurt, and a few scary-looking wedges made to resemble something vaguely edible and cheddar-like. For the record, those may *still* be in my fridge. I can't stand the thought of wasting anything, but I also can't bring myself to touch the stuff. On the other hand, I found I was quite fond of anything derived from coconut or almond milk, and I managed to stumble upon some delicious substitutes I'm still using to this day.

There are a surprising number of dairy-free alternatives

making their way to the supermarket aisles, as long as you freely indulge your culinary creative spirit. The Internet is also chock-full of recipes. (Though I advise you skip the gourmet sites you normally peruse or you'll be falling off the wagon in no time flat. Nothing says *fuck dairy-free* like scouring recipes for lobster mac 'n' cheese. And any attempt to make a salted-caramel cheesecake with rice milk is just plain unholy.)

Sure enough, two weeks after lactose and I had our insufferable breakup, my daughter started to feel better. And you know what? As much as I hated to admit it, so did I. I felt far less gassy and bloated, which may be more information than you wanted. I could even wear some of the clothes that I hadn't been able to pour my booty into before, which was an unexpected benefit. In the four months that I was dairy-free (yes, *four months*! Can I get a gold star for that? Or maybe a slice of gorgonzola?) my child-bearing hips shrank two sizes and my kid became the most content baby on the block. She was in such a state of euphoria you'd have thought I'd slipped her a Valium.

MILK DOES A BODY GOOD—MOSTLY

Here are some other important things I learned about breastfeeding.

When your milk comes in, you may find your areolae get darker or lighter, your breasts may become disproportionally engorged, and they might be big enough to feed a herd of hungry hippos. Similarly, your nipples may become firm enough to hang your car keys from, but at least you'll never have to worry about misplacing them again. That remote control key finder you bought from QVC at three in the morning has just been rendered obsolete.

Your boobs will see more action than Jenna Jameson.
As a side note, I'm overjoyed to share my first name with such a class act.

Did I mention your boobs will see a lot of action?
No, really. The cantaloupe ain't the only thing getting squeezed in aisle seven of the grocery store. And wait until your kid is old enough to start tugging your shirt down.

Kids don't know the meaning of indecent exposure, so wear a tight-fitting bra or break out the old hickey-covering turtlenecks from high school.
Rest assured, your child will choose the most unsuitable times to attempt to tear your clothes off, and it sometimes stems from boredom rather than a nutritional need. For instance, Gray used to think church was a good forum for feeling me up. Most often, this occurred midsermon. Praise the Lord, is that Jenna's breast I see? I've also experienced standing in an airport security line (attempting to juggle the baby, a "folding" stroller, and an infant car seat, while simultaneously removing my shoes), when it dawned on me that my kid was headed for second base in front of every TSA agent in the Tri-State area. Who needs an X-ray machine?

If you see men (or anyone else, for that matter) staring at your boobs, check for leakage.
Don't assume you're looking so hot that everyone you pass by is contemplating a wild romp in the hay with you. The fact

that you're toting a wailing toddler on your hip who's leaving a trail of snot and the faint stench of poopy pants behind you probably severely lessens your caliber of seduction. It's physically impossible to ooze sexuality when you're also oozing baby goo.

Breastfeeding gives you an excuse to be lazy, and what new mom doesn't deserve a few minutes to sit still?
You also deserve a few minutes to shower, comb your hair, and get out of your pajamas, but let's not get carried away. You'll have to get a bit more creative for those opportunities. Breastfeeding is honestly the cheapest, easiest, most natural source of food for your baby. As luck would have it, it also allows for *Mad Men* marathons while you dish the goods! The milk is always warmed and ready to go, and it keeps your kid from getting sick as often. Your body actually sends protective antibodies to the mammary glands, which shield your baby from infection and build immunity. How freaking cool is that? Between us, my husband and I saw several bouts with the flu, multiple colds, and a sinus infection before Gray's first birthday. We went through five boxes of Kleenex in three months, and that's no exaggeration. But despite our steady stream of maladies, do you know what Gray came down with? One slight bug that lasted for a few hours. Got milk?

As if having an excuse to embrace being lazy isn't enough motivation, breastfeeding can be a huge catalyst for losing your pregnancy weight.
Who needs a gym membership when you have a calorie-sucking newborn doing push-ups on your chest?

You need to trim your baby's fingernails frequently.

I know you're probably wondering how this pertains to nursing, but I promise you won't be asking that question when little Freddy Krueger gets going. You *will* become a scratching post! Infant nails are akin to mini tattoo needles, and they can rip your chest open like a raccoon rooting in the Sunday night garbage.

Don't be surprised if your kid is a milkaholic.

This is normal, and it doesn't require a twelve-step program. There's not much else to preoccupy him yet in this life, so he's grasping at straws . . . or nipples, as the case may be.

Even when your breasts have grown accustomed to having a fanatical booby groupie, it may not be the end of your agony.

On a good note, the new suffering brings some comedy along with it. You may find that your child's captivation with your boobs results in any number of the following practices: flesh-pinching, squeezing, smacking, slapping them like a Christmas ham, punching, poking, prodding, kneading them like pizza dough, jabbing, tugging, and tuning in to 97.7, The Nipple (playing all-day hits on your tits). In fact, you may see more titty twisters than hell week at the local fraternity. Regrettably, you're not allowed to get wasted like those boys are.

Beware of baby mind control.

Don't be surprised if you fall under the spell of breast brainwashing. Marlowe could make me lactate the second she even *thought* about food. The milk letdown was so forceful it felt like someone was taking a Taser to my nipples. And the scariest part is that I got used to it!

As with earthquakes, you will be rocked by a few aftershocks.
For example, following my booby boot camp, I wasn't aware my left nipple would decide to stand at eternal attention. Who knew the Pointer Sisters would wind up directing traffic full-time or flagging planes coming into the Nashville airport? The reality is that your breasts may never be the same again. But you know what? Suck it up. (Sorry—bad choice of words there.) Your husband isn't worried about whether your nipples are bigger or more uneven than they used to be, as long as he can still mess around with them. And that's what really counts.

Beware of getting too used to playing show-and-tell with the tatas.
Those guys . . . Yeesh! You give them an inch, and they take a yard. The more generous you are about letting them see the light of day, the more second nature their exposure becomes. And the more second nature it becomes, the better chance you have of not noticing that Lil' Miss Lefty is popping out to say "What's up?" to the sweaty UPS guy as you sign for a package from *Diapers.com*. That driver probably sees less excitement than a snail on any given day, so don't give him a reason to be equally slimy. If you aren't cautious, your neighbors may also be in for a treat. Or a teat, as the case may be. I've had to consciously stop myself from pacing in front of our giant picture window while I breastfeed, so I don't unwittingly look like I'm running a neighborhood bordello. When people start doing

drive-bys to see if the porch light is red or begin calling you Miss Kitty at the local block party, it's time to get curtains. Mundane outdoor tasks should be taken into account as well. On more than one occasion, I've caught myself retrieving the mail in a partially detached nursing bra. Swanky, I know. My point is, being on display can become all too familiar. My advice is to think of your breasts as masked crusaders. Even Superman needs to cover up in a disguise from time to time, right? It's a bird, it's a plane, it's . . . oops!

Breastfeeding can be messy business.
When your breasts are locked and loaded, be careful where you take the safety off. Let me explain. Have you ever turned on your backyard hose, only to find there's a puncture causing water to spray clear over the fence and onto your neighbor's cat? Well, milk-supplying nipples don't have just a single hole; they have many holes. Every now and then they fancy themselves a sprinkler system and, if you aren't careful, they can take someone out. Not surprisingly, insurance doesn't cover that sort of accident. If you're curious about the milk-shooting phenomenon, think of what happens when you shake a champagne bottle. The cork keeps all that carbonation in there, and as soon as you release it, it gushes out. Sometimes, if you've waited a while to nurse, the pressure builds up. A bit of prompting from your little one is enough to send that milk out like it's being propelled by a turbo booster. Pleasant thought, huh? Don't misunderstand me—it isn't painful at all. But it's like playing badminton with firecrackers every time you give your kid a snack in public. Duck and cover, people!

You will have some funky side effects.

I didn't get my period for a year and a half, which I attribute to the frequency of breastfeeding. Apparently my body was telling me to slow my roll and postpone trying for that second kid until after I'd potty trained the first one. (A word of caution: if you aren't menstruating, it doesn't necessarily mean you aren't ovulating; it just isn't consistent. In other words, you can still get knocked up and not have any clue until you're doubled over the toilet, puking your guts out. Consider that my warning.) Also, and this may have nothing to do with breastfeeding at all, my hair fell out for fourteen months like I was in the throes of chemotherapy. I'd heard I might lose a few more strands than normal, but that didn't come close to describing the gruesome scene. Every time I showered, I pulled softball-sized clumps out of the bathtub basin. If I'd started collecting it all at the beginning, I could have made myself a Hannibal Lecter–inspired fur coat. Or perhaps a really barbaric toupee.

Try and try again.

Infants can be picky about their eating habits, so that old adage is definitely true for breastfed babies. Breastfeeding requires a lot of trial and error, testing of various positions, and mental diligence. Your little one may love the cradle hold but despise the football hold. Try everything and figure out what makes both of you most comfortable. Believe it or not, the same can be true for bottle-feeding. The first time I pumped for my second daughter so my husband could have some bonding time with her, she screamed bloody murder and turned that bottle down like it was liver and onions. We discovered she hated the length of the bottle nipple. Since every nipple is contoured differently and has a specific level of milk flow, a breastfed baby tends to be naturally drawn to the ones that more closely mimic her mom's breasts.

Get ready to love it.

All joking aside, I wouldn't trade the bonding experience for a million nights of sound sleep. In fact, the thought that I'll eventually have to stop nursing already makes me want to weep, despite the fact that I'm still in the process of breast-feeding Marlowe. Moving on from breastfeeding can be emotionally challenging and draining for everyone. Gray and I both experienced withdrawals from it when she weaned at nearly two years old, even though from a maturity standpoint, she was ready to give it up. Her heart definitely belonged to the boob, and we both liked it that way! Although I knew I would be having more children to breastfeed in the future, I missed the quiet moments Gray and I spent simply gazing at one another as she ate. The special and unique relationships I've developed with both of my girls have been greatly enhanced by breastfeeding, and I've cherished every moment. Even at three in the morning, when I'm too worn out to remember my own name.

If you're having trouble breastfeeding, don't be afraid to reach out for help!

There are generally classes offered at your local hospital, La Leche League likely has a support team in your area, and (with any luck) there should also be a fabulous team of hospital lactation consultants on hand after you deliver. Their knowledge, assistance, and emotional support are there for your benefit, so take advantage while they're available!

As a heads-up, not all the lactation nurses will treat you with kid gloves, which isn't necessarily a bad thing. Nipples often have to be coaxed a bit, and some lactation nurses will endeavor to physically help that along. You may be uncomfortable with the thought of a nurse being hands-on, but the alternative is not having a proper latch. That's far more frustrating and uncomfortable, mark my words!

After Gray was born, I recall being put off by the second lactation nurse who was assigned to my room. I was so physically and mentally spent that I yearned for a gentle hand to help guide me. I just wanted my kid to eat, for crying out loud! The first nurse had been kind and soft-spoken, so the second nurse's gruff approach was nails on a chalkboard. I'd graduated from Florence Nightingale to Nurse Ratched in one hospital shift.

I mean, I'd just been poked with needles, doped up, pried open, stitched up, and deprived of solid food. This was promptly followed by seventeen hours (*seventeen*!) of not being allowed to hold my precious baby, who I was so desperate for that I was bordering on maniacal. The last thing I wanted was a rough introduction to latching on. But I wasn't there to dip my toes in the water; I was there to dive in headfirst and sink or swim. Thank God for Nurse Ratched, or I would have been at the bottom of the deep end.

Initially, I bristled at how brusquely she thrust my daughter's face at my breast. *The kid is less than a day old*, I thought. *Is she really ready to sidle up to the bar like a Betty Ford Center reject?* The answer was an enthusiastic *absolutely*. Apparently it was just what the doctor ordered, because Gray started knocking my milk back like it was Colt 45.

In retrospect, the first nurse hadn't provided us with anything other than encouragement. And while I likely required some of that too, what I *really* needed was a crash course with visual aids. In no time, Gray and I were on our way to being pros. It just entailed some experimentation and a lactation nurse who knew how to get results. I'm eternally grateful, despite her cantankerous breastside manner. My advice? Don't bite the hand that feeds, or your kid may end up biting the nipple that feeds him.

CAN I GET A LITTLE LOVE FOR ALL THE NONBREASTFEEDING MOMS OUT THERE?

I admit that I'm in the breastfeeding encouragement camp, which must be blatant by now. I believe it is incredibly beneficial for your child, and I feel the bonding is unparalleled. However, that's my personal opinion. Not everyone even has the choice to breastfeed, for one reason or another, so don't beat yourself up if you opt out of it. That's your prerogative, and *no one* should be crucified for that! The world will not end if you don't breastfeed. Exhibit A: I can think of several dear friends who weren't breastfed, and I can't imagine the bond they have with their mothers being any deeper or more loving.

Alternately, I know folks who were breastfed who don't have stellar relationships with their mothers. So don't put unfair pressure on yourself! Formula is not the root of all evil, despite what some might say. If you do what's right for you and your baby, you're doing the right thing. Case closed.

THE MORAL OF MY STORY
Breastfeeding my children has provided me with some of the most beautiful bonding time I could possibly hope for. It has also rendered me an exhibitionist and part-time taffy pull. Fun stuff.

An example of the sort of "exercise" that helped me get rid of the baby weight after I had Gray. *Photo courtesy of Mimosa Arts.*

CHAPTER 12

Survival of the Fittest: Losing Your Pregnancy Weight
without Losing Your Sanity

A SCENIC VIEW OF MY PAST

I've always been curvaceous. Some of the more polite folks
have applied benign euphemisms such as *thick* or *shapely* to
describe my proportions. Others have scrapped the sugarcoating altogether and opted for slightly more offensive versions;
I'll refrain from rehashing those, since I'm sure you are creative and resourceful enough to come up with some good ones
on your own. (That said, *thunder thighs* was a personal favorite.)

At the end of the day, I guess Hollyweird has been consistently shocked by the fact that my measurements are . . . normal.
To be frank, it hasn't always been the most supportive place
for a young girl with a bubble butt, a flat chest, and the height
of an Oompa Loompa. Still, I wasn't (and I'm still not) often
considered for the leading lady roles, given my size and stat-
ure. If you look like Malibu Barbie and you can act, or sometimes even if you can't, the entertainment industry is thrilled
to roll out its red carpet for you. If not, some doors have to be
opened. Or knocked down. Or pummeled with brute force
until they fly off their hinges. It's a good thing I know how
to deliver a joke.

It took a long time for me to embrace my figure, and I thank God for parents who made sure I knew that the rest of the world didn't necessarily mimic the views of the superficial LA scene. Going back to the East Coast during my hiatus weeks was a huge help, since I was consistently reminded that not everyone lives on coffee for breakfast, lunch, and dinner, with a side of lettuce thrown in from time to time for nutritional value. It also served me well to be on a sitcom where the lead character wasn't a tall, buxom blonde with a propensity for giggling like a schoolgirl. I didn't play the gawky sidekick to the shallow head cheerleader; I played the best friend of a nerdy, trumpet-playing, exemplar of an ordinary adolescent. I'd like to think Mayim and I were both adorable in our own right, but my stance remains—we weren't the poised, pimple-free beauty queens one might expect to grace one's television screen. Which, in my humble opinion, was a beautiful anomaly. In a sense, *Blossom* punched a hole in the industry's ozone layer, and I'm proud to have been a part of that. I'd like to think we assisted in paving the way for more average-looking, relatable teenagers on television. Maybe we even convinced a few girls out there that they didn't need to look like one of the picture-perfect *90210* chicks to survive high school! (Hell, I might have been one of those converts myself, if my former agents hadn't kept sending me on all the fat-girl roles they could find. Which was a constant morale booster. Notice I said *former* agents.)

Even so, that didn't keep me from having my share of body-image-related incidents. I've included a couple, for argument's sake.

Un-emaciatedly ever after

In 1997, I guest-starred on an episode of the poor man's *Married With Children*, called *Unhappily Ever After*. *Blossom* had ended not too long before, and I'd been a bit stunned (though I'm not sure why) by how brutal the Los Angeles auditioning scene had gotten while I was preoccupied by a full-time series. I'd gone from competing for roles as a child to competing for roles as a twentysomething, and that was a culture shock. Now my peers were prettier, the competition was stiffer, and the available parts seemed to be fewer and further between. So when I booked a bit part to play Kevin Connolly's love interest on the WB series, I was pretty stoked. I happened to be close pals with Nikki Cox, so I wasn't mad that someone was actually paying me to hang out with my friend for a week either. And who can turn down working alongside an alcoholic, chain-smoking, debauchery-devoted stuffed rabbit voiced by Bobcat Goldthwait? It was like acting opposite a cussing, unscrupulous version of Alf. I was in puppet heaven.

On day one, I showed up for work with my lines nearly memorized and my spirits high. The first order of business? A wardrobe fitting. I walked in to find the fabulous gay assistant pulling clothes for me. In a rare turn of events, I was actually playing a cute girl, so that meant sexy little numbers that accentuated cleavage. (Thank you, silicone bra inserts!) After years of Six's flamboyant style, complete with cowboy boots, baby-doll dresses, and the notorious hats we all know and love, I was finally graduating to the big leagues. Nearly nonexistent skirts and precariously plunging necklines . . .

Who could ask for anything more? I introduced myself to the costumer, and he began having me try on the garments he'd chosen.

I'd provided my sizes in advance, so I expected it to go fairly smoothly. You can't argue with the facts, right? He handed me a dress, and I promptly poured myself into it. It was snug, if snug is a hippopotamus wedging himself into a polka-dot bikini. Looking in the mirror, I admired the newer, more provocative me.

The assistant rolled his eyes dramatically and made a clucking noise that I generally reserve for know-it-all teeny-boppers and prudish great-aunts. Dismissing the ensemble with a patronizing wave, he pulled something else from the rack. It was a pair of tight pants and a bustier.

Despite an earnest attempt, I couldn't get the pants past my thighs; they were clearly made for an Amazon woman with pencils for legs. I laughed it off, shrugged, and turned to him with a rueful smile. "Guess I need to grow a little, huh?" I joked.

If I was expecting civility in return, I didn't get it. Instead, I was met with a look of sheer horror, a derogatory snort, and an exaggerated head shake. He didn't stop there. "Ugh. How am I supposed to find something cute to fit *those* hips? They should stick to casting skinny girls."

Gee, thanks, buddy. And just when my ego was climbing back down from that ledge.

The case of foot-in-mouth disease
In 2005, I guested on an episode of *Cold Case*. Being pigeon-holed as a sitcom actress had haunted me for long enough, and

I was delighted to have been cast in a well-respected drama series. It was my chance to prove I was capable of more than just a comedic assist. Because that particular episode took place in the '80s, it was also a fun opportunity to wear wigs, colorful makeup, and other whimsical attire I generally wouldn't . . . except, perhaps, on Halloween.

Case in point, I wound up sporting a skin-tight leopard-print mini dress with some perilously high heels. Having just come off of a five-year run on *The Parkers*, where our craft service table was often laden with Roscoe's Chicken and Waffles (don't knock it until you try it!) and where folks actually appreciated a woman with some meat on her bones, I filled out that little number in a way that was nearly obscene. I'm glad it was obvious I was with the film crew, because being on location near Sunset Boulevard in that getup could have earned me some side money I hadn't bargained for.

When it was time to shoot my first scene, I was called to the set from my Honeywagon, and I began teetering my way over. If I'd been smart, I might have temporarily worn flip-flops or slippers instead, but I was all about first impressions. And apparently, I was faring well in that department. Glancing across the street, I spotted a sound guy manning his cart. He took one look at that dress I had on, turned to the guy next to him, and said, "Wow, look at *that* fat ass!"

Now to be fair, he said it very quietly, never expecting me to hear him. And technically speaking, I hadn't. Unfortunately for him, however, I'd spent a summer volunteering at a deaf arts camp, so I was profoundly adept at reading lips. Better than George H. W. and his infamous new taxes.

Finding the chance to mess with a crewmember far too enticing to pass up, I called out, "I certainly hope you meant that as a compliment! That was *phat* spelled p-h-a-t, right?"

That poor blundering audio bloke started stuttering incoherently and practically peed himself. I smiled and kept walking.

CUT TO . . .

I may never qualify for Hollywood's version of thin or drop-dead gorgeous, but my German heritage gave me a love of bratwurst, a pretty formidable stubborn streak, and a solid set of birthing hips. And in the long run, aren't those more useful?

MY CRADLE CHRONICLES

Not everyone looks like Cindy Crawford a month after they give birth. Then again, most of us didn't look like her in the first place. If dropping your pregnancy weight seems more far-fetched than winning the Powerball, don't despair. I've felt your pain and the love handles too.

I'm often disappointed by (otherwise known as jealous of) the number of celebrities who show up in the press only a few weeks after having a baby, appearing svelte, toned, and well-rested. Don't they know better than to go flaunting their good looks and glamour? It's unfair to the rest of us normal folks, especially those of us who are vertically challenged, who don't have the genes to pull it off! Or, for that matter, the personal trainers, nutritionists, nannies, and/or plastic sur-geons. No one should spend nine months expanding, then be able to bounce back like a rubber band in a week or two. It's eerily unnatural.

Lord knows I didn't rebound so easily. I gained forty pounds during my first pregnancy and forty-three with my second. You may or may not find that to be excessive; I don't see much need to defend it either way. Suffice it to say that a few weeks after I had my daughters, I was still feeling like the Michelin Man's illegitimate child.

Not that I begrudge you if you're able to easily lose the weight. As long as you're doing it in a healthy manner, more power to you!

Having said that, I return to the concept that not all of us can drop our pregnancy pounds like they're a yacht anchor, and most of us don't have endless resources to help us reach that goal. Some women have to work really hard at it; others have to work even harder than that. It can definitely get discour-aging, especially when you see friends and fellow moms who make it all look easy. Keep reminding yourself the bulk of it can be attributed to body type and genetics. They go a long way toward defining how it all goes down. If you find your-self throwing your scale at the bathroom mirror, try to give yourself a break! Losing nine months of accumulated weight takes time.

It's also good to keep in mind that your body parts don't always feel like going back to the locations whence they came. Your boobs, for example, may decide they prefer being closer to your belly button than your chin, and your butt may experiment with performing its best imitation of a flat French crêpe. Mine did. I've been asked countless times how I managed to lose the rear end that so famously earned me a spread in *King* magazine years ago. The truth? I had kids. Was I looking to lose it? Not in the slightest. In fact, I'd always been quite proud of the attention my "assets" had garnered. Unfortunately, my body didn't give me a say in the matter.

DON'T WEIGHT IN VAIN

I hope you weren't expecting me to spend this chapter divulging previously undisclosed, underground secrets for pregnancy weight loss. If they exist at all, which I sincerely doubt, no one has bothered to share them with me either. All I've got for you are the following tried-and-true practices.

Exercise

It's the obvious solution, and there's a reason for that. It works! Mind you, I'd be lying if I told you I'd actually used this method. I'm not proud of it, but I absolutely *abhor* hitting the gym. I know the health benefits and yada yada, but I simply despise it. Unless my workout consists of lifting a rib eye or a glass of Syrah to my mouth, I'm not terribly proficient at making time to exercise. Hence, I'm totally ignoring my own practice-what-you-preach stance on this one. Ultimately, I realize that just because I suck at finding time for exercise doesn't mean it's a bad idea. So basically, you should do it even though I didn't. Isn't that nice and hypocritical of me?

Regardless of my aversion to going to a gym, mother-hood has made me realize that exercise comes in many dif-ferent forms. Just because you aren't running on the treadmill or lifting weights doesn't mean you aren't accomplishing the same things in your everyday routine. Try the following pro-gram on for size (not that your kid will give you much of a choice): catch a barrage of Cheerios in midair, sidestep tor-pedoing teething toys, heft baby in and out of the bathtub, lug infant car seat around Target for an hour, volley ten dia-pers into the garbage receptacle, wash three loads of laundry, bounce crying infant for twenty minutes. Repeat until you pass out. If that's not enough to tone some arm muscles, I don't know what is! Of course, you'll also need to make sure you follow your doctor's orders regarding what your body can handle and when. For example, I wasn't allowed to pick Gray up in the two weeks following Marlowe's birth, because my C-section incision needed ample healing time. Don't overdo it!

Breastfeeding

I swear this isn't my way of being sneaky and trying to force my breastfeeding convictions on you. Breastfeeding actually hap-pens to be the main reason I lost so much weight so quickly after I gave birth to my first daughter, so it would be a little strange if I didn't give it the credit it deserves. Granted, I'm sure body type has something to do with it, as does the fact that I don't eat a ton of junk food (desserts during pregnancy not withstanding). I did have that four-month stint of going dairy-free on account of Gray's awful colic, which I'm sure didn't hurt either. But I can honestly attribute most of the weight loss to breastfeeding; it burns that many calories per day. (Which means you also need to be diligent about following the proper guidelines for how many calories should be consumed per day while breastfeeding!) Now, I've had friends who breastfed that swear they couldn't lose the weight, so I'm sure it also depends on other factors, such as natural metabolism. In fact, my own experience drastically differed after I gave birth the second time around, when I found it took significantly longer to lose my pregnancy weight despite breastfeeding. Nonetheless, I'm sticking by my method. How can you go wrong when weight loss is an accidental byproduct of something you're doing for your child's benefit?

Stop stepping on the scale.
No, it won't actually make you lose weight any faster, but at least it will prevent you from losing your mind until you do. The point is to be realistic. Don't expect your skinny jeans to fit two weeks after you give birth. You have to allow your body time to work its way back down. It also takes a while to shed the excess water weight, especially if you were pumped full of IV fluids at the hospital, so don't judge yourself prematurely. It'd be great if we didn't judge ourselves at all, but I suppose we should have realistic expectations of that too.

Ignore the ignoramuses.
Disregard those offhand, glib remarks made by the insensitive ass-hats who don't recall how challenging it was to lose

pregnancy weight and who don't have a dog in the hunt. Sadly, there are a lot of those out there. For example, here's a fun story about just such a fool.

When my first daughter had just turned four months old and there was no longer any reason to see my OB-GYN every other week, I thought it might be a good idea to find a primary physician. I can only imagine how sad my gynecologist must have been that I was going to be calling someone else for every question and ridiculous self-diagnosis of the neurotic kind. And just when she was about to give me my own honorary parking space! Anyway, I hadn't seen a general practitioner for over seven years, unless you count going to the doc-in-a-box when in need of a flu shot. Which I don't.

It was still relatively new for me to be getting out of the house with Gray. I was finding my life of poopy diapers and incessantly lactating breasts far too alluring to share with the masses, tempting though it sounded. Therefore, a trip to the doctor was a more riveting outing than it should have been.

I arrived at the doctor's office early and spent the next forty minutes running the typical new-patient-paperwork gauntlet. Which, in case you're curious, is super easy to handle with a squirming, hungry infant in your arms. I felt like I was buying a house or adopting a child as I signed the mountain of forms that would merely allow me to be in the presence of someone with a medical degree. After spending significantly longer than I cared to answering questions about whether or not I suffered illnesses and symptoms I never knew existed, and never wanted to, I was brought back to the nurse's station.

A diminutive woman in her late sixties brought me over to the scale-and-height chart and did her best to obtain my measurements. God bless her, she was shorter than me and could barely reach above my head to move the sliding marker into place. I envisioned gifting her with a five-tiered step stool at Christmas and then lost myself in a funny thought bubble that involved her challenging Shaq to a friendly game of hoops. (For the hell of it, I had her win.) Anyway, as I stepped away so she could squint up at the ruler from behind her Coke-bottle glasses, she inadvertently dropped the marker by an inch. She declared me four feet eleven inches and made a note in my file.

Now, I'm no doctor, but I'm fairly certain I didn't shrink during pregnancy. According to every medical professional I've ever been to, I'm hovering somewhere between five foot nothing and five feet one inch. This may seem like a silly thing to dispute, but when you're fun-sized like me, an inch can make a huge difference.

Knowing the nurse's faux pas, but not wanting to be rude, I politely asked if she wouldn't mind measuring me one more time. Inevitably, the same damn thing happened, as she struggled to peer at the results. This time, however, her hand didn't slip quite as much, and she conceded an additional half an inch. Four feet eleven and a half inches. Yay, me!

One would think the fact that I'd suddenly shot up by half an inch over the course of thirty seconds would give her pause, but such was not the case. I opted to leave well enough alone. In the long run, what could it hurt? It's not like I had a contract with Elite Model Management hanging in the balance, and even at my size I can still clear the height re-strictions on theme park rides, so I'm faring okay. Perhaps the woman was trying to recruit me for some sort of Napoleonic bowling league. Who knows? I figured I might as well play along and take one for our precious, pint-sized team.

Now that the height fiasco was over, it was time to be weighed. I inhaled sharply and silently prepared to have my ego bruised. Drumroll, please . . . I was 130! I nearly jumped for joy. I'd managed to lose thirty-seven pounds in four months, which was far more than I'd expected, consider-ing my lack of dieting or gym attendance. I was pleasantly surprised and pretty darn proud of myself. I mean, I would have been perfectly content *not* to have lost all that weight so quickly, so I couldn't complain.

My pride and I blissfully followed the tiny nurse back to the exam room, where we sat and verbally addressed every single question that had been asked of me on the forms I'd already filled out in the waiting room. I felt like she was about to scream, "Liar, liar, pants on fire! You *do* have a family his-tory of Hippopotomonstrosesquippedaliophobia! (In case it sounds like I'm making stuff up, that's actually a real thing. It's the technical term for a fear of long words and, by virtue of my having written it here, I suppose it pretty much clears any theory that I might be afflicted with it.)

We eventually got down to the height-and-weight section of the questionnaire, and she became oddly grave. I started to get nervous. "You're four foot eleven and a half," she stated dryly. Inwardly, I rolled my eyes. Outwardly, I acknowledged her assessment. "And you are 130 pounds," she finished with a look of mock sympathy.

Color me confused. "Okay," I mumbled. "Is there a problem?"

Her next words blew me away. "I'm obligated to tell you that you are obese."

Say what? I didn't bother trying to pick up my jaw off the floor. Laughing awkwardly, I tried to locate whatever scraps of my pride had stuck around. There were none. "See that little girl down there in her infant carrier?" I asked her. "I just gave birth to her four months ago. I haven't lost all my pregnancy weight yet."

"Yes, you look great," my elfin friend said dismissively, "but you're overweight. Would you like some brochures on that?"

Brochures? Is this lady serious? They better be pamphlets about time-shares in Cabo or safari tours in the African bush, I thought. But believe it or not, I wasn't mad. Offended, sure, but not mad. In fact, I'm just dark and twisted enough to have found it hilarious . . . but only because it was happening to me.

If any other woman had been standing in my place, I would have been profoundly angry on her behalf. Can you imagine that being said to someone suffering from postpartum depression? Or how about someone who battled bulimia prior to having a child? Yikes. The bigger question is, would she have had the audacity to say the same thing to me had I been four months along in my pregnancy?

I thought for a moment and inquired, "How overweight am I?"

She glanced down at her chart. "Point one," she answered

emphatically.

I was dumbfounded. "Let me get this straight. I'm only *point one* over the standard weight measurement for my height?"

"Yes," she replied simply, "if you were a half an inch taller, you'd be all set. Are you sure you don't want those brochures?"

I rest my case. May you never experience this level of stupidity as you work to get back to your pre-pregnancy weight.

Desert the desserts.

After I had both girls, I found it difficult to abandon my new-found affinity for sweets. Nine months of packing away the chocolate éclairs and butterscotch brownies make for an arduous divorce process. If you can find it in yourself to eliminate any of the "bad" things you craved during your pregnancy, you will likely lose the weight more rapidly. Of course, if you were yearning for deep-fried donuts covered in mayonnaise and candy corns, chances are that's easy to ignore now that your bizarre cravings have subsided.

I'm not advising you to diet, as that's not something I can speak to from a health standpoint. My suggestion pertains mostly to frivolous items that are easily avoidable, such as cooking with gobs of butter and cream, or continuing your Friday night ritual of ordering one of everything at the Taco Bell drive-through. I'm not reinventing the wheel here—we all know cutting out the fat equals losing the fat. But it's nice to have a reminder now and then.

Sometimes the reminder comes in the form of how your child reflects your food consumption. If you're breastfeeding, your child may show signs that what you're eating isn't sitting well. Nothing weaned me from my dessert compulsions quicker than my daughter's tummy troubles. The constant crying and diarrhea led me to the whole dairy-free phase I've referred to on several occasions. After two weeks, Gray was finally keeping an appropriate amount of breast milk down and had ceased screaming like a feral cat after every meal. By sheer default, I'd also dropped another few pounds.

THERE'S NO CRYING IN WEIGHT LOSS

I offer all of these rather simpleminded, amateur ideas as a nudge in the right direction. If you've hit a wall greater than the infamous one in China, you may wish to seek consultation from a nutritionist, fitness expert, doctor, or weight-loss specialist. I'm no Jenny Craig or Jillian Michaels over here!

In fact, when I did the cover shoot for this book, I had given birth to Marlowe five months before, and I was still about twenty pounds heavier than I wanted to be. Instead of begging the art department to Photoshop me into a lie, I embraced it. I hope you do the same!

With any luck, you'll find the things that work for you, be it ten minutes of yoga in the morning before your baby wakes up, or hard-core boot camp while your husband sweats it out at home on babysitting duty. As long as you're cutting yourself some slack and having realistic expectations, it's all good! Slow and steady wins the race on this one. I guess we can just be thankful the tabloids aren't scrambling to snap photos of us in our bikinis!

THE MORAL OF MY STORY

Two kids later, my nipples have a mind of their own, my booty is all but nonexistent, and my belly boasts a beautiful scar over the layer of plump goodness formerly known as a flat stomach. In case you were wondering, Six no longer has a six-pack. Could I eat bland fat-free crap, hire a trainer, and bust my ass seven days a week to achieve that again? I'm certain I could. But when would I have time to be a full-time mommy or write the next book? We all have our priorities. I'm living life to its fullest, and I've concluded that I don't need to fit in with my model-looking starlet peers as long as I can fit into my beloved pre-pregnancy jeans. Someday. Maybe.

Please
wash your
hands before
touching mine

A peacefully sleeping baby Gray—at least until some crazy fool ignores my overprotective sign. *Photo courtesy of Jenna von Oy.*

CHAPTER 13

Shot through the Heart and Germs Are to Blame

A SCENIC VIEW OF MY PAST

I think we've already established that I was a bit of a mischief maker as a youngster. It wasn't intentional, mind you, but my creativity often led me to express myself in peculiar ways. Which is a polite way of admitting I was a handful. Yes, Mom and Dad, you finally got me to put that in writing.

This particular story begins with makeup, which I've always been fascinated by. When I was a kid, one of my favorite parts of booking a new show or commercial was getting to watch the makeup artist go to work on transforming me. That's certainly not to say I was motionless or calm for said artist. I fidgeted like a puppy circling his next bush to pee on. Nonetheless, it instilled a love in me that continues to this day.

One of the bright ideas I got when I was about ten was to begin my very own tackle box of supplies. Since my parents weren't about to buy me stock in Revlon, I began asking the professionals I worked with if they had anything in their kits they could spare. One lipstick, two eye shadow, three mascara, four; five blush, six bronzer, seven concealer, more. In no time, my personal stash was better than that of most rodeo clowns. There was one makeup artist I'd worked with on several different projects, and he fed my cosmetics gluttony like no one else. He'd contributed face glitter, fake tattoos, and some false eyelashes that would have made a drag queen jealous. One day, he surprised me with the crème de la crème of prized goods—special effects blood capsules. I assume this already has your mind reeling. I mean, what good can come out of a ten-year-old being in possession of blood capsules? To elaborate, the tablets were filled with some sort of powder that, when mixed with saliva, would emit a gory-looking mess. They were harmless, didn't contain real blood of any sort, and weren't at all complicated to fabricate. If I had been really enterprising, I could have made them at home with empty gel caps, some syrup, and a little food coloring. But who needs to raid the pantry when you have the real thing? And so I commenced getting myself into trouble.

Those capsules stared back at me for weeks, just begging to be used. They sat in their cozy little nook of my cosmetics caddy and taunted me like a high-strung street mime. *There must be some way to do justice to the awesomeness that is a blood capsule*, I thought. And then the light bulb went off. April Fools' Day was rapidly approaching, and who was the most gullible person I knew? That was an easy decision: my mom.

When the day of reckoning was upon me, I waited until my mom was busy handling other affairs and thought I was quietly playing by myself in my room. Which, for all intents and purposes, I was. I climbed onto the giant armoire in my bedroom, took a stack of heavy books, and threw them against the wall for dramatic sound effect. I then worked myself into hysterics, complete with tears streaming down my face (I'm an actress, after all, so this stunt is in my repertoire), and raced upstairs screaming, "Mommy! Mommy! My teeth!" at the top of my lungs.

My parents rushed in to find me covered in blood, the red liquid streaming down my face like I'd been mauled by a grizzly bear. And just when they were seconds away from dialing 911, I grinned psychotically and shouted, "Happy April Fools' Day!"

There was nothing happy about it. I'm actually surprised they let me live to tell this story. My mother nearly fainted, falling to her knees and sobbing violently. My dad was so enraged he couldn't even speak. He pointed me to my room like the grim reaper, and I wasn't allowed to come out for a long time. I've never faked tears since, except when I've been paid to do it professionally. Still, I have no doubt that karma will eventually come back to take revenge on me. I hope my daughters don't read this.

CUT TO . . .

If seeing my child toddle into a table corner is enough to make me cry, I can only imagine what I put my mom through all those years ago. Nothing is heavier than watching your baby suffer, even if the intention behind it is something positive, such as a monthly well visit to the pediatrician. I quickly discovered that watching my child receive vaccinations was more painful than attending a Justin Bieber concert. Not that I've ever been to one, thank God.

My cradle chronicles

When your child makes his grand entrance into this world, he will spend his first few months being shuttled back and forth to the pediatrician for checkups. In other words, you're about to become a glorified chaperone. Your car will become a catch-all for every distraction tool and pacifying instrument known to man, and you're likely to see more of your pediatrician than reruns of *I Love Lucy*. It's crucial to make sure you have a doctor you trust implicitly, and it helps if that doctor isn't more effectively reached by plane, train, or spacecraft.

For the most part, you will be bringing your newborn to the doctor for growth-and-development assessments. Your appointments will revolve around monitoring your baby's weight, height, health, and nutrition, with the added benefit of getting free samples of fun things like grape-scented Boogie Wipes. I love those!

Provided that you choose to have your child immunized, you will also have front-row seats to the shot show . . . which ain't a romantic comedy, I can promise you. But more on that later. Let's talk about the basics first.

Finding a good pediatrician

Ask friends and family you trust for pediatrician recommendations, and make sure you've had an opportunity to sit down with the doctor well before baby is born. Most doctors will meet with you face-to-face, which I strongly suggest, and this will get a lot of your initial questions out of the way. It will also ensure that you're more comfortable when it's finally time to bring baby in. If you're at ease with the doctor, your child will be more at ease during the visits too. I'm not suggesting he'll be jumping for joy at the idea of getting pricked with a needle or examined like he's a lab specimen, but babies can't really jump for joy about anything at that age, so they're shit out of luck anyhow.

Truthfully, the appointments will probably be more stressful for you than they are for your child, simply because you know just enough about what to expect that you can fret in advance. We stress out more than our kids do, and we don't even get a lollipop when it's all over. What's up with that?

Make sure your pediatrician is on the same page.
You need your pediatrician to be a loyal advocate for your child's well-being. If you have specific points of view on vaccinations, breastfeeding, or other health topics, make sure you find a pediatrician whose principles coincide with yours. If you go into it butting heads, it's harder for the doctor to do her job and for you to be an effective parent. To be clear, that isn't to say the doctor will never, or should never, disagree with you. If you need to be educated about symptoms, remedies, or information in general, you need someone who will be honest and up-front. You both bring different knowledge to the table. You might better understand your child's sleeping and eating habits, for example, while the doctor better

understands what might be causing those habits to be inter-rupted. It is critical that you work together to best serve the health of your baby.

Make sure you trust your pediatrician.
She's your go-to gal for all things puke, snot, rash, mucus, nonstop crying, and blood related. It's vital that you have retained someone who keeps you calm, eases your fears, and professionally explains things in terms that make sense to you. She is the one you'll be calling at 2:00 a.m. when your child is sick with something you're baffled by, or when you're comforting a screaming toddler who (God forbid) just managed to trip over her toys and split her head open. You want a doctor who is patient and kind, whose staff promptly return your phone calls, and who doesn't make your kid shriek like a cornered pig every time she enters the room.

Be as honest as possible.
Holding back isn't helpful to your doctor's diagnosis. Sometimes it's easy to automatically jump to the conclusion that you're being paranoid, especially since all of this is uncharted territory. If you think something might be indicative of a larger issue, don't chalk your suspicions up to inexperience! Let your doctor decide if the information is relevant. Alternately, try not to exaggerate, which poses its own set of problems. I'm prone to long, drawn-out stories (clearly), but I do my best to present only the facts at doctor's appointments. Spouting flowery versions of my daughter's breastfeeding habits and waxing poetic about her tummy ache

won't get me very far. Even though it's tempting.

WHAT TO EXPECT FROM YOUR CHILD'S DOCTOR

Your pediatrician will probably visit the hospital to check on your newborn in the day or two following delivery. It may be someone else from the practice instead, depending on whose shift synchronizes with your stay, but someone generally makes an in-person appearance. He'll look at your baby's chart, assess how you're both adjusting, and answer any immediate questions or concerns you may have. After that, well visit schedules can vary from practice to practice. I've found that most pediatricians like to do checkups at birth, approximately one week after birth, and then once every few months. My daughters had checkups at six months, nine months, twelve months and so forth, until the vaccination schedule settled down and they were graduating out of the infant stage.

Expect to be nervous, even if nothing is wrong.
You may find you anticipate your pediatric appointments with all the tranquility of a jackhammer tearing up a concrete sidewalk. That's perfectly acceptable, though you may want to switch to decaf on those days so you don't prattle on like Little Miss Chatterbox. Or like me. If I could remember to follow my own advice on that, it would also be great.

Ask all the questions you need to.
Your first few weeks (or months or years or lifetime) will be spent praying you do right by your child. Initially, you'll want to do everything by the book, and you'll spend a lot of time

sweating the small stuff. Your doctor won't think you're a loon for showing up with questions . . . even if your list is longer than Rapunzel's hair, and even if you're afraid that half of your questions will make you sound dumber than the invention of diet water. This isn't his first time doing this, but it is yours and he's taking that into consideration.

Why is our baby fussy every time she eats? Is this rash cause for concern? What can we do to help soothe her to sleep? What does yellow poop mean? How many hours should baby nap in one sitting? Should we wake her up to feed? I promise you'll have plenty of inquiries, and your doc anticipates that too. Ask away, and bring a notebook to write all the answers down in, because it takes a while for that baby-brain thing to subside. Don't rely on your husband to remember all the answers for you either, because even though he looks interested, he's probably daydreaming about Monday Night Football.

Take advantage of the knowledge source.
Ask for help with the fundamentals. Have your doc show you how to properly take your baby's temperature, clear his nose of gunk, and best assist your baby with getting rid of post-feeding gas. I'm a better learner when I have visual examples to follow, so I enlisted our pediatrician to give us a dress rehearsal of the essentials, which was highly beneficial when showtime rolled around. For instance, no one is comfortable the first time they have to insert a rectal thermometer, so it's marginally easier if you've had someone show you the ropes in advance. Just as long as you're not the one being practiced on.

Don't freak out if the doc asks about your daily routine and home life.

I know it seems like you're being peppered with prying questions that sound like you're being accused of a major parenting infraction, but that's not the objective. It isn't your doc's subtle way of finding out if you're violating some secret mommy code regarding how many times your child should have her diaper changed in one afternoon or what holding position you've settled on during breastfeeding. The questions don't mean that she has social services on hold, that your name is being indelibly written on some in-office patient blacklist, or that you're about to be ostracized by the entire medical community. And, in case this thought was running through your overactive imagination, she can't tweet out snarky commentary about you once you leave her office either; she's bound by medical oaths and some serious HIPAA laws. (With any luck, she's cooler than that anyhow!) Don't let your imagination run amok on this one.

Well visits are all about adjustment. Your physician is simply trying to assess baby's lifestyle thus far so she has some sort of foundation to work from. Infants aren't capable of saying, "I'm fussy because I'm already teething," or "My diaper is cutting off the circulation in my thighs," so the doc has to piece together a general picture of baby's new environment and go from there. Siblings and parents are a good indication of how baby is adapting, so don't be surprised if she asks how you are managing too!

You know your own child best.

Trust your gut. If you think something is wrong, call the doctor. That's what he's there for! Of course, if you talk to him more than your own husband, you may want to distract yourself with a productive pastime such as crocheting mini baby loafers, reupholstering the high chair, or painting life-sized portraits of every baby photo you've taken thus far.

Listen carefully.

You may know your child better than anyone else, but don't mistake that for knowing more than your doctor. There's a reason you didn't hike up your legs and deliver your own kid, and there's a reason doctors get paid the big bucks to diagnose and treat the rest of us. They aren't Yoda, Mr. Miyagi, Dumbledore, or some other fictional all-knowing being; they were educated and trained for longer than most of us can handle being in school, and they have a lot more hands-on experience with kids than we do. Maintain an open mind and heart, because if you've chosen your pediatrician wisely, you should feel secure about the information and course of treatment he's giving you.

THE SHOT HEARD 'ROUND THE WORLD: VACCINATIONS

Let me start by openly stating that my husband and I are very pro-vaccination. This is a decision we made after research, introspection, and a careful weighing of facts. Whether or not each of us chooses to vaccinate our own kids may be a personal decision, but it ultimately affects those who come into contact with our children as well, so it's important that we make the effort to get educated. I hope your pediatrician's take on it will be a strong consideration too. That said, the point of this section isn't to engage in a conversation (or all-out brawl) over whether or not vaccinating is the "right" or "wrong" path for you to take.

If you do decide to vaccinate, don't be surprised if the vaccination schedule freaks you out. There will be more shots than most people can handle in any given sitting—even at a bar. Since this is one of the first times your newborn has experienced discomfort or pain, she may scream for a minute. And since she isn't old enough to be placated by a pretzel or a Tinker Bell sticker, your boob may be working overtime for a while. If you're anything like me, just the sound of my child crying is enough to make me start lactating, so you should already be primed and ready for action. Stay calm and offer baby all of the love and affection he needs to feel safe!

Bugging out about bugs

Now that we've covered doctors' visits and vaccinations, let's discuss keeping your baby well. Unless you're planning to banish your baby to a plastic bubble, there's no way to entirely avoid germs. This is especially true if you have a lot of visitors, so don't feel guilty about making sure sick family and friends stay home until they're better. No one is going to watch out for your child more than you are, and it's better that you risk hurting someone's feelings rather than wind up with a sick infant. Since it takes time to build up a newborn's immune system, the first few months are critical. Your loved ones mean well, but sometimes their excitement over meeting the new arrival supersedes their common sense. Politely ask everyone to refrain from stopping by if they're under the weather. That is your prerogative as a parent.

Despite your best efforts, germs are inevitable, so you may find yourself at the pediatrician between well visits. It's best to consult your doctor if your little one catches something, even if it seems like a common cold to you. We can't run to the local pharmacy and throw the usual remedies at a sick newborn, so call your doctor and ask what you can do to get baby's sensitive system on the mend.

The good ol' stomach flu

Illnesses can take on a life of their own in children, since kids don't know to make a mad dash for the toilet before throwing up or politely request a tissue when their little noses start oozing. This fact might lead you to hoard a surplus of cleaning supplies and brush up on your sterilization skills. The worst of these culprits is the good ol' stomach flu. It's like some foul, twisted, graphic novel rendition of a Dr. Seuss book. "One puke, two puke, baby pukes, you puke" or "Do you like puke here or there? Do you like it everywhere? Would you like puke in your house? Would you like puke on your blouse? I do not like puke, that is true; now I'm stuck cleaning buckets and bedsheets too."

When Gray caught her first stomach bug, I learned that vomit doesn't discriminate. It doesn't care if you haven't yet cleaned up the mess on the couch before it decides to invade the living room rug. It doesn't give a flying you-know-what if you are wearing your favorite dry-clean-only trousers or if your laundry triples in under ten minutes. It's enough to make you want to call in a hazmat team. I'll ditch my fears of a populous-crushing Ebola outbreak when we can find a way to keep the simple stomach flu from jumping from family member to family member like a damn camelback cricket. And if you don't know what that is, look it up. Those suckers are *ugly*. Almost as ugly as the stomach flu.

I didn't get sick often as a child, but I recall a few doozies. When I was six years old, for instance, I caught a particularly heinous twenty-four-hour bug while filming a commercial for a Chuck E. Cheese's–like establishment in Philadelphia. We'd taken the train in from Connecticut, shown up to hair and makeup, and then I promptly began shivering and feverishly mumbling.

Even at the age of six, I wasn't willing to give up a job. I was mortified at the mere hint of having to leave set and relinquish the gig—even if that meant suffering through hours of climbing through bouncy balls infested with pathogens (which I was clearly helping to cultivate), and rocking out to interminable rounds of badly crooned kids' songs being warbled by animatronic hedgehogs.

My favorite part of the experience was when I upchucked all over the stale, grease-laden pizza I had to pretend was delicious. And I was already tortured by the fact that I had to eat pizza in the first place, since I was the one freakish kid in America who abhorred the taste of it. They had to have a bucket standing by so I could do the old heave-ho after every take of that scene. Which, I'm confident, was an absolute pleasure for the entire crew. At the end of the day, the commercial added a bit of money to my college education fund, so what's a little gagging and barfing?

I think I was less affected by my own childhood bouts with the stomach flu than I am nowadays when my girls get sick. It's miserable watching your kids endure any pain or discomfort. I'd gladly trade my own well-being if it meant my kids could go through this life injury-and-illness-free. A mom can dream.

As a side note—and this is important to file away—sympathy puking is nothing to be ashamed of. When Gray got sick for the first time, I'd just gotten over the crud too. On night one of the dreaded spectacle, my sweet girl sat up in bed, called out for me in the pitiful way only a feverish and nauseated child can, and then instantly vomited all over herself and her bed. I rushed into her room just in time to catch my kid and half of the aforementioned vomit in my hands, and that stench brought me over to the dark side. I wound up taking a field trip to the toilet right afterwards. Twice.

The only positive spin I can put on all this is that kids don't usually throw up for days on end. Relative to an adult, the symptoms are generally milder in nature . . . at least in my experience. In our house, flu vomiting has lasted only a few hours before subsiding. Thank God. Because a few hours of corralling wayward bodily fluids and aggressively pushing replenishing liquids on your baby like a Times Square street vendor hocking bogus Rolex watches feels like an eternity.

The common cold

I hate to say it, but colds are equally miserable. They are equivalent to the little dive bar leeches who just won't quit sending cosmopolitans your way. They seem to show up so often you might think they're stalking you and, unlike true dive bar wack jobs, you can't make a cold go away by scribbling a fake name and number on a napkin. *WebMD* statistics say a preschool-aged child will get an average of nine colds per year, which is staggering. And true. If you think that's bad, wait until they start attending elementary school, because the average supposedly goes up from there!

The beastly part about colds is the congestion. Coughing fits are bad, puking is no picnic, but congestion is downright evil. In my opinion, there's nothing more disturbing than worrying your child can't breathe. Marlowe had a recurring cold that wouldn't go away for the first few months of her life, and we lost a lot of sleep over that. It was such an awful one that even my breast milk wasn't enough to combat it. Infants can't blow their nose or cough up a phlegm globule the size of an atlas, so prepare yourself for some anxiety-filled and wakeful nights spent being a very keyed-up hall monitor.

You want some peace of mind? Get a NoseFrida. The idea of sucking snot out of your child's nostrils may sound disgusting, but that thing saved my little girl from a lot of additional discomfort. When your kid is suffering, you'll do damn near anything to make it go away.

Ear infections, colic, and rashes, oh my!

There are so many illnesses you might vicariously experience during your parenting adventures that I'd need a degree to even discuss them all with you. The closest I get to that distinguished honor is a brief stint at the University of Southern California's film school, which helps you about as much as your car mechanic showing you how to host a Tupperware party. My goal certainly isn't to get you paranoid about the possibilities of what your child might contract, as I'm sure you'll manage that all on your own. Hell, if you want to jump-start your neurosis, go spend ten minutes surfing the Internet. Actually, don't.

HONING YOUR MANAGEMENT SKILLS

You'll note that I haven't offered any remedies in this chapter. This would firmly reside outside of my jurisdiction, especially since we may have completely different methods of nurturing and medically treating our children. However, here are a few simple tricks that have helped me in the thick of it.

Don't be an alarmist.

This is also commonly known as *don't freak out every time your kid tumbles, stumbles, scrapes his knee, or stubs his toe*! Calm is key, even when your insides are churning and your nerves are threatening to give you away. In other words, put on a show and act calm in front of your child. It doesn't need to be an Oscar-worthy performance, just one that will help your kid to stop screaming, crying, squirming, and being frightened.

Symptoms can be scary for children, since they have zero medical knowledge or awareness and no prior experiences to draw from. Initially, they won't have any concept of what a bruise or illness really means. Every pain and scratch is a new sensation, so their reaction may not be equal to the extent of their injury. I've found that my kids respond to actual pain rather than the appearance of a wound or what it might imply. My daughters cry because they've hit their head on something and it hurts; they don't cry over the egg that's forming at the site of impact.

But since you're able to assess damage based on the visual aftermath of your child's accident, you might have a tougher time recovering than they do. Blood may not trigger the same fear or repulsion for your child that it does for you, for example, so your child may be less inclined to overreact at the sight of it than you are. I can't tell you how many times I've wanted to scoop Gray off the floor and shout, "Oh my God, are you okay?" and excessively dote on her until she can't stand it anymore. Instead, I wait to see her reaction before I offer any of my own. If your child is physically hurt, she won't be shy about it—I promise! The quickest way to make a child start howling is to extend knee-jerk feedback.

It's also important to remember that not all crying indicates physical suffering. Sometimes tears are the only form of expression your child knows to give. You'll be stuck translating pain levels through nonverbal cues until he can offer explanations and answer questions like "Did you get hurt or scared?"

Don't oversearch the search engines.
I've said it before and I'll say it again . . . The Internet is not part of your inner circle. Don't let it become your pediatrician, guidance counselor, mom, confidante, or therapist. I hope you have at least a few of those options in human form to call upon. If not, unearth your little black book and get to work!

Don't hesitate to call your doctor.
I've joked that you shouldn't have your pediatrician on speed dial, but that's just my way of saying you shouldn't call 911 when the cat is stuck up in a tree. While you don't want to clog the phone lines with questions that can be answered with a little common sense, you also don't want to regret having made matters worse for your child out of sheer self-consciousness and medical immaturity. In a psychological battle of "burdening" your doctor versus ignoring warning signs or your intuition, bothering the doctor should be the least of your concerns. The professionals are there to answer questions and provide you with remedy advice. If there's nothing to fret about, they'll tell you that.

This is especially true if your newborn gets sick. Older children have already begun to build their immune systems so they can more effectively ward off germs. If you fear that your newborn is coming down with something, let her doctor decide whether or not there's anything to worry about. You don't need to carry that burden on your own!

Do dole out an abundance of those magic mommy kisses.
Nothing says "You'll be okay" better than hugs, kisses, and cuddles. Sometimes a little love makes the difference between a child who's willing to let you administer prescribed medication, or one whose refusal of it causes a fever to spike even higher. When it's all over and your kids are sleeping peacefully and illness-free, you can rest easy knowing you did your part to cure them with love and affection. That's also a good time to cure yourself with a hearty glass of wine and binge watch *The Bachelor.*

THE MORAL OF MY STORY

Pediatrician visits and vaccinations often leave me feeling like I'm sending my child into battle, even though I *love* our physician and it likely hurts me on a deeper level than it does my girls. When the day is done, I wind up needing shots too, and we're no longer referring to the sort dispensed in sterile medical equipment. I'd bet that you, too, would choose dealing with the repercussions of a tequila bender over watching your child cry. Even if that bender involves spiked green Jell-O or quarters being pitched into mason jars while some teenybopper sorority sisters chant a chorus of obnoxious cheers. On second thought, that might be a step too far.

Apparently we're kissing and telling. Brad and I sharing an intimate moment while I'm pregnant with Marlowe. You know, "intimate" save for the fact that there's a photographer in front of us, a dancing baby in my belly, and a two-year-old gallivanting in the yard. *Photo courtesy of Micah Schweinsberg.*

CHAPTER 14

Bringing Sexy Back

A SCENIC VIEW OF MY PAST

Six stood outside of Blossom's house, seconds from indulging in a serious game of tonsil hockey with Stevie, played by actor Jonathan Brandis. Clearly, Jonathan was an old pro at making out. He'd already had some recent film success and, you know, being a relatively famous Hollywood actor probably wasn't hurting his luck in the girl department. I, on the other hand, was greener than a St. Paddy's Day lager. Six may have looked like she knew the promiscuity ropes but, at fourteen years old, I sure didn't. This was not only my first on-screen kiss; it was my first-ever kiss. My insides were churning so violently I thought I might throw up a little in my mouth. Which probably wouldn't have endeared me to Jonathan.

I'd been freaking out all week in anticipation of this moment, and now it was finally upon me. I'd already depleted the craft service station of every Altoid, Binaca spray canister, and gum pack they had. I was convinced it still wasn't enough. What was expected of me here? Should I just close my eyes and pucker up?

My question was abruptly answered. No sooner had I heard the director shout "Action!" than I felt a tongue push into my mouth. Oh. Action, indeed! I hadn't really prepared myself for tongue, but when in Hollywood . . . Jonathan must have known how these kinds of scenes were done; this certainly wasn't his first romping rodeo. I did the only thing I could do and went with it.

When the director called "Cut!" on our rehearsal, I blushed ten thousand shades of red and stared at the floor. Suddenly, my shoes had become the most interesting thing in the room.

And that's when I heard the snickering from behind camera three. A few of the crew guys were laughing their asses off, and I suspected it was at my expense. I made the mistake of looking up and locking eyes with one of them.

"For God's sake, Jenna," one of the crew guys scoffed. "Don't you know you aren't supposed to French kiss on a sitcom? This isn't Cinemax." He might as well have said, "Amateurs. Thanks for forcing us to watch you swap your nasty, cootie-filled teenage spit."

So much for playing it cool during my first kiss. I decided to make myself look even cooler by hiding in my dressing room for a while.

On a more positive note, Mayim and I secretly exchanged coded messages for the remainder of the afternoon, discussing my newfound smooching skills. At least someone thought I was the bee's knees.

Cut to . . .

Who has time for public displays of affection when you've got a baby to take care of? For that matter, who has time for private ones? Good-bye, sex life. Hello, bedroom bedlam.

MY CRADLE CHRONICLES

Bet you never dreamed you'd be in a conversation about sex with "that girl" from "that show," huh? I know I played somewhat of a girl-next-door on *Blossom*, and it's tough to see beyond that perception, but you'd better get over that nonsense quickly, because this section is a doozy. I'm all grown-up now, and there's only one way to make a baby outside of a lab, unless you know something I don't.

Let's be frank, any curiosity about my virginity, or lack thereof, probably ended back in the '90s. Once my hat-wearing, Joey-obsessed alter ego questioned whether or not she should sleep with a random high school crush on a "very special episode" of *Blossom*, I'm sure the novelty wore off. Or at least I'd like to think that's the case. Nowadays, I hope the only folks who truly give a damn about my sex life are my husband and I. That said, I feel I'd be ignoring a very crucial point if I didn't at least introduce a discussion about how one's extracurricular bedroom activities can be drastically affected by pregnancy and children. And that's going to involve some relatively revealing confessions on my part. Yep, this is a chapter on everything you never wanted to know about me. Stick around and find out how fun it is to spit take that unleaded latte you're drinking. You know, if you didn't already do that during my mention of flatulence in the hospital chapter.

Pregnancy sex . . . or lack thereof

My husband has ever so graciously granted me permission to disclose some very personal information about our nonexistent midpregnancy sex life. You may find yourself hankering for more action than a Jean-Claude Van Damme flick, or you may find yourself on a self-imposed intercourse interlude. In other words, you may be discovering that you wouldn't want to grope your husband even if he looked like Clive Owen, sounded like Barry White, and had moves like Mick Jagger. Either way, it's totally normal.

I, for one, was hornier than a rhinoceros in heat. Before you start thinking, *Quit bragging, Jenna!* I'll let you in on a little secret: about three months into my pregnancy, sex became so painful that I had to take a hiatus. A *very* miserable and extended hiatus. Just when I was thinking of doing the nasty more often than an adolescent boy and his favorite gym sock, my body screwed it all up. No pun intended. How unfair, right? But, alas, fair is for people on *Leave It to Beaver* episodes. And technically, to be blunt, leaving it to the beaver was doing nothing but making me sexually frustrated. (Yeah, I really just said that.) I got to deal with bodily dysfunction that benched me from the horizontal mambo and made me wonder if I'd ever see my feet past my belly button again in this lifetime. Yay, me.

If your sex drive is shit-out-of-luck the way mine was, breathe easy, friends. Your hormones will even out again at some point and you'll be able to ease back into sex. And *ease* is the key word there, at least in my case. If you're fortunate enough to adapt to your body changes a little more successfully than I did, stop reading this *right freakin' now*, grab your lasso and cowboy hat, and go get 'em, girl! Your husband will thank you, and I'm all for encouraging the debauchery. Though in case you were wondering, this is one instance where I really don't want credit for any assistance I may have given.

Before we go any further, I feel it necessary to speak on behalf of your significant other for a moment. If you're experiencing vaginal pain similar to what I did (for argument's sake, we'll call it collateral coochie damage) and sex isn't on your weekly or monthly agenda, please don't leave your husband totally in the hole . . . or out of the hole, if you know what I mean. Intimacy is a vital part of marriage, even when maternity miseries are making it seem as enticing as licking pool tables. I'm sure you have the most understanding spouse in the world, just like I do, but keep in mind that he's already braving your midnight cravings, your sudden mood swings, the onslaught of impending fatherhood panic, your dire need to buy baby clothes even though you don't yet know whether it's a boy or a girl, and the fact that his mother-in-law is moving in for two weeks once the kid is born. To quote the famous words from *Jerry Maguire*, show him the money. Oh, and while you're at it, help him help you!

If you're one of the coolest people on the planet, you may find that you have no trouble with sex during pregnancy at all. (Other than, you know, the fact that you're trying to maneuver around a belly the size of a waterbed.) I hope this is the case, for your sake. Still, you'll probably notice that things feel different. For instance, you may find your breasts are so sore you can barely wear a bra; hence, your husband will not be touching them with a ten-foot pole. Plus, the stimulation may cause them to leak, which is *totally* hot and erotic. I hope the sarcasm is coming through loud and clear there. Alternately, you may obsess over your new voluptuous figure in a way that makes you want to rock the obscene, smutty lingerie you've been saving for a rainy day.

You'll also find certain sexual positions aren't so easily attainable. As your belly grows, the old standbys don't always work. Propping yourself up on pillows is often a helpful trick when finding a comfortable position becomes impossible. That really worked well for me. It should be noted, however, that five pillows later I looked like I'd robbed a Bed Bath & Beyond outlet, and I couldn't have gotten up from them even if I'd seen a tray of double-chocolate brownies across the room.

As a side note, if you're someone who likes to surprise your hubby at the office so you can frolic on his desk, you may want to tell him to get a sturdier one in anticipation of your visits in month nine. And you might need a step stool. I'll give you a moment to contemplate that visual.

Postpregnancy sex
Kids don't appreciate the meaning of a red bandanna on the doorknob, so discard any grandiose thoughts of sneaking off to do the deed. My husband and I spent months trying to figure out a plan that didn't result in hearing our baby cry at the most inopportune moment. And let's be honest, when

you're finally able to enjoy some intimacy with your spouse after months of being too weary, too smelly, too covered in spit-up, and too distracted, *any* interrupted moment is inopportune. Eventually you'll find a system that works for you; it may not be foolproof, but it'll be a step in the right direction. For instance, my hubby and I finally figured out that Gray slept most soundly when she napped in the car. After a short ride, she was visiting Never-Neverland for at least an hour. We started planning road trips left and right, and our weekend "errands" became significantly more intriguing. The coffee wasn't the only thing brewing at our local Starbucks!

Once Marlowe was born, finding time for sex became exponentially more difficult. I'll tell you right now, two babies napping simultaneously is a fool's paradise. One afternoon, in a turn of events that made us scamper like a couple of guilty teenagers fooling around under the high school bleachers, Gray woke up exceptionally early from her naptime and walked in on us. Thankfully, her eyes didn't have time to adjust to the dark before we'd thrown robes on, but it was a close call. We couldn't stop laughing for a good hour after that, as we relived our panic over nearly traumatizing our three-year-old.

I should also mention—and please don't flip out here— that you *still* may find yourself uninterested in lovemaking, even after your baby is born. After all, your body just went through a bit of internal turmoil. And that's putting it mildly. Following Gray's birth, it took several months before I was truly up for some hard-core fooling around. Serving drinks at the all-day booby bar, coupled with immense exhaustion, doesn't always leave much stamina for other things. The only recommendation I can give is to be patient with yourself and make sure you're openly talking to your husband about what you can and cannot handle. Believe it or not, he may be experiencing similar issues. Stress and financial woes can affect a man's libido drastically, and having a baby certainly puts some pressure on. Much to his (and your) dismay, he may not be in the mood as often as he used to be either. This, too, shall pass.

I had friends who warned me that having a kid would change things in my marriage, and I refused to accept that idea. I loathed any suggestion that my husband and I might put sex on the back burner, and I took their warnings as a personal affront. The implication that my husband and I might not find an immediate groove in our ability to manage everything left me feeling supersensitive, so I concluded that those who brought it up were presumptuously passing judgment about business they shouldn't stick their noses in.

Until I realized they were right. Kids make it tougher to find time alone, and that's just part of the deal. It truly has nothing to do with whether or not your marriage is stable or secure; it's that sex tends to fall a few notches on the priority list when you've worked nine to five, you're trying to get dinner on the stove, the house is a wreck, the dogs are howling to be let out, and the baby needs a diaper change before glomming back onto your nipple for another hour. That's the way it goes, even with great intentions and killer sexual chemistry.

Turns out those friends were coming from an

all-too-knowing, been-there-done-that kind of place, and they had a good inkling about what was in store for us. The fact is, there's nothing easy about raising children. It's hard enough to find five minutes of peace and quiet to eat a sandwich, much less a long enough stretch to get down and dirty with your significant other. And sometimes sex requires more planning than sex ever should. I mean, isn't it supposed to be spontaneous and exciting? What's so freakin' spontaneous about penciling your spouse in after a breastfeeding, during the first ten minutes of the naptime window, before you have to leave for a meeting?

The reality is that having a baby brought an entirely different mind-set to our sex life. It's not always easy to concentrate on getting to third base when you can't stop wondering if you've just heard your child sneeze, cough, coo, cry, or—God forbid—turn the doorknob. Lord knows I've done my share of stopping in midaction to check the damned monitor, which is why Brad and I have really had to step up our game. Creativity has become our best friend, and we're willing to schedule our time together if that's what it takes.

We've also had to be really careful not to make our life all kids, all the time. We love our daughters so deeply that it's easy to get wrapped up in them and wind up neglecting our own needs. It's a balancing act that involves work and thinking outside of the box (no, not *that* box, though I like your spirit), but my husband and I realize we are entitled to quality time together without the pitter-patter of little feet. It's equally important to being a good parent, as far as we're concerned.

Marriage needs nurturing too!

Making a love connection

A friend once told me, "As impossible as it seems, make sure you have date nights—even if all you discuss is the latest and greatest about your baby." I couldn't agree more. The first time Brad and I left Gray at home so we could enjoy a dinner out, my mom was in town visiting. Obviously, I trust my mother implicitly. She has raised four kids, and her love for both of our daughters is so full of warmth and light it could overshadow a disco ball. Still, we were devastated to walk out the door. My tears started falling as soon as we hit the driveway, and by the time we were at the main thoroughfare I had mascara halfway down my face. Alice Cooper would have been impressed.

You can't put your motherly instincts on a shelf just because you want a date night with your spouse, but it's perfectly acceptable to think of your baby throughout dinner. You can bemoan teething trials during appetizers, discuss changing your diaper brand over drinks, and whip out the brag book after dinner so you can show it to the waitress. Indulge yourself; you're a new parent!

But I feel like it's equally important to go ahead and take that step, tough though it may be. Your marriage deserves it. For that matter, if you can find it in your heart to prolong the meal enough to enjoy dessert and coffee, do it! If you're feeling particularly frisky, cop a feel or cram a shag in the backseat of your car while you're at it. It's all about improvising.

The good news is that most of us wind up having more than one kid, which means we've figured out a way around the scheduling conflicts. If we've managed it, you can too!

THE MORAL OF MY STORY

Having a baby made finding time for sex about as easy as swimming laps in a pothole. Who knew sneaking in time for foreplay would require keener artistic sensibilities and more creative license than writing this book? On that note, you'll need to excuse me for five minutes so my husband and I can squeeze in a make-out session . . .

Tutus and table-eating. Gray decides to test her taste buds on the furniture during a particularly rough bout with teething. *Photo courtesy of Jenna von Oy.*

CHAPTER 15

Whining and Dining:
Adventures with Separation Anxiety and Teething

A SCENIC VIEW OF MY PAST

It was my first day of work on *The Parkers*, and I was ready to dive headfirst into a brand-new show. It had been a few years, so I was itching to feel that thrill again. I couldn't wait to meet the cast and crew, dig into a funny script, and be back at work doing my favorite thing—making people laugh. In anticipation of such an illustrious gig, I'd spent the day thus far showering, spending way too much time applying makeup and primping, and picking out the perfect ensemble to help me leave a lasting first impression on my costars and the network execs. Since I was boasting my twenty-five-year-old body and booty back then, I chose tight pants that zipped up the back and a fitted top that left little confusion as to what was (barely) contained underneath. It was the first and only time in my life that I've consistently maintained a personal trainer and made a serious effort to get myself in prime physical condition, so I was eager to flaunt it. Perhaps a little too eager.

I'd tucked my new studio pass into my purse, my script was patiently waiting in the front seat of my car, and all that remained was the drive across town. But first things first, a stop at Starbucks. Because no job was important enough to break my cherished breakfast ritual! I mean, what good is a girl without her morning cup of joe? Take it from me, I'm way funnier when I've had my coffee. Actually, I'm funniest when I've had my wine, but better that I wasn't drinking *that* before my workday began. And so it came to pass that I was Starbucks-bound.

As with most Starbucks junkies, I had my comfort zone. There was a branch about two blocks from my house (I'm shocked I had to travel that far, considering there's one on virtually every block in Los Angeles), and it was my prevailing caffeine command post. I knew every barista by name. It was my Cheers, only the brews had froufrou names like Sumatra and Cinnamon Dolce Frappucino instead of pilsner and pale ale. Nonetheless, I was a regular. As I made my way to the front of the line, I nodded hello to my fellow daily devotees and dwellers. We were all partaking in the same Starbucks Kool-Aid, so it was customary to offer some sort of acknowledgement to one another. Every now and then I even got a smile out of someone, though I can't say Los Angelenos are always known for their cordiality.

On this particular Monday morning, the shop was extraordinarily busy. Let me rephrase that. There was utter pandemonium at my Starbucks. I'd never seen so many people packed into that place, but perhaps I'd been taking too much advantage of my unemployment by sleeping through the morning rush. I watched a group of moms tussling with their young'ns (read: very transparently counting down the minutes until school drop-off, while not-so-discreetly slipping Kahlúa into their Americanos), and a cluster of boisterous actor types admiring their new headshots. Ah, the charm of narcissism. Did I mention how much I love LA?

Speaking of narcissism, back to my story. It took me twenty minutes to reach the counter, but I finally ordered my latte and stepped to the side to await my energy-stimulating masterpiece.

That's when it started to feel a wee bit drafty. I looked around to see if I'd stationed myself under an air vent. Nope. Oddly, the breeze seemed to be affecting only my backside. What the hell?

I reached behind me to touch the waistband of my pants, which was still clasped by a hook and eye. No problems there. And that's when the realization hit. I quickly ran my hand down my pants zipper, which was located right up the middle of my rear end. Sure enough, it had busted open, exposing my butt to the massive mob of jittery java guzzlers. Apparently, there were buns available at Starbucks that morning, but they had nothing to do with pastries.

Do you recall what I said earlier about my desire to leave a lasting first impression? Well, I accomplished that and then some. And did I mention I was wearing skimpy, lace thong panties underneath my peekaboo pants? Those baristas will never forget me (parts of me, anyway), and the day care moms were probably gossiping about my indiscretion for weeks. Thank God social media wasn't so prevalent yet, or I might have earned myself some sort of infamous hashtag, such as

#bottomsup, #bootyisonlyskindeep, #pouringitonthick, or my personal favorite, #Starbutts.

I held the sides of my britches together for dear life, waited out my drink preparation (you didn't think I was embarrassed enough to leave without it, did you? That's crazy talk!), and didn't make any unnecessary eye contact as I dashed out to my car. Needless to say, I immediately rerouted back home to change clothes before work. My career as an exhibitionist was officially over.

The next morning, before heading into the studio, I returned to my beloved Starbucks, kept my head held high during my walk of shame to the counter, and ordered my usual drink. This time, no patrons were there but me. Just in case, I'd worn less hazardous clothing. If I'd owned protective gear, I might have worn that too.

The same barista, a teenage boy, was behind the register. His eyes grew rounder than my post-honeymoon waistline, and he stared at me for a minute before speaking. "I can't believe you had the guts to show your face in here again!"

I suppressed my mortification and answered nonchalantly, "Oh, did anyone notice that?"

"Are you kidding?" he said. "*Everyone* noticed. People were talking about it for hours!"

Clearly, the fates had not spared me at all. Nonetheless, I responded, "It's a butt; everybody has one. Besides, what fun is life if you can't laugh at yourself?"

With that, I grabbed my beverage and walked out the door.

Glancing back, I saw the kid shaking his head with respect. He may also have been contemplating my sanity, which is fair.

Still, I left smiling. I felt I'd pushed past the awkwardness and found a silver lining, which made me pleased and proud.

And let's be honest: desperate times call for desperate measures. There's no way in hell I was going to start driving an extra two blocks to a different Starbucks branch every day.

CUT TO . . .

Sometimes in life you just have to grin and bare it. Literally and figuratively. The public humility of displaying my rear end at my favorite Starbucks establishment was unfortunate. The private humility of not being able to calm my children down in the throes of teething or separation anxiety has been far more unfavorable. It makes that silver lining a little tougher to locate. And sadly, it doesn't include being rewarded with an endless supply of high-maintenance lattes.

MY CRADLE CHRONICLES

When you get to the teething and separation anxiety phases of parenthood, you're really off to the races. One day your kid seems a bit crankier than normal; the next day you're jumping hurdles worthy of steeplechase and praying you don't get bucked off. You can almost hear the starting pistols fire and the bets being placed over the course of your fate. But I digress. My point is that this stage really tests your patience and the decibel level your eardrums can handle. It can be a game changer.

For some children, teething and separation anxiety can

cause a complete temperament turnaround. A kid who was easygoing may suddenly whine about everything. And I do mean everything. As in, you may start thinking your kid needs to be checked for bipolar disorder. He may act like the sky is falling every time you pick him up. Or put him down. Or change his poopy diaper. Or don't change his poopy diaper. Or hand him to his daddy. Or don't hand him to his daddy.

Not to worry. He should mellow out by the time you send him to college. If nothing else, at least he'll be potty trained by then.

Despite the drama that teething and separation anxiety introduce, you'll find they are also a good excuse to offer extra hugs, kisses, and cuddles. Because unlike a college student, most babies will let you love on them when they're in pain. Or when they feel insecure. Or whenever you damn well please because you had the distinction of carrying them in your belly for nine months and that's your prerogative. Teething and separation anxiety can get prickly, but they have their up-side—they also mean your child is growing. And progress is a beautiful thing!

TEETHING

You've just gotten used to feeding schedules, learned how to change a diaper without messing up yet another change of clothing, and figured out the quickest way to get your kid to go down for a nap. (God bless that weird, vibrating, bouncy seat thingamajigger!) You're finally sleeping for longer than a two-hour stretch at night, have created a new repertoire of ten-minute meals that can be prepared before the tiny human has lost interest in his bumblebee rattle, and have perfected the art of one-handed e-mail writing. Now your world is turned upside down just because some itty-bitty incisor is threatening to poke through the surface of your baby's gums? It's simply unjust! My advice? Man up, and have a good glass of wine close by. Just think how much worse it must be for your kid, who feels like his mouth is suddenly boycotting.

Having a teething infant isn't that unlike having a teenager. They won't go to bed until three in the morning, and then they want to sleep until odd hours of the day. There's endless whining, excessive drooling, facial acne, and they may refuse to eat anything that's healthy for them. Essentially, the only difference between a teething infant and an angst-ridden adolescent is the former doesn't come home from college on the weekends just so you'll be tricked into doing her laundry for her. Also, your infant can't surprise you by bringing along her creepy new boyfriend with the fake British accent and ironic hipster mustache. Man, I'm not looking forward to the first time that happens.

In case you aren't sure what to blame Miss Cranky's bad mood on, here are a few indications that a new tooth might be the culprit.

1. All-around irritability
In my experience, when I started looking at my husband and saying, "Who is this little fusspot, and what did she do with our good-natured kid?" teething was the cause. If all

you contend with is a pout here and there, you're getting off easy! I feel for those of you who will be weathering a more tempestuous storm. Get out your umbrellas, ladies; you may be in for the big, badass, mother of all torrential downpours. May it be as fast as it is furious because, depending on your proclivities, twenty-four-hour whining can also drive you to twenty-four-hour wining.

2. Trouble sleeping

Slumber tends to take the brunt of all things that deviate from a baby's normal, uneventful, healthy day, and teething doesn't help. It downright massacres a sleep schedule, if you're lucky enough to have a consistent one in the first place. Your child is a tad warm? His sleep may be affected. He has gas? His sleep may be affected. Some congestion? A damp diaper? There's an errant sound in the room? An additional light on? He can smell that the milk dispenser is within arm's reach? In all those cases, his sleep may be affected.

And, of course, in all those scenarios, *your* sleep isn't just affected; it's totally nonexistent. It's an antislumber party.

3. Constipation

Teething can severely cut down on your baby's ability to . . . ahem . . . move things along. Bet you never thought you'd be worried about changing fewer diapers than normal, huh? Don't be surprised when your little one isn't having bowel movements as frequently as you've become accustomed to and you start to pray for a monster-sized poop. Of course, you may find the opposite is true instead. See number 9 for that!

4. Mouth and gum hypersensitivity

Your baby suddenly has sharp objects protruding from his gums. Expect some inflammation and tenderness.

5. Facial acne

It will likely look like a rash around your baby's lips and chin, and it doesn't mean that he's prepubescent, so don't go signing him up to be the youngest Proactiv spokesperson ever. The blemishes are usually short-lived. In my experience, there's no need to treat them with lotions or creams; it's best to leave them alone. They'll dissipate once the teething has run its course.

6. Food refusal or loss of appetite

Would you want to bite down on something as painful as an erupting tooth? It's probably like trying to eat a Jawbreaker immediately after a root canal. Which makes me hurt just thinking about it.

7. Comfort nursing

Even if your baby can locate your breasts like a heat-seeking missile, he may get agitated during feedings. He may also start doing a lot of what I refer to as booby bobbing, without actually consuming very much. My girls both spent a lot of time nursing for comfort when they were in pain. Simply being against your skin can be a soothing reliever. Just be careful that your nipple doesn't start becoming a teething-toy substitute. Yikes.

8. Drooling

If your child is leaving puddles of saliva on the floor that would give my basset hound a run for her money, she's likely teething. Get that girl something to gnaw on, and keep a roll of paper towels handy. And maybe a pair of galoshes, just in case it gets out of hand.

9. Diarrhea, fever, runny nose

I lumped these three bad boys into one point because there seems to be some disagreement among the experts as to whether teething can actually cause these symptoms. All I have to go on is my own experience. Gray never ran even a low-grade fever while teething, but the runny nose was prevalent. It didn't just run—it jogged, sprinted, dashed, and had its own marathon racing bib. The diarrhea was present from time to time too, but I never knew whether to chalk that up to my diet instead. Infants who are exclusively breastfed tend to have pretty soft stools anyway, so it's not always easy to determine the responsible party. I'm still suspended out there in teething limbo with Marlowe, so I'll let you know how it goes. Provided I survive it.

10. Biting

This one is the kicker. Or rather, the chomper. Every now and then teething can evoke a scene straight out of The Twilight Saga. Your child may gum everything in sight, including you. You may be left to wonder if you should dress in full-body padding, peruse the real estate market in Transylvania, or begin toting garlic to ward off the next attack. If you've bitten off more than you can chew on this one, don't freak out. Apparently, it's a very typical phase children go through as they learn to communicate, try things on for size, and experiment with appropriate ways to express themselves. Social graces aren't necessarily built in.

I think you'll discover that most parents have received a "love bite" or two. It's generally more innocuous than it sounds, since it usually stems from your child testing the waters rather than biting you out of sheer spite.

Kids don't always have an extensive enough vocabulary to explain themselves with words alone. My little Dracula wannabe, Gray, once randomly leaned over and bit my leg. (I mean, I know my thighs are beefy, but come on!) In part, the act was done out of frustration. Still, I don't imagine she would have attempted the ambush had teething not been involved. Employing the art of distraction really helped in that instance, as it curbed her curiosity and didn't draw too much attention to the unwanted act. This may or may not work for you, but it's worth a shot! I also found a simple but firm "Ouch!" was enough to startle her into understanding it didn't feel good to me. Kids don't always comprehend the physical repercussions of biting until you let them know.

Alternately, if your child is a serial biter, isn't responding to your attempts to stop him, or is getting progressively more aggressive, the issue shouldn't be taken lightly. If you find yourself in that situation, I hope you'll call your pediatrician before you wind up with baby hickeys covering 90 percent of your body!

Words and gestures may be preferable to being gnawed on, but babies don't necessarily know or care about that. The trick is finding a constructive way to discourage the behavior without unwittingly emphasizing an act you don't want your child to repeat. May the force (and patience) be with you!

ANOTHER ONE BITES THE BUST

Before we move on to the joys of separation anxiety, here are some fabulous fang factoids you might be interested in knowing.

1. The two bottom teeth in the front of your baby's mouth will usually come in first, but don't be surprised if you have trouble finding them right off the bat.

Even after our pediatrician told me, "Oh! Gray has two teeth coming in; I feel the nubs," I was clueless. Nubs, schmubs! I could have run my finger along Gray's gum line for hours, and all I would have come up with was a whole lot of slobber and a pissed-off baby.

2. Teethers aren't overrated.

Wouldn't you prefer to give your kid a clean object that's meant for her mouth, rather than find her nibbling on the remote control? Or the dining chair leg? Or the dog toys? Or your nipple? There are some pretty cool teething toys out there, including bracelets or necklaces that double as bling for you. My girls were also fond of baby gum massagers, which resemble a mini toothbrush. Sooner or later, someone will devise a teether that also babysits while you run to the restroom. Hell, I'd invest in *that* Kickstarter campaign!

3. Despite my praise for teethers, you don't necessarily need to purchase fancy toys.

A friend of mine put a clean, wet washcloth in the freezer, then gave it to her son to munch on. It worked wonders! My parents used to give me black licorice to go to town on, though I can only imagine the mess I made. Of course, since I'm a '70s baby, they also rubbed brandy on my gums to numb them. I'm not proposing either of those as a solution, though a candy-and-brandy combo doesn't sound half bad as your own personal kid-free nightcap.

4. Remedies for a teething infant can run the gamut, depending on which way you lean regarding medication.

My husband and I always prefer to try the more holistic options before any over-the-counter pain relievers, so we did everything in our power not to introduce Baby Orajel as a new food group. We even went so far as to try the trendy amber necklace, for argument's sake, though I personally felt it wound up being more of a fashion statement than an effective antidote.

SEPARATION AND STRANGER ANXIETY

These guys are a force to be reckoned with, and there's a subtle difference between the two. They're like twins with differentiating moles on their tushes. The way I see it, stranger anxiety causes your child to be afraid to interact with folks he doesn't know. With separation anxiety, he will be afraid to be anywhere but where you are. Which is amazing. And then not. He will be more cemented to you than Jimmy Hoffa purportedly is to Giants Stadium. The term *clingy* will not cover it. We aren't talking a scenario where an unruly dryer sheet has to be pried off a random sock; we're talking about octopus tentacles brazenly suctioned to a helpless mollusk. If you experience this issue, I'm sure you'll easily come up with your own analogy for it. It may or may not be describable by polite words alone. Because as nice as it is to have your child act as though you're the best thing since the invention of the Snuggie, it's also good when your child knows you aren't the only person she can count on for comfort, contentment, and consolation. It isn't realistic to think we can always be there to hold, help, or offer the breastaurant to our babies.

If your child develops either or both of these anxieties, you may find it somewhat intimidating. Before you start begging to be put out of your misery with an elephant tranquilizer, let me assure you that this stage doesn't last forever. It can, however, be a whopper. In a crowded room, Gray could hunt me down with the enthusiasm of a Tyrannosaurus rex pursuing a mountain goat.

I have friends who have never experienced this particular issue, and who are under the impression that separation anxiety merely involves a few tears being shed during day care drop-off. This is not the same thing. A few tears are a child's way of saying "I'll miss you, Mommy, but feel free to run errands to your heart's content with no guilt whatsoever. In fact, spoil yourself by sneaking in time for a pedicure, because our parting will hurt you more than it hurts me."

Separation anxiety is when you walk out of the room

simply to put pants on and your kid starts screaming at the top of her lungs like you've subjected her to watching *Gigli* over and over again. Separation anxiety is when your child freaks out every time the FedEx guy knocks on the door, because she thinks a babysitter is coming over. Separation anxiety is when you feel like the best parent in the world because your child adores you so much that she doesn't like anyone else, but also like the worst parent in the world because your child adores you so much that she doesn't like anyone else. It's a double-edged sword, and sometimes you may want to take that sword and plunge it into your eye.

Stranger anxiety is slightly more comprehensible, because children shouldn't be expected to feel comfortable around people they don't know . . . until you realize the anxiety includes *everyone* but you. Gray went through a lengthy phase where she refused to go to anyone else including my husband, who clearly wasn't a stranger. I reluctantly became a staple presence in our first two years of Christmas photos, when a quick holiday visit with good ol' St. Nick erupted into severe fits of panic. I guess I should have known Gray would fall apart when we got close enough to smell Mr. Local Mall Santa's aftershave. (Which, predictably, was Old Spice.) For the record, I didn't blame her; if I were forced to sit on a stranger's lap I'd be pretty freaked out too, especially if the guy were surrounded by little men with pointy ears. It's not exactly a scene that implies safety and security. Not to mention, my husband would probably have something to say about my spontaneously leaping onto another man's lap.

Admittedly, it's heartwarming to constantly feel wanted by your child and to be considered the center of her universe. It's what we mommies live for. And you know what? We're *supposed* to be the center of their universe! But as nice as it is to be needed, it's also nice to be able to get dressed in the morning, wash your hair, take a pee break, or sip from a cup of coffee while it's still hot. I've jokingly blamed the magic power of the boobies for this magnetic attachment, but I know there's more to it than that. Breastfed children certainly aren't the only ones who struggle with separation or stranger anxiety.

We moms spend the first few months making sure our children feel safe, comfortable, and unconditionally loved. We give them unwavering attention and encourage snuggly naptime in our arms. Then, all of a sudden, we ask them to stay with someone they've never met before while we go out to enjoy a movie with Daddy. It must be terribly confusing! In some cases, it probably even feels like abandonment, which is why it's best to gently ease into the transition. Asking your baby to accept strangers cold turkey is equivalent to having someone drop you into the depths of the Peruvian jungle, expecting you to Bear Grylls your way out of it.

Here are the rules I've tried to live by when leaving my children in someone else's care.

Sharing is caring.
As hard as it is to pry yourself away from your newborn, let other folks have a turn. When friends or family come to visit and offer to hold the baby while you fix lunch, take them up

on it—even when you know you can simultaneously handle food prep and infant care like a pro. No one doubts that you can masterfully multitask! You are a mommy, after all, and Multitask is our middle name.

Start early.

Make sure your baby begins having some one-on-one time with her daddy, grandparents, and other close family or friends from a young age. In my house, the girls were at home with me 100 percent of the time while Brad was at work. This meant they saw a lot more of me than they did him. Because Gray's separation anxiety was so substantial, we made a point to really enforce Marlowe's special Daddy time as soon as she was born. Whenever possible, Brad holds her, soothes her, and changes her diaper. That way, she's used to being attended to equally by both parents. There's no guarantee that it will completely obliterate all future issues, but it's certainly helping to cut down on them. Not to mention, it's never bad to remind your husband he's just as equipped as you are to care for your children! Minus, of course, the lactating boobs.

Take it one step at a time.

Initially, you may want to try making use of the Pack 'n Play or swing while you do something simple nearby, such as folding laundry. This way, your child becomes used to an appropriate amount of autonomy. Next, graduate to accepting an offer from a friend who is willing to help out. Have the friend hold little man while you get a few things done around the house, and be sure to make brief trips in and out of the room. Baby needs to start understanding that you may leave for a short period of time but you always return.

Start small.

Don't wait until you have an office retreat in Wyoming to try leaving your kid with someone else for the first time, even if it's a family member your baby is familiar with. There's a big difference between being in the next room over and being a plane ride away. Family members don't need to be guinea pigs for your inaugural travel adventure! It's never fun when everyone who's blood-related and lives within driving distance starts breaking out in hives every time you say you have a conference to attend.

Don't leave immediately after the babysitter arrives.

Even though you're itching to get to that wine tasting with your girlfriends, spend some time going over pertinent details with the sitter and take a few minutes to play on the floor with her and baby before your departure. Or at least long enough that baby knows you're comfortable around the person you're leaving her with. If you've already started the car and you toss the kid into the sitter's arms on your way out the door like some sort of fumbled football pass, you're probably not taking enough time to help your little one ease into the transition before you go.

Don't be tempted to practice your ninja skills by sneaking out of the room.

I'm a huge proponent of earning my children's trust. They

need to believe I mean what I say, whether it pertains to following through with the rules I set or leaving them in someone else's care. If I book out of the house like a fugitive and fail to inform my kids I'm going, they're less likely to believe I'm a reliable presence in their lives. Showing them they can trust me enforces the concept of honesty!

Don't invalidate baby's feelings.
Trying to tell her, "Big girls don't cry!" probably isn't going to do anything but make her cry harder. Leave that phrase to Fergie or The Four Seasons, and try for soothing words instead. The fact is, your child *isn't* a big girl yet, nor should she have to act like one. You know the whole crawling-before-you-walk thing? Babies have to cry before they know how to properly express themselves. It's perfectly understandable for your child to be upset when you leave; you are the biggest source of *all* of her basic needs, including love!

Don't dillydally.
When I have to say good-bye to my kids, I try to make it short and sweet. I've found that prolonging the transaction just gives my kids the impression that I don't want to leave. I try to kiss them briefly, say my parting words, and then do my best not to look back. Which is harder than it sounds.

Make sure baby naps and eats before you leave him with someone else.
You know how it's a bad idea to go to Costco on an empty stomach because you wind up buying a cart full of things that will sit in your pantry well past their expiration dates? The

same is true for leaving an infant in someone else's care. When baby is hungry or tired, things are more likely to hit a fever pitch. Do everything you can to make sure baby isn't already fussing over other issues before you hand him over.

Make sure the sitter comes to you, not the other way around.
It really minimizes the trauma when your child is able to be in surroundings that are comfortable for him. Change is always stressful, even for us adults. When my kids have their own toys and naptime space nearby, it tends to cut down on their uneasiness.

Let baby know you aren't abandoning him and you are coming back.
Kids understand a great deal more than we realize or acknowledge. Even if they don't comprehend the explanation for why we have to leave for a few hours, they get the sentiment behind it. Go ahead and tell baby that you're on your way to the library, that you'll return shortly, and that he's going to enjoy some quality time with his dad in the meantime. The tone of your voice will be reassuring even if all baby hears is sweet-sounding gibberish.

Be honest about how long you'll be gone.
When I'm leaving for a two-hour meeting, I don't tell my girls I'll be back in five minutes and hope they don't have any concept of the time that has elapsed. All that does is give them a reason to doubt what I say. Kids may not be able to stalk the clock, but they aren't oblivious to the passage of time either.

Try not to make yourself feel bad about walking out the door.
This tends to be the toughest rule to abide by, but half the battle is convincing yourself it's okay to leave your child with someone else. I hate being away from my girls, even if it's only by twenty feet. And you know what? They know it. If I wear my heart on my sleeve, it just makes things worse.

It's overly sappy, but each wail and teardrop will be a dagger in your heart; it's just part of the deal. As much as it may tug at your heartstrings, will yourself to stay strong. Continually going back to console your child will only prolong the inevitable. The amount of time your child spends crying will eventually lessen.

Wait until you get to the days of preschool drop-off! At first, even the biggest and baddest toy won't be able to distract your little one from falling to pieces over your departure. It'll be like Armageddon up in that joint. But the next thing you know, you'll be on the receiving end of a wave good-bye and the words, "I don't need you, Mommy. I have to go make a castle out of Play-Doh now." Which, of course, will hurt your heart almost as much.

Don't let anyone make you feel like something is wrong with you or your child.
Thankfully, I have supportive women around me who reminded me that it was perfectly normal and age-appropriate for Gray to have mini-meltdowns when I left her. Having a child with separation or stranger anxiety is nothing to be ashamed of or embarrassed about. It means your kid is maturing and

growing. It signifies that she's learning the difference between people in her inner circle and those outside of it and making the conscious decision to remain in safe territory. It's such a common part of the growth process that I believe every child experiences it to some degree.

As with anything else, however, the intensity of it differs from kid to kid. If you were to throw a bunch of unfamiliar adults into a room together and instruct them to have a party, you might get similar results. The gregarious real estate broker might come up and shake everyone's hand, while the librarian hugs the wall for dear life and wills herself to become invisible. We can't all be extroverts.

You may run across a parent who doesn't even remotely understand your predicament. That's her cross to bear, so try to let it slide. I had Gray with me at a friend's baby shower, and a woman I'd never met asked if she could hold Gray for me while I decorated a Onesie. I thanked her for her kind offer but explained that Gray probably wouldn't take to it very well due to her intense stranger anxiety. Though she had several children of her own, her feathers got ruffled and she haughtily replied, "Thank God *my* daughter doesn't have that problem."

I'm here to tell you it isn't a *problem,* so don't let it torture you. Your kid will most likely experience it at one point or another, and that's perfectly okay. Don't let anyone tell you differently!

Don't put time limits on the phase.
From my understanding, kids can begin having anxieties at

around six to seven months old, but ten to eighteen months is when it crescendos. Every kid will work through it at his own pace, so I don't feel it's fair to rely on the numbers. Your eleven-month-old might have been fine with you leaving her with a sitter last week but reach new levels of hysteria over it this week. You just never know when anxiety will rear its pretty little head.

Gray still had trouble well into year one, so we were on that adventure together for a good long time. Enrolling her in day care a few days a week certainly helped get her used to being with other people, but her increasing comfort level didn't directly translate to anyone and everyone who asked to hold her. And you know what? I'm happy about that. I can only hope she's as skeptical of strangers when she gets older!

Honesty is the best policy.
Make sure you discuss your child's anxieties with a sitter or caretaker ahead of time, and find people who are willing to appropriately help you. Positive encouragement is a must. When the person watching your child isn't willing to put any effort into finding distractions, doesn't extend patience while everyone works through the transition, has their feelings hurt by the fact that baby wants his mama instead, or can't remain calm during any meltdowns that ensue, they aren't the right person with whom to leave your child. Your baby will sense if the sitter is upset by the situation, and that's completely counterproductive.

Unfortunately, separation anxiety can affect family

members as well, which sometimes gets touchy. We have extended family who expressed their sadness and disappointment during Gray's anxiety phase. They were bothered by her unwillingness to let them hold her during visits. It isn't that I had no sympathy for them, but if family members are only able to stop by every now and then, they're technically strangers to your child too. Just because you know someone is related by blood doesn't mean your child understands it. We can't control how our children react to others, family or not, and we shouldn't have to apologize on their behalf. A one-year-old isn't setting out to hurt anyone, and he is incapable of grasping that he's doing so. The fact is, helping a child through separation and stranger anxiety is a lot for anyone to deal with, including you. And you've got the biggest stake in the game! Make sure you rely on folks who are willing to climb into the trenches with you.

P.S. Embrace this time and appreciate it for what it is. If you think the separation anxiety is bad now, just wait until your kid is a teenager. This doesn't come close to the separation anxiety he'll experience when you ground him from using his iPhone during dinner!

If you don't want to leave your child with someone else, don't.
Not every mom is comfortable with the idea of leaving her kids with someone else, and I respect that. If you are in a position that allows you to stay home and avoid all manner of day care or sitters, there's nothing wrong with that either! It's all about trusting your instincts and doing what makes you

comfortable. What works for someone else won't necessarily feel right to *you*, so don't feel pressured! You and your child will know when you're ready to take that next step.

THE MORAL OF MY STORY

Teething and separation anxiety bring their fair share of tears, but they don't last forever. If you're daydreaming about slipping Benadryl into your kid's sippy cup or drinking yourself into a state of nirvana, take a deep breath and get your hands off the medicine and liquor cabinets. Pretty soon you'll be chauffeuring your kid to the dentist and dreaming of the days when your daughter refused to open her arms to strange men.

The crawl that launched a thousand messes. Gray learns to make her way from room to room, where trouble eagerly awaits. *Photo courtesy of Jenna von Oy.*

CHAPTER 16

Cruisin' for a Bruisin'
And Other Mobility Melodrama

A SCENIC VIEW OF MY PAST

As with every other adolescent in America, I waited for my sixteenth birthday with bated breath. Getting a driver's license meant something very meaningful . . . I could cruise around Los Angeles with my convertible top down, blasting hardcore rap music I had no business listening to, much less singing along with. It meant I could cram my car full of fellow child actors, loiter around Sunset Boulevard, and do crazy things like go through the drive-through at In-N-Out Burger to get a double-double with grilled onions, wrapped in lettuce instead of a bun. I'm telling you, we were really living on the edge. But you know what? I wasn't drinking (yet), and I wasn't doing drugs, so it could have been much worse.

A driver's license meant freedom, and I couldn't wait for it. Until it dawned on me that all the truly fun places in Los Angeles required identification that indicated one was over the age of twenty-one, so that brand-spanking-new license wasn't going to do me a damn bit of good. The weight of the unjust world came crashing down like a cartoon anvil on my tiny, teenaged, hat-wearing head. My all-important sweet sixteen came and went, and I realized all that coveted ID card gave me was my own parking space in front of the *Blossom* soundstage and the ability to drive my older friends to clubs they could get into and I couldn't.

By the time my nineteenth birthday rolled around, I was over my part-time gig as weekend chauffeur. It was time to see and be seen, get a little raucous, and dance the night away, as nineteen-year-old college students are wont to do.

I was ready to leave the burger joints behind and ponder major life-altering decisions, such as which club would let my underage friends and me sneak in, whether or not we'd run into Paris Hilton while we were there, and how long it would take before the paparazzi would catch a shot of any of us drunkenly making out. My parents must have been very proud. But being nineteen seemed eons away from twenty-one, and who wants to wait another two years for the privilege of showing the world just how young and inordinately stupid one is? Moreover, who needs to wait on something as dumb as legality when one's friend has the hookup on Olvera Street, where one was capable of finding everything from homemade tortillas, to Day of the Dead trinkets to, apparently, high-quality phony IDs.

But this Goody Two-shoes didn't have the guts to don a ridiculous incognito getup and hold some clandestine meeting by the piñata kiosk. I was certain the cops would see me for the impostor I was, rip off my overpriced baseball cap, cuff me, and charge me with spearheading some young Hollywood bogus identification distribution ring. So instead, I borrowed an old license from someone's sister's friend, who supposedly looked just like me. This might have been true if you were a nitwit, three sheets to the wind, or as blind as a cave cricket, but I went along with it anyway. I wasn't about to spurn my meal ticket. Besides, the card had a certain je ne sais quoi that spoke to me . . . namely that it said I was five foot four, and I was beguiled by the fact that anyone thought that might be a credible height for me. Flattery will get you everywhere.

We were in business. That Friday night, my new ID and I met up with a group of friends so we could attend a charity fashion show at an upscale bar. I know that sounds slightly less magical than unscrupulously finessing our way into The Viper Room, but I was still an outlaw-in-training. It qualified as proper rebellion in my world.

When we arrived at the red carpet, a burly bouncer was stoically manning the door. We're talking Buckingham Palace–guard stoic. He was daunting, to say the least, and my harmless little plan to score entry into a twenty-one-and-over establishment suddenly lost some charm. This guy had guns that shamed the Incredible Hulk, and I was just a spunky pip-squeak who was five feet on a good day. Five foot four, if you believed my new ID. Nonetheless, I was in it, and I wasn't about to back out now. What's that whole thing about holding your head high in the face of adversity?

I watched as each of my friends, who also had fake IDs, showed their cards and gained access past Rambo. Easy breezy. Now it was my turn. I flashed a disarming smile, handed over my license, and waited for the go-ahead.

After a moment of careful inspection, he peered down at

me (way down) and raised an eyebrow. "What's your name and birthdate?" he grilled.

I recited the information I'd been practicing since the precious card had been put into my possession. I knew I'd answered correctly, but the guy gave me no reaction whatsoever.

"Driver's license number?" he continued.

I chuckled nervously and silently cursed my lack of preparation. "Who memorizes their license number?" I joked, hoping it might fly.

He shook his head. "I'm sorry, but I can't let you in with this." He seemed genuinely apologetic, which was almost worse.

"I can tell you my address and my height," I offered desperately.

He shook his head again.

And then I went for it. When all else fails, I thought, try righteous indignation. (Do not attempt this at home.) "What's going on here?" I demanded. "I can't believe you're questioning my identity!" I held my poker face like a champ, until the guy broke out into a disturbing grin that made me step back a little.

He leaned in and quietly whispered, "Nice try. I know who you are, Jenna. I love your show."

Leave it to me to find the one thirty-five-year-old meathead in Los Angeles who was a *Blossom* fanatic.

CUT TO . . .

Forget passing a driver's ed test in order to sneak into lame Hollywood parties; my kids should've had to pass a hard-core balance test to freely navigate my house. Nothing leaves mass destruction and ruin in its wake quite like a newly mobile baby.

My cradle chronicles

If the idea that your child could accidentally roll off his changing table has you jumpy, you might need to find a therapist before this is all said and done. As your child works his way toward the one-year mark, pivotal developmental milestones lie in wait around every corner. Obviously, your baby's first step is one of the most monumental of them, and you'll find yourself waiting for this achievement with both trepidation and elation. It's a rite of passage that will cause you to break out the video camera while simultaneously wishing you could mummy-wrap both your child and your home in scads of protective gear. The house formerly known as organized is about to look like it was invaded by the zombie apocalypse. Behold, the days of paper plates and Dixie cups are upon you, as you relegate your precious wedding china to storage tubs and pry curious fingers off Grandma's heirloom tea set. Flower vases get moved to higher shelves, and lit candles are a thing of the past. You'll say hello to baby gates and drawer locks and bid farewell to the treasured family stemware. Let the games begin.

When your baby becomes mobile, the "easy" part of his infancy is over, and your stint as professional kid-chaser officially begins. It's time to break out the Band-Aids and Boo-Bunnie ice pack, and mentally prepare yourself to dry some tears. You'll start extolling the practicality of a minimalist lifestyle and dreaming of days when you aren't haunted by every table corner and staircase you see. You'll quickly become best friends with those really awesome fellas named superglue and duct tape, and you'll contemplate extreme safety measures such as lining your walls with foam and strapping cushy pillows to your baby's bum. Your mommy radar will launch into overdrive, and you'll master the arts of gasping, cringing, flinching, wincing, and reminding yourself that breathing is supposed to be involuntary.

You know those extreme obstacle courses where race cars have to take curves without slamming into strategically placed orange cones? Your home will suddenly resemble one of those tracks, making items like a wine rack and utensil drawer look more like a wall of razor blades and an open cage of Bengal tigers. Your nerves will be shot all to hell and, in no time flat, every room in your house will appear to have been ransacked by the Tasmanian devil. Because it has. Good times.

THE BABY STEPS TOWARD WALKING
Here is a breakdown of some of the steps on the road to your baby becoming ambulatory.

Tummy time
This is technically the precursor to crawling, and the royal *they* say to start it when your baby is a newborn. (Though I would recommend waiting until he's lost his umbilical cord stump, or it can get prematurely ripped off. Ouch. And ew.) Babies spend a lot of time on their backs now that the American

Academy of Pediatrics recommends to always put infants to sleep that way (it reduces the risk of sudden infant death syndrome). Add to that the time spent in a swing or car seat, and it's probably good to provide a little change of position here and there. Tummy time allows for that.

Babies need solid leg, neck, and back muscles to walk, and tummy time also gives them an opportunity to build and strengthen those areas. It will encourage your baby to lift his head, push up on all fours, roll over, practice the kicking he'll need to swim the English Channel someday, and if you're lucky he'll even face-plant onto the tummy time blanket like a drunk chick at a KISS concert. If you're extra lucky, you'll catch it on camera so you can show it to his first girlfriend behind his back.

Your baby may not enjoy tummy time right away. Gray actually never liked it, while Marlowe took to it immediately. When Gray fought it, I sometimes laid her belly-down on my own chest, so her tummy time was spent skin-to-skin. She preferred this method, which seemed to provide her with the comfort she needed. Truthfully, I preferred that method as well. Any time spent cuddling with my girls gives me the warm fuzzies!

If your baby isn't keen on the whole tummy time thing, try adding a little stimulation. You can purchase infant floor gyms for this purpose, complete with all the bells and whistles (some actually even have bells and whistles), though we never invested in this sort of entertainment venue. We put a few colorful toys out and made sure the dogs stayed away. That was about as high-tech as we got. Many of the books and articles I've read suggest putting toys just out of your child's reach, since it forces them to stretch and move in order to get to them. This seems a bit like dangling the carrot, but I get the theory behind it. I'll admit that when Gray crawled for the first time, it was because she saw a ladybug rattle at the other end of her blanket and decided she was getting it come hell or high water. When Marlowe was learning to reach for toys, she figured out how to turn in circles. And let me tell you, it's endless fun to watch your three-month-old spin like a gyroscope.

I know tummy time is supposed to take place daily, but our efforts were somewhat erratic. When we had our heads on straight enough to remember, we did five to ten minutes of it. Fitting it in every single day was definitely never our strong suit and, as far as I can tell, our girls are turning out just fine. Nobody's motor skills have been stunted, and the baby police never showed up to ticket us for indecent tummy-time exposure.

A couple tips: You may want to reserve this activity for a time period when your baby doesn't have a full stomach. I certainly wouldn't want to do belly flops after consuming a large milkshake, so I don't suppose our kids do either. Another suggestion is to get a waterproof pad (my favorite is the Conni Kids wee pad, because it's sturdy and easily washable) and combine some diaper-free time with tummy time. Now we're really getting ambitious! We opted to go this route with Marlowe, and she absolutely adored it. It cut down on her diaper rashes because it allowed her bottom to have a break, and she thoroughly loved the freedom to move around with no restrictions. As a side benefit, it also gave her a glimpse into what life at a nudist colony might look like, should she ever give it some thought. Which I pray she doesn't.

Crawling

Get those eyes in the back of your head adjusted properly, because you are one step shy of employing them full-time. Crawling is the baby step right before baby's step, so to speak. It's like the moment in a horror film just before the dumb girl races up the attic stairs to her doom. You know the terror that's about to ensue, but all you can do is brace yourself and keep watching.

There's no other way to say this—some kids come up with weird-ass ways of getting around. Where there's a will there's a way, and not every child opts for the traditional crawl. If your kid suddenly starts sauntering down the hallway like an erratic spider monkey, go ahead and tout her as *inventive* and praise her form of crawling just the same. Gray did a quirky, one-handed, boot-scoot boogie until she got the hang of crawling on all fours, and we have one friend whose little boy would only slide backward from room to room. After that he went straight to walking, with nothing in between.

The fact is, not all kids crawl. Yes, it's a common phase before walking, and the majority of children manage to do so, but some kids skip it altogether. So don't panic if your baby is not as far along as some of his peers (don't forget that nobody is handing out awards!) or if he has a bizarre method of moving around.

The crawling stage will likely offer a lot of comic relief as you watch your baby eagerly making his way toward everything you've ever wanted to keep him away from. Every. Single. Thing. Fortunately, at this stage of the game you can still make your way to objectionable items before baby reaches them. Enjoy this while you can. And no joke: If you haven't babyproofed your house yet, you'd better initiate Operation Put That Shit Away pronto! If you still think I'm kidding, read the section on babyproofing.

Moving along the furniture

This was one of the funnier phases my girls went through, namely because they bobbed and weaved like those goofy, puffed-up, inflatable wind dancers you see at used-car lots. It was highly amusing to watch them work their way across a room, pausing every few seconds to regain their balance and grin back at me like they were getting away with something.

Once your child discovers how to pull himself up into a standing position, he'll take advantage of every coffee table and TV stand he can find. Playing sideshow spectator becomes more interesting by the day, as your kid gleefully blazes trails from furniture piece to furniture piece, until he misses his intended target and keels over. You think The Three Stooges had a good schtick going? Wait until you get a load of your kid! It's slapstick at its best. (I think it goes without saying, but this is funny only when your kid doesn't get hurt on his way down. If he does, it's no laughing matter at all.)

During this phase, we found our girls really took to push toys. Apparently there's something strangely alluring about a little lawn mower–looking thing that sounds like a retro pop-corn maker when it rolls along. I don't get the attraction, but

I don't have to. The beauty of push toys is that they give kids something to hold on to while still enabling them to explore the world around them and work their way up to walking. Of course, it also gives them the false sense of security that they can start racing across the living room like they're Mario Andretti, which sometimes leads to spontaneous and unsolicited somersaulting. You'll want to watch your kid closely and make sure you've cleared a football field–sized path for him to totter down.

If all else fails, they make baby knee pads. Seriously—we own a pair.

Standing up

Much to some parents' dismay, standing up doesn't always directly translate to moving forward. A lot of kids learn to stand without holding on to anything ("Look, Ma, no hands!"), then proceed to squat, bounce, sway, and even dance, all without taking that much-anticipated next step of . . . well . . . a step. There's plenty of time for roaming later, so I say let the dance-a-thon continue! Hell, if you take him to a mall, you might be able to start an impromptu flash mob.

Walking

They say most kids take their first steps between nine and twelve months, but this is totally a crapshoot. My little sister walked at eight months, and by nine months she was practicing for half marathons (my poor mother). Alternately, friends of ours have a son who hasn't walked yet, and he's sixteen months old. The little guy is taking his sweet time. For those quick to say, "There's something wrong with him," there isn't. It doesn't necessarily mean anything if your kid doesn't walk until a little later than his peers do. Sometimes it's by choice. Some children take a very laissez-faire attitude about the whole process, because they've got nowhere else to be and nothing they are aching to get to. If you have a baby who was born prematurely, don't forget to take that into account as well. A lot of premature babies progress on the timeline they would have been on had they been born on schedule. For example, a child born two months early may not walk until a few months after his fellow toddlers, because his developmental age is younger than his true age.

WALKING IN A STRESS-FREE WONDERLAND

Here are a few tips regarding your kid's efforts to walk on the wild side.

Barefoot is better.

At least while inside the house. I found that shoes kept my girls from balancing properly and added yet another new obstacle for them to overcome. Bare feet also kept them from slipping as easily on our wood floors. My inner fashion maven desperately wanted to pair that itty-bitty plaid skirt with its matching pair of baby UGGs, but it just wasn't terribly practical. I believe that learning to walk barefoot gives kids a stronger sense of their own bodies, improves their coordination, and doesn't weigh them down in the name of style.

Great adventure

Some kids are Dora the Explorer, and some are content to gaze at the world from afar. Either is normal and fine; just be sure to figure out which path your child is on. And quickly. Before you know it, your kid might start leaping off steps or doing the patented Spider-Man move up your living room walls. It's better to have some idea about what you're in for. When I was on an episode of *Celebrity Wife Swap* in 2014, my swap's grandkids were swinging from her glass staircase, if that gives you any idea. Kids are fearless!

Get ready to get your exercise.

Once kids start moving, they never stop. And I truly mean *never*. Not to mention, after learning to walk comes learning to run and navigating the stairs and jumping on beds, so . . . your work is cut out for you. Your kid is about to have you sweating more than Jack LaLanne.

Let it go.

And I'm not referring to the overplayed song from *Frozen*. When your kid transitions from crawling to walking, he'll be a one-man demolition derby. Picture Godzilla taking down Tokyo. By the time you clean up the toilet paper he managed to drag through four rooms (someday he'll be magnificent at TPing your nasty neighbor's house), he'll have already torn apart your underwear drawer and dumped three-quarters of your shoes into the bathtub.

First of all, don't freak out. Sometimes kids teach us lessons the hard way . . . like the fact that closing any extraneous doors, especially those leading outside, is smarter and safer for everyone involved. Including our underwear and shoes.

Your house has officially become Romper Room, and it's going to stay that way for a while. Chances are you won't be able to keep up with all the mess, because kids can tear a room apart faster than you can say, "What special form of hell is *this*?" The best thing you can do is adapt.

Gray was particularly fond of putting her magic touch on our DVD collection, for example, which started out being alphabetized and wound up in a box in our basement. Sometimes you have to let go of your prior opinions regarding tidiness and organization, or give up the fight altogether, in order to avoid risking your own sanity. If you're anything like me, you'll start dreaming of dust-free floors more than making out with Brad Pitt. Sadly, that still won't make those clean floors a reality. I've never been on that Brad Pitt bandwagon myself (I'm more of a Jon Stewart kinda gal), but I definitely wish that robot housekeeper from *The Jetsons* would show up at my door and mop my house on a daily basis. With five dogs and two kids, I need all the help I can get.

The cool thing is that your friends will understand. They no longer expect your place to look spotless (if they ever did in the first place), because everybody else with kids has a house that looks like it was invaded by creatures from *The Walking Dead* too.

Get those magic mommy kisses ready.
As difficult as it is to wrap your head around, accept that there

will be bruises . . . on your kid *and* on some of the household items you treasure. No child makes it out of this phase without a few scrapes and tumbles, and there are often a few casualties of war where your collectibles are concerned too. The good news? Your kid will probably fare better than your antique lamp. Most bruises aren't beyond repair, thank God, and kids tend to have thicker skulls than we give them credit for. They are exceptionally resilient.

None of us want to see our kid hit the ground (or anything else, for that matter), but they all have to stumble before they can walk. That said, there are some bruises that kisses and an ice pack can't cure. I was taught that I should call the doctor if our child starts acting abnormally after an especially hard fall, gets strangely sleepy, or begins showing signs of a concussion such as vomiting or having dilated pupils. So far, we've avoided that scary scenario.

Learning to walk is hard work.
My advice is to try not to get too ahead of yourself or your little one. In our excitement over each new milestone, it can be easy to get too assertive with our encouragement. Our babies will crawl, stand, walk, and run when they're ready. I've learned that breakthroughs occur only on my children's own terms—not when I have the camera out or the in-laws are around to see it. I try to give as much praise and support as possible, without the pressure. (This philosophy comes in handy later on during potty training too.) The fact is that it takes a lot of energy for baby to focus on simply remaining upright, so he needs to go at his own pace. It takes a lot of energy

for you to keep him safe too, so do what you can to prep in advance! Which brings me to the sheer hell that is babyproofing.

THE BUSINESS OF BABYPROOFING

Babyproofing will, inevitably, be more work than you envisioned. If you're anything like I was, you're thinking, *It's no big deal. I just have to put a few things away and get a couple of those plastic cupboard locks.* Well, I'm here to tell you, you shouldn't underestimate the curiosity of a baby on the loose.

Here are some tips to aid and abet your home "redecoration" plans.

Make a preemptive strike.
Begin your babyproofing early, because you'd be surprised how involved it can get. Sure, it's fairly simple to install outlet protectors, put a temporary gate in front of the stairs, or cover the bathroom doorknob. But what about all those wires you've got lying around your home office desk? And how about that heirloom hutch with flimsy glass doors that was passed down by your husband's beloved great-aunt? Not everything can withstand the hurricane that is a toddler. Obviously, closing doors to rooms that don't need frequent access is a must, but not all areas of the house will have that option. At some point your bambino will understand what "No" and "Don't touch that!" mean, but that will take a little practice and a whole lot of trial and error.

The first time I attempted to teach Gray not to touch certain things around our house, she found my scolding to be wildly hilarious. I've told jokes written by professional sitcom writers that have gotten less laughter from the audience. It's a complicated parenting moment when you try really hard to wear your stern face, only to wind up being mocked by someone who isn't old enough to ride the tea cups at Disneyland, which causes you to laugh even though you shouldn't, which completely obliterates any authority you might have had but more likely didn't. Not my finest hour.

Bench your breakables.
This is also known as, *Move anything and everything you love to higher ground like you're preparing for a tsunami.* Murphy's Law states that your child will find a way to annihilate the things nearest and dearest to your heart. In other words, put up the expensive bottle of champagne you got on your wedding day if you don't want the kitchen floor to drink it. Which begs the question, why didn't you and your hubby drink it yet? What are you waiting for? (Unless, of course, you're reading this while you're still pregnant, in which case you are exercising some impressive restraint.)

The main idea here is there's no sense in giving your little one the opportunity to shatter your great-grandma's perfume bottles or the tapas platters you paid way too much for in Spain. A balsamic vinegar carafe I bought on a trip to Italy years ago was our first real casualty of war with Gray, and I learned my lesson.

My mom, on the other hand, took a bit longer to learn hers. My brother, Pete, was a bull in the china shop when he was little. He somehow managed to crack four glass tabletops before my mom gave up on replacing them. Depending on the stamina of your kid, you may find yourself diving for every plummeting gravy boat, decanter, and coffee mug before it smashes to smithereens. And that's just the warm-up.

Think like a child.
When you examine your house for weaknesses, survey it at the level a baby would. If that means getting on your hands and knees and crawling around for a while, do it! It will be amusing (and possibly a turn-on) for your husband, at the very least.

It may be some time before baby can reach doorknobs or pull down cords, but you'll get there sooner than you think. My husband spent hours frantically hiding computer and lamp cables when we realized our daughter was making a bee-line for them. Go figure. A roomful of colorful, fascinating toys, and she heads straight for the wires of doom. Nothing jump-starts your heart quite like having your kid try to pull herself up on electrical equipment!

Stairwells are particularly dangerous too, so this is where those childproof gates come in handy. At some point, having a banister for support is helpful, but not all kids can reach. If you have munchkins like our girls, most railings are too high up to do much good. Hell, I can barely reach some of them.

Corner bumpers aren't a bad idea for particularly sharp

table corners, and make sure to stow away flimsy furniture or secure any heavy items that fall easily.

Lid locks for your toilet seat are a must. Can you say, "How did my toothbrush wind up swimming in the potty?" Somehow kids always manage to contaminate things that generally belong in your mouth.

You may want to keep a lock on your stove so no one accidentally pulls the oven door open while it's hot, and plastic cabinet and drawer latches are crucial for any space where you keep cleaning supplies or toxic items. I recall the neon-green Mr. Yuck stickers from my childhood, which peppered every Comet and Clorox container we owned. In theory that's a good idea, but no one-year-old will let her mischievous merriment be thwarted by some silly sticker. That really works for kids who are slightly older. To avoid catastrophe, it's best to restrict baby's access altogether.

Babyproofing = adultproofing

Evidently the safety gear designers of the world have a sense of humor and think we parents are a lot smarter than we really are. Or maybe they just wrongly assume if we can manage to keep a kid alive long enough to get her to the babyproofing stage, figuring out a piddly little toilet latch should be a piece of cake. Not so much. Deciphering the installation and subsequent use of all our babyproofing gadgets was almost as difficult as trying to decode DNA sequencing. You know, because I do a lot of DNA sequencing in my spare time. But if you're a big fan of puzzles and brainteasers, conquer away! And if you ask your husband to handle it all, at least be kind enough to put a beer in his hand first.

Spoiler alert: babyproofing isn't foolproof.
Please don't kill the messenger, but your safety efforts may not be entirely effective. Foam corners can be peeled off, gate latches require some strength and discipline but they're do-able, and toilet padlocks are merely an unspoken challenge for your child to find toys small enough to finagle underneath the lid. It will take you hours to figure out how to set up and apply everything, and then somehow your kid will figure out how to dismantle it all in twenty minutes. It's pretty impressive.

Don't get overly paranoid.
As much as it sucks, we can't watch over our children every minute of every day, and we can't protect them from every single disaster that's waiting to happen. There's not enough bubble wrap in the world to cover every surface of our living space, and it would be downright evil to force our kids to wear body armor until they're eighteen. Though the thought has clearly crossed my mind, however fleetingly. In a sense, getting injured is a rite of passage for babies who are learning to walk. I don't wish bumps, bruises, cuts, stitches, or scars on any of our children, but I acknowledge a certain number of them come with the territory. As parents, the best we can offer is to create a zone that's as safe as possible for them.

The moral of my story

Your days are numbered. You may never sit down, eat lunch, or go to the bathroom by yourself again once your kid learns to walk. But at least you get to witness the beauty of watching him stagger around your house like a drunken sailor!

Yawns truly are contagious—especially when Mommy is getting less sleep than Gray. *Photo courtesy of Mimosa Arts.*

CHAPTER 17
Chatting, Chowing Down, and Chasing Mr. Sandman

A SCENIC VIEW OF MY PAST

When I was ten or so, I became enamored with *Willy Wonka & the Chocolate Factory*. I mean, who doesn't get off on watching two hours of an eccentric Gene Wilder cavorting with absurdly tanned little people? I couldn't get enough of it. I imagine the filmmakers intended for the majority of us to connect with the lead boy, Charlie, who was the model of all things pure and good. However, they didn't account for my budding dark side. I managed to take on an odd preoccupation with Slugworth, the rival candy manufacturer who sends in spies to steal Mr. Wonka's innovative confections. I wanted to have what he had—the mystery, the intrigue, the candy he so cunningly pilfered. So, in all of my ten-year-old wisdom, I set about finding a way to attain this lofty and inspired goal. As luck would have it, Halloween had just passed, so there were plenty of tasty sweets floating around our house. None of it belonged to me, of course, since I'd already mowed through every Kit Kat and Butterfinger I could get my filthy little hands on, but that didn't matter to me. Where there's a sinister streak, there's a way—and my poor, innocent, five-year-old sister got caught in the crosshairs.

I started by writing a ransom note. It wasn't just any old ransom note, mind you; it was a thing of beauty. I cut letters out from back issues of *Highlights* magazine and put them to good use. What's the point of having *Highlights* to expand your mind if you can't also reuse the pages to plot nefarious schemes? At least I was recycling. Next, I snuck into my sister's room and stole her favorite stuffed animal, Ruff the Raccoon.

I know, I know. You're probably thinking, *This girl was Satan's evil spawn!* In my defense, I didn't intend to be cruel. I was obsessed with Nancy Drew and Hardy Boys books, had a detective agency that I ran out of the cubbyhole beneath our stairwell, and actively sought ghosts in our historic town library. I was spellbound by thrillers and whodunits, so my pursuit of chocolate may have gotten slightly more creative than it should have. It doesn't make it right, but I suppose my ten-year-old moral compass needed a little more directional work.

Anyway, I took Alyssa's raccoon and hid him away in a safe location, otherwise known as my sock drawer. In his place, I left that ransom masterpiece I'd constructed, demanding all my sister's Halloween spoils in exchange for her beloved companion. As if that weren't bad enough, I pretended to find said letter, read it aloud to her in mock horror, and then suggested we wait out in the snow until the thief returned to collect his goods. After all, we couldn't just let him get away with it. A bonbon burglar *must* be caught!

We'd been camped outside in the bitter cold for an hour or so when I declared my desperate need for a restroom. In a stroke of sheer genius, I ran inside to change into a dark trench coat and fetch the kidnapped, cotton-stuffed varmint.

Tucking my hair up under a fedora, I raced around to the opposite side of our house and made my way up to the mailbox. Keeping my head down for anonymity's sake, I hastily removed my ill-gotten cache of treats and jammed the raccoon into the cold, metal vault. I darted away before little Alyssa could see my face or shout for help, and let myself back into the house. By the time I'd taken off my coat and hat and made my way back outside to resume my position on the stakeout, my sister was bawling.

That night, I was bawling too, courtesy of my punishment. Since I'd been such a visionary in my kidnapping ploy, my dad was equally imaginative in his discipline. I was tasked with deveining several bags of shrimp for dinner. Which is, for those who may not know, the process by which one cleans out the poo-poo track. Talk about a shitty punishment. And learning the hard way.

CUT TO . . .

I didn't know the true meaning of *learning the hard way* until I had to engage in a battle of my child versus the three *S*s: speaking, sleeping, and snacking. You think seeing the Virgin Mary on a slice of Wonder Bread is a miracle? Try sleep-training your kid. That debacle will be closely followed by the first time your child repeats something she shouldn't in front of your in-laws. And don't get me started on the introduction of solid foods. My wardrobe will never be the same. Neither will my walls.

My cradle chronicles

Offhand, it may seem like there's no correlation between your baby learning to talk, graduating beyond formula or breast milk, and learning to take naps on his own. But all three come with their own manner of chaos. And guess who's tasked with cleaning up the mess?

Look who's talking!

Who: Your kid.

What: God only knows. Your child's first words can range from common ones such as *no*, or *Mommy*, to off-the-wall things like *tickle*, which was my first word. (I'm not sure what that says about me.) Other kids wait until they have something important to say before bothering to utter anything. We thought my little brother was mute until he was two years old, at which point he called out, "Mommy, I bumped my head!" He's in good company. Einstein was supposedly several years old before he spoke as well, and the water-cooler gossip is that he said something akin to, "The soup is too hot." Of course, that's probably a tall tale, but it's a fun one.

When: Anytime from roughly six months old on and, if you're lucky, while you have the video camera at the ready. There were countless times we thought Gray said things that we can never prove, because we weren't recording her at the time.

Sadly, babies don't have rewind buttons or closed-captioning options. I'd swear up and down, for example, that she said "turtle" at six months old, but only the bathtub and the rubber duckie and I were privy to it. And they still refuse to support my claims, those cheeky bastards. The fact is, sometimes a baby's first words are a bit on the muddled side, leaving you to wonder if she said "Goo goo ga ga," or "Look, there's Lady Gaga!"

Where: You name it. The pantry, the dog park, the kitchen-ware aisle at Target . . . There's really no telling where you'll be when baby decides to start chatting it up. If good fortune is on your side, you won't be in front of a crowd of people, because you're likely to get misty-eyed about it. And weeping in front of the masses is a little embarrassing, unless you're winning the Super Bowl. As a side note, once your child starts actively talking, there's no filtering what he comes out with. This includes brilliant things like cuss words, explicitly detailed talk of poop and flatulence, what you and your husband heatedly said to one another during your last argument, and what you recently compared your stepmother to. Don't let that angelic face fool you—a talking kid is a dangerous one!

How: Your kid finally decides he's had enough wailing, grunting, gurgling, and squealing to last a lifetime and opts for something that sounds a little less like *Planet of the Apes* and a little more like something in the dictionary. That doesn't mean you'll necessarily understand it any better, but at least you're all on the right track!

Everything in our lives revolves around words. Words can build relationships and tear them down. I once read that the average person says approximately sixteen thousand of them per day. Some folks, like a certain former speed-talking best friend I played in the '90s, are probably spitting out significantly more than that. But words are the cornerstone of our relationships with one another, so when your baby starts speaking, it opens up a world of possibilities—and a seriously giant can of worms. Your child has spent months understanding far more than he could articulate, and suddenly he's figured out how to interact with you on a completely different level. It's equal parts fascinating and frustrating. Here's my take on the drama, pitfalls, and violations (please don't hate me) associated with it.

Cracking the code

Your child won't wake up one morning and miraculously be able to quote Thoreau or take phone messages for you. There are various phases between newborn babble, Toddlerese, and what one might consider an effective conversation. I'll just go ahead and cut to the chase—not all of them are decipherable. In fact, each time you think you've conquered your baby's lingo, he'll introduce a new and improved set of words that baffle you. You'll ask baby to repeat himself a few times while you secretly wrack your brain for what an "Argpham" might be. It's clearly something important, since he's repeated it forty times in a row. Meanwhile, he's busy gesticulating wildly, repeating that incomprehensible word *another* forty times in a row, and pitching a fit because he thinks you've turned into a moron during the last minute and a half. Cue the meltdown. No one enjoys being misunderstood! The only thing you can offer in this scenario is patience. Or a baby translator.

Talking back (the good kind)

Even if the only language your baby seems to be fluent in is something that sounds like Klingon, don't be afraid to converse with him anyway. You don't have to mimic his noises to join in; simply speak the way you normally would. Whatever you do, just don't leave him hanging! I've seen a lot of parents fail to engage their baby because they forget those grunts and coos are his first attempts at eliciting a response. Even if your child can't yet reciprocate with answers, she's absorbing your cadence, vocabulary, and the sentiment behind your words. So tell her about your exciting day doing the laundry, making chicken pot pie, taking the trash out, and changing dirty diapers. Hell, recite some poetry or a scene from *The Princess Bride* if you want. She won't really care what you're saying, but she'll enjoy hearing it!

Learning to listen

In observing a plethora of mothers talking to their infants, I've noticed a fairly common habit—what I've termed "the mommy monologue." This consists of parents directing a series of statements or questions toward their child without ever pausing for a response; they just keep on talking. And talking. And talking. They deliver longer run-on sentences than my old *Blossom* character, which is downright freaky. I'm sure baby is thrilled to have the focused attention, but sometimes he wants a chance to participate too.

Even before our kids are capable of uttering coherent replies, I think it's important to leave room for them to smile, gurgle, shake a rattle, or offer whatever form of answer they wish. Words aren't the only way of saying important things like "I love you" and "I'm hungry!" Leaving a space in between sentences encourages them to respond in their own way. With that idea in mind, I made a point to curb my chatty nature (as much as that's possible) when my girls were infants, because I wanted them to learn early on that conversations are a two-way street. I started posing questions and waiting to see what would happen. You know what I discovered? They instinctively knew I was leaving them an opening for feedback. By the time Marlowe was three months old, she would begin jabbering away and testing out new sounds each time I would address her!

Bye-bye, baby talk

I'll just go ahead and state that we are *not* fans of baby talk in our house. We aren't having esoteric discussions over cognac or anything, but we abide by the Dr. Seuss quote, "A person's a person, no matter how small." We've always spoken to our girls as equals (within reason, of course), while exercising care not to sacrifice our position as their parents. We don't broach adult issues with our children—we stick to material that's age-appropriate—but we try not to dumb down our vernacular or imitate childish voices in order to "be at their level." I think you get the gist. Sure, we made tons of funny facial expressions and exaggerated our vocal inflections when they were infants, because babies respond to that. It gets their attention and lets them know we're trying to connect with them. But I'm a firm believer that parents can encourage social development without emulating baby babble and without oversimplifying the way they speak. I always get a little cross-eyed when I hear parents raise their voice a few octaves, affect that strange syrupy tone, and say things like "Penelope no want to go bye-bye with mommy?" or "Mommy kiss Penelope's yucky boo-boo?" I find it to be excessively patronizing, and I think kids deserve better. Why set them up to have to relearn proper grammar and sentence structure a few years down the road? At some point, speaking in choppy, simpleminded baby talk is no longer cute or appropriate. Interviewing for her first job by saying "Violet want to give grumpy Mr. CEO her résumé" probably won't go over very well. I strongly feel there's a happy medium somewhere in there, where we can speak to our kids in a way that reaches them without challenging their intelligence.

Adopting errors

It's easy to fall into a pattern of unintentionally endorsing the words our children say incorrectly by using them ourselves. For example, a parent might say, "Look at the big 'ephalant' at the zoo!" I think it's cute as can be when my kids accidentally mispronounce something; there's serious entertainment value in it. Gray called bananas "debabas" for almost a year, and she coined the term "lasterday" in place of "yesterday," which still makes an appearance from time to time. I've found both to be endlessly charming, and I haven't always been quick to correct her. But I've had to make a concerted effort to use the proper version of those words when speaking to her, because it's just too easy to say them incorrectly myself. I've done my best to let her figure out the correct pronunciation on her own. This allows me plenty of time to enjoy the overwhelming cuteness of it all without reinforcing the wrong thing.

Word dwarfism

I've heard many a parent employ condensed or simpler words when their child is present, even when carrying on a conversation with a fellow adult. Why not go ahead and break out those SAT words? Our kids learn multisyllabic words the same way they learn monosyllabic ones—through context and repetition. It might be a while before your child can use them in a sentence, but so what? They'll pick things up at their own pace. And you'd be surprised which words manage to sneak into a child's dialogue. When Gray was two, during a car ride to her day care, she informed my husband, "We're going to have a fire drill again at school today, and I'm going to be traumatized." Not sure where she picked that one up, but kids absorb everything!

GUESS WHO'S COMING TO DINNER

Who: We're still talking about your kid.

What: It usually starts with a pureed vegetable of some sort. Regardless of what it is, it's about to adorn the walls like some vicious serial-killer massacre, so expect to be wearing it and dress appropriately. In other words, keep your raincoat handy. Even better, invest in a biohazard suit.

When: Timing is everything. The appropriate age for transitioning children to solid foods differs for everyone, but I'm all for waiting as long as possible. Just because your baby has teeth doesn't mean he's ready for food. The American Academy of Pediatrics website essentially states that breastfeeding is a child's ideal nutritional source through the first year of his life: "The American Academy of Pediatrics reaffirms its recommendation of exclusive breastfeeding for about 6 months, followed by continued breastfeeding as complementary foods are introduced, with continuation of breastfeeding for 1 year or longer as mutually desired by mother and infant."* Believe it or not, I'm on the side of authority on this. (But just this once; I wouldn't want to mar my reputation.)

Where: Anywhere that doesn't contain white walls, dry-clean-only clothing, or strangers who are within spitting distance.

How: Get that food in any way you can, whether it's by coaxing, playing airplane, pretending you're eating it too, or using a slingshot. I'm just kidding. No, I'm not. Yes, I am. I think.

There's nothing cuter than a baby's expression when she tastes

---

*"Breastfeeding and the Use of Human Milk," *Pediatrics: Official Journal of the American Academy of Pediatrics*, published online February 27, 2012, accessed April 28, 2015, http://pediatrics.aappublications.org/content/129/3/e827.full.

carrots for the first time. Her little nose scrunches up, she starts working the food around in her mouth, prepares to swallow, and . . . kapow! You're hit right between the eyes with chewed-up orange mush. A professional archer couldn't possibly have better aim. Unless you happen to be a fan of squished banana facials or chewed-up-Cheerio hairspray, prepare to need a shower 24/7. You've got a pretty messy future ahead of you!

Here are some questions you might be asking about your new assignment as super-duper food-pusher extraordinaire.

How will I know when it's the right time to try solid foods?
When I first considered giving Gray a taste of nourishment beyond breast milk, a friend said something that made me hold off a little while longer. She mentioned that a lot of folks decide to start their kids on solid food because it's captivating to watch (which you'll find it is) or more convenient to their lifestyle (which you may also find to be true) and not necessarily because their child is truly ready. She told me the right time is often later than parents think it is.

Gray was about ten months old when she first tried solid food, and I wound up basing my decision on her age combined with some obvious cues. When she was getting ready to try something more than breast milk, I noticed she was showing signs of still being hungry after feedings, and she also began gravitating toward my dinner plate. I'm not referring to a minor curiosity; I mean she was stalking it like my pug stalks a morsel of steak. (Or cheese. Or anything edible, really.) Your baby will likely begin to show immense interest in what you're eating, and breast milk may no longer seem to satisfy her. She might even try to grab food off your plate, mimic your chewing motions, or open her mouth like a baby bird.

Regardless of the signal, kids are pretty easy to read when it comes to food. Just don't mistake the random curiosity of a two-month-old as a sign that you have a child who's old enough to handle a three-course meal. Other important things to take into consideration are making sure your baby is able to steadily hold her head up as well as sit up by herself so she has less of a chance of choking. Because choking isn't fun for anyone.

What foods should I start with?
A lot of folks are big on beginning with rice cereal, but I've never been a fan. Because I breastfed, I didn't feel the need to give my girls anything beyond fruits and vegetables until they were ready to have food that wasn't pureed into the consistency of a muddy puddle. They were already getting their nutrition via my milk, so I supplemented with whatever healthy produce I had on hand. If you aren't breastfeeding, you may want to look into which foods will impart the most well-rounded nutritional value for your baby, whether store-bought or homemade.

Should I make my own food?
This sounds like something only the granola moms might do, but I beg to differ. I didn't find it to be as intricate or

time-consuming as I would have thought, and I didn't need a degree from Le Cordon Bleu to figure out what to do. If you have a blender, I promise you can make it happen! Nobody's looking for you to make a culinary extravaganza for your eleven-month-old. Even Gordon Ramsay has to draw the line somewhere.

I'm a foodie, so I was gung ho about immediately getting my girls acclimated to the kind of fare I was putting on the table for my husband and myself. It certainly made it easier than prepping an entirely different spread for the kiddos! My girls spent only a short time strictly eating purees. After that, I began introducing very small pieces of some of the items we were having for dinner that night. Our pediatrician told me most foods were okay, such as salmon, as long as it was cut to the size of our daughters' pinky nails, and as long as we weren't giving them foods that posed health risks, such as honey. Nonetheless, that isn't to say I was offering bacon-wrapped scallops right off the bat. I'm not *that* radical. I opted to delay the introduction of certain foods that required a lot of chewing, or that might have posed allergy issues, such as shellfish. Just to be on the safe side.

While still in the puree stage, I made very simple versions of whatever vegetables we were having for dinner that night. I started with fresh produce such as carrots, kale, sweet potatoes, or peas. I first steamed or boiled them, sometimes using a combination of several, and then pureed them in the blender or food processor. I'm big on flavor, so I also doctored up the mixture by adding a dash of spices or herbs such as vanilla, cinnamon, dill, garlic, basil, or lemon zest. I believe exposing a child to natural seasoning early on develops a more complex palate and makes it easier to broaden his culinary horizons down the road. Sometimes I also added a bit of plain nonfat yogurt or a fruit, such as apple, to thin it all out. You can even mix in breast milk, which may help get your baby accustomed to the new taste profiles. Once I was done, I put the concoction into little resealable puree pouches with twist-off caps (they are wonderful space savers in your refrigerator), and voilà! Homemade baby food.

In case you're curious, here was my reasoning behind making my own baby food rather than purchasing the store-bought stuff.

1. I knew exactly what went into it.
In other words, I didn't have to scour the ingredient list to make sure there were no unrecognizable additives. Or even, for that matter, additives that I could easily recognize, such as that wicked bad boy: sugar (and all of his alien life forms that like to go incognito as something that sounds healthy). I found relief in knowing precisely what was being put into my child's body. To clarify, I'm not saying jarred food is bad for your baby. The contents vary from brand to brand, and some brands may be as pure as Mother Teresa. Some even offer organic options. I can't speak to the nutritional value of commercially made baby food, since I skipped it altogether. I am, however, saying the only way to truly know what your child is eating is to make it yourself.

2. Fresh, in-season produce equates to higher nutritional value.
We've all been told that fresh fruits and veggies are healthier than processed ones, so that's not a new concept. Fresh produce is healthier than the jarred stuff too, for exactly the same reasons; the nutrients don't get lost in the shuffle. That may start a civil war, but I'm a big believer in eating what's fresh and in season, whenever possible. And so ends any chance I had of being sponsored by the major baby food companies.

3. It prepares your child for the true taste of solid food.
I personally feel my daughters transitioned to solid food more easily because they didn't eat jarred food first. They got used to the true flavor of what they were eating, since it was made to order. I've tasted plenty of baby food in my time (don't ask), and while I find it generally carries the flavor of the vegetables and fruits that went into making it, it doesn't taste quite like the fresh stuff. Commercial baby food is cooked at very high temperatures because it has to be stored for a greater length of time. Any bacteria also has to be killed off. Consequently, some of that yummy flavor is killed off too!

4. It's significantly less expensive.
Baby food adds up—quickly! You don't need a whole lot of fresh food to produce the equivalent of one jar of baby food, so I found the cost difference to be tremendous. Not to mention, we were already buying fruits and vegetables at the grocery store for ourselves, so grabbing a little extra wasn't a difficult task.

Even though I've presented my case for making one's own baby food, my biggest suggestion is this: don't do it because of peer pressure! If you feel like it isn't conducive to your lifestyle because it's too time-consuming, takes up too much space in your refrigerator or freezer, or just isn't your cup of tea, go a different route! You are *not* a terrible mom if you don't make your baby's food from scratch.

Let me tell you a little story. When Gray was just shy of a year old, I brought her to her friend's birthday party. She was the youngest attendee, so she was the only one who couldn't partake of the pizza during lunchtime. Knowing this in advance, I'd brought a packet of food along for her in one of those resealable bags I spoke of. As I opened it up to feed her, one of the dads asked, "I've never seen baby food like that before. What do you have in there?"

I answered, "It's a parsnip-and-apple mixture I made."

His wife happened to walk up at that moment and frowned. She turned to me and said, "Oh, you're one of *those* moms. Well, I couldn't do that because I had to work. I didn't have time to fool around with food."

I was flabbergasted (and a bit insulted, to be perfectly honest), so I kept my mouth shut. I didn't bother explaining to her that in no way did I believe making my own food made me a better mom than her . . . But I should have. Perhaps it would have inspired her to let herself off the hook.

I think we parents tend to get most defensive about the things we feel guiltiest about, and there's absolutely no need to feel like a delinquent parent over choosing not to make your own baby food! If you opt to make your own purees, then great. If you choose to buy commercially made food, then that's fine too. I'm all for whatever keeps your kid well fed and healthy. Which, I imagine, is your goal as well. Do your own thing, and don't let anyone else put you down for it.

What changes should I expect when I introduce solid food?
I'll tell you what I found the biggest change to be: the diaper evolution. More complex foods mean more complex poop. This isn't a subject I really want to elaborate on, but let's just say the BC (Before Cuisine) poop is downright dainty compared to the AC (After Cuisine) poop. Your baby's Pampers contents are about to hit critical mass.

Choking can be a hazard even with breast milk or formula, but the stakes go up with solid food.
Properly chewing and swallowing (or gumming and swallowing) are things your child will have to get used to, which is why mushy foods are introduced first. While I was never paranoid about the choking issue, my husband and I did take a first-aid class that included infant CPR. I highly recommend it!

Sometimes there's no rhyme or reason when your kid won't eat something.
You may wind up with a picky kid or one who eats anything. Your baby may also prefer certain textures and flavors, while others turn him off. For instance, Gray despised bananas as a baby but obsessed over them by the time she turned eighteen months. Just because your ten-month-old isn't into broccoli

doesn't mean he won't develop a taste for it later, so there's no need to force-feed him those brussels sprouts!

Naptime ain't for sissies

Who: You guessed it . . . your kid.

What: The hell that is naptime training.

When: Preferably before your kid moves in with his first girl-friend.

Where: Initially, anyplace you can get him to pass out, whether it's a swing, a Pack 'n Play, the car, a bassinet, a crib, a cosleeper, or a makeshift couch cot. In a pinch, even the bathroom rug will do.

How: With a lot of patience and creativity on your part.

First off, let me say I realize the subject of sleep training tends to be a controversial one. To cry it out or not to cry it out? That seems to be the eternal question and the generator of mass mommy hysteria on the Internet and social media. I've honestly been torn about my stance on this issue for quite some time now. In theory, I thought I would be fine letting my children cry until they fell asleep. In reality, the cry-it-out method went over like a lead balloon; it just didn't work for my husband and me. Moreover, it wasn't effective for our daughters, especially Gray. We tried to transition Gray into her own crib countless times during her infancy, and it failed miserably. Every time. It wasn't for lack of patience, diligence, effort, or creative tactics on our part; our kid just *hated* her crib. Which may be the biggest understatement I've ever made. She felt abandoned, and she viewed that crib as a jail. A pretty-in-pink, beautifully carved, cushy-mattressed jail. During the screaming and bawling intermissions (not that there were many to speak of), I'm fairly positive she was plotting ways to fashion a shiv out of the wooden bars and break out of the joint.

Unless you count being home to stuffed animals, extra blankets, and clothes waiting to be hung, the crib wound up being a nonfunctioning showpiece in the nursery until Gray's sister came along. Marlowe didn't mind being in there at all. I didn't even have to consider the cry-it-out method with her, since she never made a fuss to begin with. To put a slight spin on the *Forrest Gump* quote, "Kids are like a box of chocolates; you never know what you're going to get." Consequently, your sleep training methods may require some adjustment.

Since sleep training tactics are such a personal choice, I'm going to stick with what I'd like to think are some loose observations and universal recommendations for you.

Choosing the technique that works for you
The fact is, there are countless methods for sleep training, and many of us would disagree on which one we deem most appropriate and acceptable. The good news is the only people

who really have any right to weigh in on it, as it pertains to your children, are you and your spouse. (Assuming, of course, that you've chosen a safe method.) As with any other tough parenting decision, it would be outstanding if we could all respect one another and try to be nonjudgmental. However, I acknowledge that's like expecting Sarah Palin to ace a social studies class. There is no best way to teach your child to sleep independently; there's only the way that feels most comfortable to you. All you can do is work toward finding the arrangement that sets the appropriate boundaries you want for your child, keeps your head and your heart happy, and—wait for it—gets your kid to *sleep*!

Making sleep training work for you

The sleep training method that works for your child may be very different from the one that works for you, so flexibility is key. I quickly learned that a child's personality tends to influence which approach is successful despite any preconceived ideas a parent may bring to the table. For instance, I discovered there were options that were better suited to our lifestyle and Gray's disposition than the cry-it-out method. I wholeheartedly want my children to respect the parental boundaries I set, but I have to draw the line when those boundaries start bordering on becoming traumatic for them. Sometimes the line of separation is muddy, so you just have to go with your gut. Sleep training your child may never rest solidly within your comfort zone, no matter how hard you try. As a dear friend whose advice I implicitly trust once said to me, "It's not all or nothing, it's not a linear process, and it's not boot camp." Be loving and gentle to your baby and yourself.

Why sleep training is important

First and foremost, babies need sleep. Their little bodies are expending so much energy on both mental and physical growth that it's crucial they balance it with solid rest. Truth be told, you need it too. Sometimes you'll be overwhelmed, completely behind on your work, or in desperate need of more alone time with your husband. Baby's naptime gives you some breathing room and allows you to reenergize as well.

Crying: when is it too much?

Despite the fact that I wasn't comfortable employing the cry-it-out method with my children, I'm not out to prevent them from ever crying. I respect that it's a natural and important way for them to express themselves. My girls need to experience tolerable frustration (my very PC way of saying my girls will get royally pissed off every now and then), because it's a fundamental part of life and growing up. Nonetheless, I found it took some time to learn their limitations as well as my own; everyone has different parameters. You may feel ten minutes is too long to allow your child to cry, for instance, while another mother may feel perfectly comfortable waiting longer. You may recognize that your child escalates to a certain type of crying when she hits her emotional limit, indicating you need to immediately shut the sleep-training venture down for the day. Alternately, you may find certain noises or movements signify your baby will be winding down sooner rather than later, so you're willing to stick it out. It isn't an exact science. You'll figure out the proper approach for you and your baby, and you'll help each other set your own guidelines.

Develop a routine.

No matter how you teach your child to sleep independently, I find establishing a naptime and nighttime routine of some sort is imperative. It can be as simple as singing a lullaby and kissing your baby good night or as elaborate as you wish. Many sleep routines include activities such as bathing, diaper changing, swaddling, turning on white noise, reading a story, or massaging baby's feet with lotion. The idea is to provide a calming ritual that baby associates with preparing for bed. Just make sure you set a routine that you're able to follow through with daily, and choose things that contribute to a soothing atmosphere that encourages sleep. If you travel often, you may find it necessary to create a program that isn't location-based. We opted for activities that could be repeated regardless of where we were, so the pattern wouldn't be interrupted if we were visiting grandparents or staying in a hotel. You'll customize a system that works for you.

Think outside the bassinet.

You can try out every sleep training method known to man and discover none of them are effective or practical for you. I encourage you to let those creative juices flow. Sometimes parenting is about coming up with innovative ways to make your kid think it's his idea to do what you've been trying to get him to do from day one. For the record, sometimes that works with husbands too.

THE MORAL OF MY STORY

The writing is on the wall, and so is the applesauce I gave my kid for lunch. Thank God I have five dogs who can clean up faster than a Hoover vacuum! Sadly, they weren't much help when it came to sleep-training my girls, and it wasn't terribly believable to blame our basset hound when my daughter loudly announced, "Mommy, I want booby!" in the middle of Easter mass. I wish you luck.

Crybabies. I resort to the if-you-can't-beat-'em-join-'em rule during Gray's one-month photo shoot. *Photo courtesy of Mimosa Arts.*

CHAPTER 18

Supermom Has Left the Building

A SCENIC VIEW OF MY PAST

When I was a toddler, my parents rented an apartment on the second floor of an elderly couple's home. Mom and Dad were working hard to make ends meet, and they made do without many modern conveniences, such as a washing machine and dishwasher. (I can barely imagine a day without my iPhone, much less years without those guys!) I'm sure bringing me into the world didn't make it easier to get by; as you know, babies can swallow your paycheck faster than an anaconda can consume a crocodile. Nevertheless, my parents did the best they could with what they had. As it happens, one of the items they weren't in a position to purchase at the time was an electric coffeepot. Since they found the idea of going without coffee preposterous (now you know where my addiction originates), they percolated their daily dose in a pot on the stove the old-fashioned way. And that's where our story begins.

One afternoon, my mom had a friend over for caffeine and conversation, which I imagine she desperately needed. I'm sure she wasn't getting out all that frequently to socialize, since I was a handful! No, really. I was a forty-year-old in the body of a one-year-old, with enough energy to power the Las Vegas grid. And little did she know, she was about to be pregnant with her second child. It's probably advantageous that she snuck in a little grown-up time while she could.

Anyway, the coffee was brewing and the two women were catching up. While they chatted, I was on a sightseeing tour of the living room. Since I was newly mobile and still finding my equilibrium, I was toddling around like a seasick Bobblehead. My mom kept glancing over to check on me, ensuring I was as far away from that piping-hot coffee as I could be. When it was ready, she noted my whereabouts and brought it over to the table. After pouring her friend a large portion, she turned around and headed to put the pot back on the burner.

It's nothing short of amazing just how quickly a baby can make her way across a room. In no time flat, I'd stealthily slipped under the tablecloth and ambushed my mother's friend. Before the woman could react, I'd gotten up on my tippy toes and grabbed for the saucer beneath her cup. I then proceeded to pull it toward me, the contents of the cup raining down on my arm and splashing onto my chest.

For those of you who don't know, a pot of coffee made on the stove is significantly hotter than it is in most electric coffeemakers, since there's no way to control the temperature. I managed to give myself second-degree burns and was rushed to the hospital for treatment. After that incident, it's sort of fascinating that coffee didn't become my arch nemesis rather than my best friend and energy ally!

I still have a scar on my wrist to show for the accident and, while I can joke about it now, nobody was laughing back then. My mom's friend felt awful that she couldn't stop me in time, but no one felt worse than my mom. She wouldn't let herself live it down and still has nightmares about it to this day . . . almost as many as she has over the time I flipped out of my baby carriage. Which may explain my affinity for roller coasters.

CUT TO . . .

After all these years of making fun of my mother's mishaps, I now play a starring role in my own accidents and foolish mistakes. We mommies might be able to leap the baby swing in a single bound and change diapers faster than a speeding bullet but, sadly, I've discovered our kryptonite . . . ourselves!

My cradle chronicles

It's *Call of Duty*, Mommy-style. Forget the Xbox version— this is real life, ladies! You may find your new child-friendly existence is somewhat reminiscent of a video game, chock-full of action and adventure. I, for one, put the Super Mario Bros. and Sonic the Hedgehog to shame as I dodge projectile sippy cups, slide across the kitchen floor on fallen cereal, scramble to stop the canine cartel from baby toy thievery, rescue Marlowe from the villainous coffee table corners (which are padded but still scarier than a back-alley run-in with Voldemort), and defend our fragile glassware from a potentially catastrophic fate at the hands of our resident tiny humans.

Who needs a demon-hunting, tomb-raiding, galaxy-fighting heroine when there's a kick-ass mom around? We may not be saving humanity from intergalactic destruction or the forces of evil, but we perform feats of derring-do on a daily basis as we deftly handle our workload, family life, and social calendar. Lara Croft seems significantly less cool when you're a baby-carrying, snot-wiping, coffee-wielding, laundry-tackling mommy on a mission to tame tears and restore peace to the planet, right?

Okay, maybe I'm getting a little carried away with this metaphor. The point is, we are pretty darn capable of juggling everything. Everything, it seems, except the pressure we put on ourselves to be perfect. Sometimes there's an antagonistic, sinister evildoer that enters the picture and wreaks havoc. And all we have to do is look in the mirror to find her.

Introducing . . . The Nag

We all possess our own internal judge and jury. I refer to mine as The Nag. The Nag tells me I would be a better mom if I made different decisions, had more patience, or handled things like a remotely competent parent would. She's the inner critic who badgers me with phrases like "Your child is too old for a pacifier" or "You should never have so much to do that you can't take the time to read a third bedtime story" or "All of the *other* day care mothers remembered today was the teacher's birthday." The Nag is one snarky little wench! She doesn't show up every day, but she's in there. She's been known to heckle, pester, and patronize me, and she knows just when I'm feeling vulnerable. I imagine you have your own version of her, and she (or he . . . I wouldn't want to discriminate) probably lives inside you like a cancer. Because guilt is a bright-red, fire-breathing, foulmouthed beast that can crush your spirit. *If* you let it.

Your Nag may have been present for years, but prepare for her to get even more vocal once children are in the picture. Motherhood inflates The Nag's ego like she's just made the cover of *InStyle*. She'll get off on instructing you how to parent your child. For instance, she might begin by telling you that you're being selfish by going back to work after the baby is born. She might condemn you for choosing formula over breast milk or threaten all-out war over the fact that you've taken a five-minute break in front of the TV. Eventually she'll start hassling you about how your child has four fewer words in his vocabulary than he's "supposed to," how his inconsistent eating habits must be your fault, and how you should already be potty training him, even though he's clearly not ready yet. Her opinions never end.

My personal Nag hounds me relentlessly about my house not being clean enough and the number of items left on my to-do list when the day is done. She gets after me for paying less attention to my dogs now that I have kids and for spending less alone time with my husband. She occasionally tells me I'm not funny enough, not pretty enough, and not a good enough parent to be writing a book on the subject of motherhood—even one that's not meant to be a how-to. I've come up with some creative ways to ignore her when she climbs atop her soapbox, but she's extraordinarily resilient. She keeps showing up after I think she's been killed off—much like a soap opera actor.

I've recognized this issue within myself for a long time, and I know I'm not alone. Insecurities can creep in for even the toughest and most confident of us, so why shouldn't we be honest about it?

The prevailing complaint among my mommy friends is "I'm worried that I'm screwing my kid up." No one's harder on us than we are on ourselves, and it's a hard mind-set to break! I encourage you to start resisting the self-contempt early on. Sometimes you have to bind and gag The Nag so the positive thoughts have enough room to take hold. If you don't, she'll start to rule the roost. She'll collect your imperfections and blow them up into billboard-sized posters that call you demeaning names like "a second-rate mom," "an unsupportive wife," and "a failure." The name-calling doesn't help you, your children, your marriage, or your self-esteem. Don't be afraid to tell The Nag to take a hike! Stuff her in your sock drawer, flush her down the toilet, or lock her in the hall closet with the board games and dust bunnies. I don't care what you do with her, as long as she knows she isn't welcome in your heart or in your head.

Here are some ideas to help you fend off The Nag:

The Nag will try to be a Debbie Downer.
Though she's a persistent little tart, keep thinking positively. Make sure she's overshadowed by The Dreamer, The Believer, The Faithful, and The Mom Who Loves Above All Else. I know it sounds like I'm sanctioning multiple personality disorder here, but I hope I've gotten my point across.

The Nag will try to compete with your inner advocate.
Sometimes it's easy to blur the lines between your helpful sub-conscious voice and the one you should ignore. We all have an angel on one shoulder and a devil on the other; we just have to decipher which is which. Learn to recognize your gut, and hold on tight!

The Nag will tell you you're too distracted while entertaining your child.
Don't feel guilt-ridden over being a multitasker; it's a prereq-uisite for being a mom! You may find yourself mentally cross-ing off the next chore on your list while reading *The Cat in the Hat*, or typing an e-mail while you breastfeed. Most of us have so much to take care of on any given day that we can't help but mentally jump ahead to the next thing. Try to refocus and appreciate the time with your baby, but don't feel like you're a bad mom for acknowledging your workload at an inopportune time. Kids demand our attention nearly every waking minute of the day. If we didn't get other things done simultaneously, we'd exist only for their amusement. I don't know about you, but if I'm going to be a full-time play-ground, merry-go-round, and puppet show, I at least need to eat a sandwich and make sure the mortgage is paid while I'm doing it.

The Nag will say you should be able to fix all things, do all things, and be all things.
That's a load of crap. It's perfectly acceptable to ask for help, and you should! I still need this reminder myself every now

and again (like every day), because it's second nature for me to handle everything on my own. The checklist-making, *i*-dotting, *t*-crossing control freak in me wants to be able to accomplish everything I've set out to do and still have time to take a bubble bath before bed (fat chance).

Sometimes it's tough to wrap your head around the fact that asking for help doesn't mean you can't do something by yourself; it means you're strong enough to know that assistance makes a task easier. Or faster. Or just downright more enjoyable. Since feeling overwhelmed can be a very real part of being a new mom, it's important to allow others to lend a hand. For instance, don't be afraid to ask your husband to vacuum the living room floor or make a dinner here and there. Go ahead and blame it on me if he gives you pushback! Let your best friend babysit so you and your hubby can have a date night, and let your mom do the laundry when she offers. If you don't want her folding your husband's safari-printed boxer shorts—and I don't blame you—set those aside for a later load.

My girlfriends had the right idea when they put out a meal plan sign-up at my baby shower. Anyone who wanted to assist us by bringing a meal filled their name in on a calendar and then, while dropping off a lunch or dinner, got to take a sneak peek at our new baby girl. (Online services are available for this as well, such as *MealBaby*, which rocks!) I'm telling you, this was my saving grace. I didn't have to worry about meal preparation for two solid weeks after having each of my girls!

Cooking is generally my therapy, but who wants to make

a pot roast in lieu of staring at that stunning little face? I bet even Paula Deen wouldn't have given up a chance to cuddle with her boys just so she could whip up a peach cobbler. So buck up and let someone be there for you. You can find a way to return the favor down the road if you're uncomfortable feeling indebted. And you know what? I bet your friends would be satisfied with a heartfelt thank-you. A homemade card can do wonders.

The Nag says you should take to motherhood like a fish takes to the ocean.

I'm calling her bluff. To stick with the fish metaphor for a moment, not all of us are born with gills. Be patient with yourself! You may find yourself bogged down by the everyday tasks, because even the daily grind can be difficult to handle at first. That's okay! You have to grow into your fancy new motherhood shoes. And sometimes those shoes are harder to walk in than a pair of freaky-looking, high-fashion, runway stilettos with an aquarium in the heel. In other words, it ain't easy, friend. We all walk a little too close to the edge of the sanity cliff from time to time.

The Nag will tell you to entertain everyone who stops by to meet your new baby.

Don't fall for it. The only people you need to take care of right now are your child, yourself, and to a certain extent, your husband. You don't need to serve guests or worry about whether your floors are polished. Visitors are coming to marvel at the beautiful child you had, not to be treated to freshly baked scones and hot chocolate. As long as it's the kind of organized chaos *you* can live with, that's all that matters.

The Nag will tell you not to cut corners.
Cut those corners anyway, as long as they aren't imperative to anyone's welfare. For example, I'm a firm believer that meals should be eaten off of paper plates during the first few weeks after you come home from the hospital, just so you can eliminate the additional work of dishwashing. I'm pretty green-conscious, so my recommendation is disposable but biodegradable dishware. That said, you do what feels right to you. I'm not here to be the recycling police!

The Nag will conduct a rude running commentary and throw it in your face.
Fun fact: I have a tendency to say things to myself out loud, so sometimes The Nag speaks through me like I'm a ventriloquist's dummy. But an inability to filter your dialogue is hurtful, even when you're the only one in the room. You know the saying, "If a tree falls in the forest and no one is around to hear it, does it make a sound?" Well, I can definitely tell you that if you talk to yourself, *you're* around to hear it, so it resonates and reverberates like a kettledrum in a football stadium bathroom. When you call yourself stupid, even in jest, or lament how big your thighs are getting, you're doing yourself a disservice. Express yourself in a way that reflects kindness and confidence—even when it's directed toward *you*! In other words, treat yourself the way you want others to treat you. What you project institutes the code of conduct and the values your

child will be following later in life, so go ahead and promote that self-love early on. Let it seep into your child's consciousness as well as your own.

The Nag will compare your parenting to everyone else's.
I'm notorious for doing this. At some vulnerable moment, you'll meet a mom who seems like she really has her shit together, is wise beyond her years, and knows every parenting trick you can only dream about. Know that she has her demons too . . . They just didn't surface during that particular outing to Macy's. Maybe the only reason she's calm is that Valium she took an hour ago. You don't know everyone else's story.

The Nag will want you to be a psychic.
This is, of course, a ridiculous notion, but there are times you'll curse yourself for not having enough foresight. As my childhood scalding coffee mishap proves, you can't always prevent disaster. At some scary and unfortunate moment, your child will skin his knees on pavement, smack his head on a doorknob, or burn his hand on a hot casserole dish. Not even a crystal ball can save our children or us from those circumstances. We can't always second-guess when our kid will have a major meltdown in the middle of Home Depot or refuse to take a nap before our trip to visit the in-laws. We can't predict when they'll have a leaky diaper on a friend's white couch, throw their bottle across a restaurant, or spontaneously lick the filthy shopping cart handle. Don't beat yourself up when you can't prevent accidents from happening!

The Nag will brainwash you into trusting everything you read on the Internet.

The Internet is a petri dish of horror stories where women congregate to share, get things off their chest, and defend their own insecurities. And since most of us have enough of those on our own, we probably don't need to add to the list. The Nag will lead you to believe too much of what you read. The fact is, there are a million sides to the motherhood story, and not all of them are going to coincide with, or reflect, your own experience. Filter through the advice and tales of woe, then follow your heart. It also helps to find a comfortable, non-judgmental, dependable, and safe friend to talk to when you're having trouble sifting through the information on your own.

The Nag will try to say you're a bad parent simply because you aren't teaching your baby to play chess while in the womb.

Don't get me wrong, I'm all for a solid education and a well-rounded child, but your kid isn't slow to learn just because she wasn't reciting Shakespeare during her ultrasounds, isn't multiplying and dividing cheese puffs on her high chair tray, and won't be learning a new language for each day of the week. There are some brilliant kids out there, and yours might be one of them. But he might not be, and that's okay too.

Hell, when we were teenagers, Mayim used to spend her days on the *Blossom* set listening to Elvis Costello and doing the *New York Times* crossword puzzle in indelible ink. Meanwhile, Joey Lawrence and I were in deep existential discussions about which member of Boyz II Men was the better singer. Mayim went on to earn a degree in neuroscience, and

I . . . well . . . I wrote this cheeky, sarcastic book you're reading. Not all of us were put on this planet to be a brainiac. Still, I'd like to think we've both been successful in our own right.

I'm not discouraging your child's education. I want Gray and Marlowe to be intelligent and thoughtful too, and that requires a certain amount of at-home stimulation on my part. Education is a combined effort between parents and teachers—we need to work hand in hand. And I thoroughly believe you should motivate your child in a way that makes you comfortable. If your four-month-old is ready for calculus, more power to you (I think). But there's a reason those introductory alphabet cards say "A is for Apple," "B is for Balloon," rather than "A is for Antidisestablishmentarianism," "B is for Biochemistry." I suspect most of us don't really believe little Johnny or Betty need to be the next Madame Curie or Louis Pasteur-in-training, and there's a lot of pressure out there without us piling on more. It's fine if your son or daughter is playing with sock puppets instead of reading Dostoevsky and spouting Molière! Don't let the crazies (including The Nag) make you feel like you aren't challenging your child enough. And don't start writing off that college scholarship just because the next-door neighbor's kid was talking two months before yours.

There's a lot of pressure to fill our children with knowledge. I worry about it too, but I try to remember that the knowledge I'm imparting won't all come from books and extracurricular activities. It comes from the time I spend with my girls, introducing them to the world around them and helping them appreciate it. Not all learning comes from a textbook or is done inside of a classroom, and *everything* starts out as a new experience for babies! I was reminded of this constantly in the first few months of my girls' lives. It was thrilling to watch them discover the joys of mastering simple tasks, such as clapping their hands or shaking their heads . . . We take so much for granted! If your child is a prodigy, I'm appropriately impressed. But I'm even more impressed by the kids who'd rather climb trees than play video games or who say "please" and "thank you" without being prompted.

When Gray was ten months old, we spent Easter dinner with a friend and her family. Her daughter and son, who were seven and four respectively, came up to Gray on several occasions throughout the evening and offered her baby-suitable toys. They tried to include her in all their activities, despite the fact that she was so much younger. At the end of the evening, the little girl approached Gray and said, "Maybe a hug before you go?" It brought tears to my eyes that this sweet seven-year-old thought to show affection to a child she'd just met. This was followed by the little boy coming over to hold Gray's hand while he bid her farewell. Neither of them had been instructed to do so. Now *that's* what I'm talking about! Being intellectually advanced has its merits, but so does being polite, kind, and generous with one's heart.

The Nag will want you to be everything to everybody.
If your mother is anything like mine, she probably used to say, "You can't please everyone." And you know what? She was right. To someone out there you are too rich, too poor, too

cynical, too optimistic, too outspoken, too quiet, too lenient, too strict, too conservative, too liberal, too forgiving, or not forgiving enough. I've been called all those things at one time or another, and some of them are even true. My point is that no matter how solid and noble our parenting efforts may be, someone out there will vehemently oppose them. This tends to be a never-ending struggle for me, because I'm a people pleaser by nature. Like most folks, I dislike being judged, unappreciated, or misunderstood. But all of that is overshadowed by the fact that I want to be a good parent to my kids. At the end of the day, we have to remember that no one else's opinions should define how we parent.

In the eyes of the flaw

Not one of us is infallible, especially yours truly! I'm far from perfect, and I do mean in a galaxy *far, far, far* away from perfect. Just because we feel good about our choices and convictions the majority of the time doesn't mean we never falter. Some days you'll feel like you've got the whole parenting thing down; other days you'll wonder who that delirious woman in the mirror is. Any mom who tells you she's never questioned her own parenting decisions—or felt ashamed, flustered, remorseful, humbled, humiliated, had self-doubt, or sold herself a white lie—is full of bologna. (Or pulling the wool over her own eyes!)

We moms can be our own worst enemy, even regarding things that are beyond our control. I'm the first person to stand up and say that I make mistakes. All the time, and sometimes more than once! I don't see any way around that, because parenthood is all about living and learning . . . and then, in my opinion, laughing at yourself later. So tell The Nag within you to get a freaking sense of humor!

THE MORAL OF MY STORY

My superhero cape and tights are on permanent back order. That said, I've realized one of the most important things I can do as a parent is to forgive myself when giving my best backfires. We may not be able to rescue the world from the brink of destruction, but we can raise our kids with love and integrity while still giving ourselves the freedom to make mistakes.

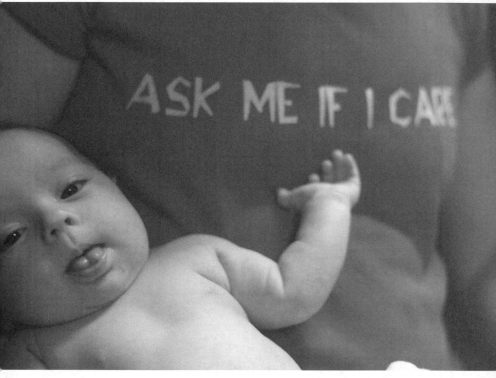

Gray demonstrates that we're embracing a carefree attitude toward those Mommy Wars. (On her grandma's lap.) *Photo courtesy of Jenna von Oy.*

CHAPTER 19

All's Fair in Love and Mommy Wars

A SCENIC VIEW OF MY PAST

Los Angeles is infested with millions of actors. No joke, we run rampant like the H1N1 virus over there. Some are brilliant at their job, some are abysmal, and most of us are somewhere in between. Some get into the industry because it's their passion, some stumble into it because they're in the right place at the right time, and still others are destined for greatness courtesy of nepotism. Some folks are too big for their britches; some are humble and normal. (Well, as humble and normal as we actors are capable of, given the vain nature of what we do for a living.) Some are seeking fame and fortune; some wouldn't dream of doing it for anything other than a true love of the art. There are those who are never given an excuse to quit waiting tables, those who unknowingly give up right before their big break, those who work consistently, and those who consistently pretend they're working. (Which, I suppose, could technically be considered an acting gig of sorts too, albeit an unpaid one.) And ultimately, the town either chews us up and spits us out or it helps us to nurture a career we can write home about. If it takes all kinds to make the world go round, you can't imagine how intensified and overdramatized that melting pot is in a kooky place like Hollywood.

Lord knows I've dealt with my share of fruitcakes (hell, I've probably been the fruitcake someone else had to psycho-manage a time or two), but I've also been fortunate enough to encounter my share of fellow actors who are in it for all the right reasons and happen to have a good head on their shoulders. In fact, I'd like to think that's the majority of us. Not all of us are out to have our names splashed across the front page of every tabloid, punch out the paparazzi, or make some poor, burned-out assistant fill our dressing room with bowls of nothing but the green M&Ms. I've always prided myself on aligning with the folks who don't buy into the notion that working actors are better than nonworking actors, the crew members who made their show possible in the first place, or the parents who gave birth to them and raised them to achieve their dreams. My friends don't have "people who call my people." If we want to schedule a lunch together, we pick up the damn phone and work out the details ourselves. That isn't to say we're without our quirks, but actors have a tendency to get a bad reputation in the press, thanks to the more neurotic and nasty ones out there. And the industry has its share of those too, believe me. This is a story about one of *those* actors. This is what happens when someone rises to fame too quickly and loses sight of reality.

About a decade ago, my best friend, Kal Penn, called me up and asked if I wanted to attend his upcoming movie pre-miere. I was honored to share such an exciting time with him and jumped at the opportunity to be supportive. He *seriously* deserved it. After years of busting his butt and getting only bit parts, he'd finally booked a movie that would put him on the map! I'm not suggesting any of us thought this particular film, which was campy, was going to earn him an Oscar or reward him with a Barbara Walters interview, but it certainly got him noticed. Granted, that may have had something to do with the fact that he bared his ass in one of the scenes, which I'm still trying to wipe from my mental hard drive. (Thanks for warning me about that one, Kal! Your mom and I were squirming in our movie theater seats like an atheist at a Southern church revival.)

Nevertheless, despite my being forced to see more of my best friend's rear than I cared to, I was thrilled to be a part of his special evening.

It also happens that I knew several of the other actors in the film. In fact, I'd become friends with one of them years before when she'd first moved to Los Angeles to pursue her career. Back when she was still green and hadn't caught a break yet, she would call me to go over soap opera scripts with her. Since I was on a successful series at the time, she was eager to have some direction and dialogue guidance, which was super flattering. We hung out in the same circle of friends, would grab lunch from time to time, and I'd even met some of her family members, including her sweetheart of a brother. It had been a few years since we'd seen one another, and I was looking forward to saying hello. A premiere after-party isn't always the appropriate time to catch up on old times, but I was excited to congratulate this woman on her recent string of movie roles; she was definitely movin' on up, and I was elated for her. It's always nice to see someone you know join the 1 percent of working actors in Hollywood. She was also making a rather notorious name for herself on the red carpet, thanks to a few risqué nip slips, but I wasn't going to hold that against her. I mean, plumbers show crack all the time and we're still paying them to fix our leaky faucets, right?

Before I could make my way over to reconnect with said actress, I heard a familiar voice calling my name . . . her brother's. He gave me a huge hug, told me how great it was to see me, and generously said, "Man, my sister is going to be so happy to see you! She's over there with some friends. Go say hi."

I took his advice and strolled toward her table. She was surrounded by an entourage worthy of P Diddy, but that was to be expected. It was her night to shine—everyone should have a support group around for strength and encouragement. I suppose I'd come with Kal for similar reasons, even if we weren't keeping vigil at a prominent table like melodramatic mobsters. To each their own, I say.

I stood there patiently while she continued chatting with her peeps, as I didn't want to interrupt. A minute or two passed and I started feeling a little uncomfortable. *She must not notice I'm standing here*, I thought. *I mean, who would just ignore someone? That would be terribly impolite.*

I lingered a while longer and she finally glanced in my direction, a marginally revolted and unreservedly annoyed look on her face. "Yes?" she asked in a tone that made me shrink a little.

Everyone at the table looked at me expectantly. I was clearly bothering the girl, but that didn't make any sense. After all, her brother had just finished telling me how excited she would be to see me. Obviously things just weren't registering for her yet, which would inevitably change any second. I mean, you don't just go and forget someone you've known for years, right? If this girl could memorize a movie's worth of lines, surely she could recall my face. And yet, here she was still staring at me like I was wearing a donkey costume and belting out show tunes at the top of my lungs.

I gave her the benefit of the doubt. "It's Jenna," I offered, "Jenna von Oy. We haven't seen each other in a while and I wanted to congratulate you on all the stuff you've got going on."

At this point I knew she recognized me, and I waited for her to jump up and hug me or invite me to sit down for a few minutes or, at the very least, say it was good to see me. Instead, she threw me a fake smile and dismissed me with, "Yeah, thanks." Turning back to her friends, she didn't even wait for me to walk away before she rolled her eyes and said, "I have no idea who the hell that is." Cue the sound track from *Mean Girls*.

I shuffled away from her table feeling perplexed as to why someone would pretend not to know me. Did I forget to wear deodorant that night? Did I have massive boogers hanging out of my nose? Had I suddenly been blacklisted amongst the Hollywood elite? (I know the *Blossom* hat trend was pretty dreadful, but c'mon!)

I felt embarrassed. Moreover, I felt insulted beyond belief.

Care to know what I didn't feel? Surprised. As pitiful as it is, I've witnessed the phenomenon time and again. Someone gets a small dose of fame, and they start walking around town flaunting it like a thirty-carat diamond ring. Which, I imagine, must seem like such a cumbersome weight to carry . . . Because as we all know, ostentatious rings and fame are both such heavy burdens to bear.

I was being shunned because now I was a lowly sitcom actress, while she'd emerged as a big movie star. I was a mere mortal, still scaling the lower rungs of the success ladder. She was destined for stardom, and I could no longer do anything to help her on her way up. I'd become a victim of Hollywood's lamest game, Trivial Pursuit: The Tear Someone Down to Make Yourself Feel Better Edition.

Yes, it's as petty and gross and hateful as it sounds. Now, is there an infinitesimal chance that this woman had recently been struck by lightning and developed an acute case of short-term amnesia that ousted any memory of me from her brain? Sure, it's possible. It might even explain her propensity for baring those boobs in public every other month. But then again, lightning is a fairly noticeable event. I should think someone in her enormous entourage would have noticed that. Color me catty.

CUT TO . . .

If I thought auditions, red carpets, and movie premieres were an epic battle of bragging rights, gossip, and wardrobe mal-functions, I was really in for it when I became a mom. Every arena is contaminated by its own special brand of pollutants, but wait until you experience mama drama! A roomful of fellow parents can get bloodier than UFC Fight Night.

MY CRADLE CHRONICLES

Something wicked this way comes and it's sporting heels, a designer diaper bag on its shoulder, and a snarky smile that would melt an ice sculpture of Donald Trump. Before you accuse me of blaspheming the king of comb-over or your beloved Louis Vuitton luggage, I'm not saying you're guilty of anything just because you own an expensive purse, send your kid to a fortune-telling acupuncturist Yogi, or feed him caviar with a silver spoon. I'm not even saying you're evil if you employ two nannies, six housekeepers, and a live-in masseuse who looks like Fabio. Whatever floats your boat is fine by me. I'm here to joke; I'm not here to judge. But the point of this chapter is—drumroll, please—neither are you. Motherhood has become a political war zone, and I wish we would all set aside our weapons and word grenades. I mean, can't we all just get along?

If I wanted a good old-fashioned brawl, I'd roll up my baby-drool-soaked sleeves and head down to my local Irish pub. That way, I could down a pint of Guinness before getting the smackdown. At least I'd get some satisfaction from the beer buzz. Instead, the buzz seems to be in my ears, and it's the constant chitter-chatter of millions of gladiators . . . er, moms . . . who are turning our playgrounds and parks into a battlefield. If you think you're hard on yourself, just wait until your hackles are up in front of the other Montessori mamas! Beware of the folks who claim their kids are signing *political globalization* at ten days old. Kids can't even throw gang signs that early, much less dictate when they want to eat or need a diaper change. Worse yet, watch out for the women who are constantly campaigning for mother of the year. News flash: that distinction is only in our minds.

Lately, there seems to be a comparison around every corner.

"Your kid walked at eleven months? Well, *mine* walked two weeks before that!"

"Your kid's first word was *Daddy*? Well, isn't that cute? My kid's first word was *precocious*."

I think every parent deserves some bragging rights, but c'mon, ladies! Quit the carnage! We aren't comparison shopping for flat-screen TVs here. I know there's a secret thrill when your child does something brilliant in a roomful of other moms whose kids appear catatonic. It gives you a sense of pride to see proof that your child is smart and special. But guess what—chances are those moms feel the same way watching their kids around yours too! We all see the best in our babies; it's the beauty of being a mom. But judging someone else's child based on our (slightly biased) views of our own sons or daughters isn't fair to those kids. Moreover, it isn't fair to our own children, who may eventually treat others the same way. We introduce how our children view the world, and I believe the behavior education begins immediately after birth. If I say "please" and "thank you," my girls are more likely to do the same. If I hold the door open for the elderly, extend common courtesies, and respect the people I deal with on a daily basis, my daughters will have a better chance of doing that too. And imagine how cool it would be if we threw in the towel on our judgments and doled out endless encouragement instead! It's wishful thinking on the grander scale, yes, but I believe we get back what we give. So why not start the kindness crusade on your own? Your children, not to mention the other mommies out there, will thank you. In fact, let me be the first to extend my gratitude.

If you're one of those people who have innocently been thrust into the thick of the mommy war by default, I feel for you. There's nothing like showing up to your child's swim class only to discover that the club has a new nickname and it's Vindictive. You signed up for an extracurricular activity to stimulate your baby, not your temper, right? I have no cathartic words of wisdom about how to handle the women who have it out for you. All I can really suggest is that you try to avoid adding insult to injury, as difficult as that may seem. Just keep reminding yourself it's for the sake of your child, who'll eventually learn to take the high road because he saw you take it so often.

Invasion of the kindness snatchers

If you're new to the whole mean mamas concept, here are some examples of what to expect and what to avoid becoming at all costs. Mind you, I see a little of myself in some of these, so this is all in good fun even if it's rooted in the truth!

The Guidance Counselors

Mother knows best. Evidently, so does the woman at the dry cleaner, your hairstylist, and the waitress at your local watering hole. The second your belly starts showing, miscellaneous women everywhere become a swarm of vultures on roadkill, and they all have their own ideas of how the motherhood business should go down for you. I'm fine if this is done tastefully; after all, I did write a "guide" of my own here. But I figure you can put my book on a shelf if you don't feel like listening to me anymore. On the other hand, some women will back you into a corner and cram opinions down your throat until you choke on them.

On several occasions, for instance, I've found myself trapped by random women who think it's their right to make sure I breastfeed. It happens that I do, but did I miss something? When did formula become the Antichrist? Yes, I may very solidly belong to the breastfeeding camp, but I'm not out to make you feel crappy if it's not the right thing for *you*. I have plenty of friends who opted to solely bottle-feed their breast milk or to go straight for formula and bypass breastfeeding altogether, and I think no less of them. I have my principles and convictions, but they are just that . . . mine.

You will run into women who worship their stance on certain issues like it's a religion and who'll do anything to convert you. To be fair, this doesn't pertain to breastfeeding alone; that just happens to be one of the more prominent points of contention. Know your own level of comfort, while still doing your best to respect differing points of view. You probably won't persuade someone else to change their beliefs, but don't let it make you question your own either. You know what's right for you and your baby.

The Mock Mamas

Similar to the Guidance Counselors, there will be the strangers who insist on becoming your honorary mother-in-law. (This is probably a good time to add that I totally hit the mother-in-law jackpot, so I'm referencing the common stereotype rather than personal experience here. Linda, you are a rock star!) Mock Mamas will randomly appear with a wet wipe to erase the schmutz off your child's face or tell your kid to use her indoor voice when it's entirely unnecessary. These intruders could care less that they've never met you, don't even know your child's name, and have no right to interfere.

While traveling to the East Coast with Gray when she was about twenty months old, I had a woman at the airport yell at me for having my child on the Jetway in cold weather. Now we're not talking sixteen below, polar region, penguins-frolicking-on-the-ice-caps cold, we're talking a balmy forty degrees. I've been known to wear flip-flops and still drink iced coffee in this kind of weather. Never mind that I had no choice, as we were all required to wait our turn in line for strollers and suitcases to be brought up to us, or that my little girl was appropriately bundled in her winter coat and hat. (It wasn't like I was letting her crawl around in her birthday suit!) I was also holding her with a blanket wrapped around her, so I'm pretty sure I had the situation under control. Still, this woman decided it was her place to loudly proclaim that I needed to "Get that baby out of the cold air!" This was followed by a look around to make sure all the other passengers were supportive of her opinion. She practically pushed me toward the terminal as I struggled to drag my stroller, purse, and child. Of course, it's not like she was offering to help me carry anything; she just wanted the last word.

Thank Mock Mamas for their input and try to distance yourself. If you don't feed their busybody frenzy, they tend to lose steam and move on to someone else. With any luck, your offender will make the world a better place by refocusing her sights on that dude who's talking at the top of his lungs on his cell phone.

The Gossip Girls

These women are friends without benefits. They like to sit around sipping upscale cappuccinos while their kids terrorize yours on the playground. They listen to your stories while mentally picking them apart, then whisper behind your back about how they really feel. They roll their eyes every other sentence and go out of their way to make you feel like you'll never be a better mom than they are . . . which might just mean you already are.

The Conservative Coalition

As odd as it may sound, I can be fairly conservative about my parenting decisions. However, these moms take it to another unprogressive, reactionary level altogether. Don't get me wrong—we all have our own ideas of what is and isn't okay for our own children, and many of us disagree over something here and there. You may think it's okay for your kid to have an iPad, for example, and someone else may vehemently oppose the idea. That's not what I'm driving at here. The Conservative Coalition is bound by a stringent set of rules that exist in their own heads, which tend to exclude every other parent on the planet (including themselves, if they were to be honest about it, which they won't be). These women act like you're toting your kid to a raunchy Mapplethorpe exhibit if you suggest you let him watch Saturday morning cartoons. And God forbid you mention sugar! If you make mini chocolate cupcakes to serve at your kid's birthday party, it's the equivalent of secretly dealing their four-year-old Mountain Dew and jelly beans behind the jungle gym.

Honey Boo Boo Syndrome (aka Smotherhood)
I used to think stage moms were restricted to the show business arena. I've crossed paths with many a mother who claimed her child was the next Shirley Temple, Mozart, or Doogie Howser, M.D., and I'm noticing an even greater number of pushy parents out there these days. Fame has become more accessible thanks to the Internet and reality television. One need only "redneckonize" the success of *Honey Boo Boo* for proof of that! In fact, stage moms seem to be coming out of the woodwork like a termite infestation. Damn near anything becomes a contest, including whose kid makes the poopiest

diaper. I can appreciate a friendly wager here and there, but kids aren't hockey trophies, Olympic medals, or Miss America sashes. If you want to pursue your long-lost modeling career, may I (somewhat) politely suggest that you buy the tiara and sequined bloomers for yourself? I promise you'll feel more fulfilled in the long run, and your kid might hate you a little less when she's a teenager. If nothing else, maybe she'll be less likely to tattoo Marilyn Manson's album cover on her face out of spite.

I'm not a proponent of pushing kids into the spotlight. That said, I know it can be hard to separate our own dreams from those of our children. It isn't that we set out to live vicariously through them; it's that we want the best for them. And you know what represents "the best" in our minds? Our own dreams and aspirations. Our ideals tend to be the measuring stick for what we desire for our kids. I encourage you to tread carefully there and respect what your child asks of you—even when they don't have the words to spell out how they feel. I was incredibly passionate about having an acting career at a very young age, and my parents were clueless about how to help me get into the industry. I begged until I convinced them it wasn't a passing phase. One thing led to another, and they ultimately figured out the ropes so they could support my dream. However, I acknowledge that I was an exception to the rule, as I've run across more parents who've forced their children into the business than those who haven't. Not all children with magnetic personalities have the desire to pursue a career in entertainment, nor do they have the maturity to handle it appropriately!

When I was six years old, I knew a little girl who pulled her own eyelashes out in an effort to keep from being sent on auditions. She was afraid to tell her mother she didn't want to be an actress. It was terribly sad. Little kids don't always say, "I'm uncomfortable" in the same way an adult would, so please listen to the heart of what your child tells you, and observe his behavior carefully. While I'm at it, I'd like to take the liberty to say we should all watch our own behavior carefully as well. None of us needs to be dancing on the sidelines at the Lil' Miss Tater Tot beauty pageant. Put away those tap shoes and give your kid an extra hug instead!

The Label Makers
This is a somewhat fascinating phenomenon to me—the need to classify a type of parenting, as if each of us falls into one specific category of tactics and techniques. What ever happened to good ol' parenting the way we see fit and giving others room to do the same?

A few years ago I attended a baby shower where I didn't know any of the other moms. There were more characters than one might find at a Star Trek convention. I wound up in a conversation with a woman who was trying to classify my parenting style as if I should be attending some sort of Motherhood Anonymous meeting. Hi, my name is Jenna, and I'm a helicopter-tiger-mom-attachment-breastfeeding-cosleeping parent. It was absurd! Every time I opened my mouth to say something, this woman felt the need to assign me to a new subspecies.

I'm frustrated by the idea that I should choose sides,

constantly defend my convictions, shun women who don't think the way I do, or decide if someone is an adequate parent based on whether she's a "working mom" or a "stay-at-home mom." I want your baby to be healthy in every way, and I trust you'll make every effort to find the best way to achieve that. What do I care if you don't serve your child strictly organic produce? That's your prerogative. And does it really turn your world upside down if my husband and I love safely cosleeping with our girls? Is it fair to assume my marriage will inevitably fail because of it? What if I wear pajamas to Target this afternoon? Do I need to get your permission for that too? Nah . . . I'm sure you'll be one of the kindest mommies out there. But I've heard plenty of those judgments flying around.

It never ceases to amaze me just how many people are willing to offer cruel critiques of other folks' personal business—people they don't know and will never take the time to get to know.

When people question your integrity, even though you know it isn't justified, it can leave a mark. You'll find your own method of dealing with the antagonism, whether you defend yourself, laugh, casually walk away, or write a blog about it. When all else fails, I find that breaking into an impromptu song-and-dance routine really throws those labeling mommies for a loop. If you can't beat 'em, you might as well freak 'em the fuck out.

Playing nice in the sandbox

A few other things to take into consideration . . .

Sharing is caring.

Instead of elbowing one another to see who can send their kid down the slide first, let's try this really cool concept called courtesy. How can we expect our kids to learn to share when we're doing the exact opposite? I'm not asking to braid your hair or debate the most talented Jonas brother; I'm just looking to be cordial. How hard is it to enjoy a glass of wine with someone? I mean if you drink enough of it, anyone's flaws can be ignored, right?

Don't be overly sensitive.

Don't bring a knife to the water-gun fight! In other words, try to give people the benefit of the doubt. Sometimes, when a fellow mom asks, "Is your son tall for his age?" she's really just curious if he's taller than average. She isn't subtly suggesting he's a mammoth man-child destined for a second career as Bigfoot.

For the number of people out there who are quick to judge, there are as many who will quickly conclude that *you* are judging, even if you're just making an observation, a joke, or friendly conversation. Some folks wear their insecurities like a muumuu. The cliché is true: words can heal, but they can also hurt. When it comes to our children, our overprotective instincts engage big-time. And sometimes they overwhelm our ability to remain calm, cool, and collected. Or reasonable. I've found myself instinctually getting defensive over small details from time to time, and I've witnessed other women take offense over odd things too. For example, when my first daughter was born, I wrote a blog about her birth. I happened to mention my surprise over the amount of dark hair she was born with, since I wasn't anticipating it. Both my husband and I were born blond. I received an e-mail from one furious mom berating me for acting like my child was God's gift just because she was born with a full head of hair. She went on to tell me there's nothing wrong with bald babies and that I should watch what I say.

Which, of course, led me to ask myself, *What did I say?* I wasn't suggesting she order spray-on hair from QVC or paste on high-end toupees like her kid is a William Shatner wannabe. I think bald babies are just as beautiful as babies with hair, and I don't think my kid is better just because I can get a barrette to stay put. How vain was this woman assuming me to be? (I know I'm an actor, and vanity tends to be our middle name, but that might be taking it a step too far.) I guess the more pertinent question is, what had her so worked up about the fact that her own child was born bald? Somewhere deep down, she already had an insecurity about it. Maybe I accidentally managed to push some sort of invisible phobia button? A predisposed anxiety over Mr. Clean, perhaps? I digress. I'll let the woman burn me in effigy or hide a voodoo doll of my likeness under her couch cushions if it makes her feel better. The bottom line: motherly oversensitivity is alive and well out there.

If someone says something crappy or patronizing to you, the hatred is hard to brush off. But new mommy exhaustion can also make for a short fuse, so try to be honest with yourself about people's intentions. In the grander scheme of things, most women are simply trying to make conversation or find common ground to walk on with you. Even if some of us suck at it.

Don't be a party pooper.

Oddly, birthday parties can be treacherous turf. On the one hand, I'm not sure why some parents feel the need to host elaborately themed soirees for a one-year-old who will never remember that the Backstreet Boys performed while the three-tiered LEGO cake was served. On the other hand, I'm also not sure why other parents get so up in arms about attending one of these shindigs. Let your kid go have fun, get serenaded by someone they could care less about, and go home with a little sugar high. It doesn't mean you have to top these people when your own kid has his next birthday. It's nearly impossible to keep up with the Joneses, the Smiths, or the Kardashians anyway, so why try? Put away the glue gun, throw out the phone number for the pony ride rental, and stop stressing. If you're throwing birthday parties to one-up the neighbor, it's likely for your own benefit and not your kid's. That said, if you're a burgeoning DIY Network star, go ahead and do your thing; far be it for me to stop you! To hell with the folks who think the immaculately edited GoPro video montage of your kid exiting the womb (complete to Diana Ross's "I'm Coming Out") is a teensy bit excessive.

As a side note, I highly recommend honoring your child's first birthday by going to a romantic dinner with your spouse. When Gray turned one, we had a few friends over to watch her smear frosting all over her face in the charming way that only a toddler can. We made sure she felt special on her big day, then turned her over to my mom for a few hours of baby-sitting and did what I think every parent deserves—we went out to commemorate one year of being on the parenting band-wagon. Sometimes it's nice to celebrate the efforts that led up to that first birthday too!

Don't be a pooper party either.

I swear someone needs to write a book on parenting social media etiquette. Who knows, maybe they already have. Face-book alone is the front line for stories that should never be made public. I beg you (and by that I mean I'm on my knees pleading and groveling) to resist the temptation to post about your child's daily evacuation habits. Especially via Instagram, which I hope needs no further explanation. (Writes the gal who published a photo of her daughter's exploding diaper in chapter 6. Apparently, I, too, could use a copy of said book on parenting social media etiquette. Then again, there's a reason I had the art department blur the mess in question like it's straight out of an episode of *Cops*!)

Everyone is relieved by a good bowel movement, but not everyone wants to hear about someone else's. Even if we're talking about your adorable kid. Please spare the masses from discussions about what color it is and what you or your kid ate to make it that way. I'm certainly not squeamish about my daughter's diaper contents, but I'm also positive no one wants me to post a running commentary about it for every-one else to give a thumbs-up on. I'm a fairly open person, but

I also recognize that not all friends and family will find excitement in my baby's excrement. They already have to put up with cuteness overload via photos and stories, so I'm sure a little class is welcomed by our buddies who have weaker stomachs, aren't parents, or simply aren't interested in the intricacies of baby poop. Try to walk in your old single-girl shoes for a moment, and think about what you would or wouldn't have wanted to be needlessly subjected to by your suddenly blunt and oversharing comrades with kids.

Friends in apropos places

In short? Know who your true friends are. Discard the catty, petty junk, and surround yourself with strong women who will love, support, encourage, and be real with you. There's nothing more crucial than honesty when you're becoming a parent! My most treasured relationships are with the women who haven't been afraid to rip the Band-Aid off and tell me the truth. Sugarcoating won't help you cope with the tough times; it sets you up to be disappointed by unrealistic expectations. It can also result in making you feel more isolated and invalidated in the long run. The true friends are the ones who take you to lunch, slide a glass of rosé in front of you, tell it like it is, then give you a free therapy session when the truth hurts.

Breaking bad

I can't keep you from falling victim to the vicious warfare out there, but I'd like to do my part to suggest you don't become public enemy number one either. It's easy to tumble into the trap if you aren't careful. It's hard not to get caught up in comparisons, because everything a new baby does is just so darn novel and exciting! I'd like to think none of us sets out to make a fellow mom feel uncomfortable; it just seems to be an unfortunate byproduct of our eagerness to share how sensational we find our own kids to be. I'm sure I've been guilty of that without realizing it, and you probably will be too. But none of us should have to continually walk on eggshells either.

When something as innocent as asking whether or not a child has started teething prompts an insecurity avalanche, it can be tough to come up with conversation starters. I'm not suggesting you clam up where anything baby-related is concerned; I'm just suggesting you proceed with caution and consideration. In my opinion, having a little awareness goes a long way! More often than not, and sadly, other moms will expect us to behave badly. Let's do ourselves a favor and disappoint them.

THE MORAL OF MY STORY

Reserve the sparring for your kickboxing class, and don't let motherhood become a competitive sport! Handle things calmly in front of your child, even when you want to remove your earrings and go all Jerry Springer on that other mama's ass! Let kindness be the punch you throw; it will make your heart happier in the long run. Oh, and you're a lot less likely to get sued.

Reading with Ruby, back in the prekid days. My Kindle hasn't gotten much love since. *Photo courtesy of Jenna von Oy.*

CHAPTER 20
Mommy Me-Time:
The Management, the Myth, the Legend

A SCENIC VIEW OF MY PAST

When I was about seventeen, a celebrity trainer acquaintance managed to arrange a weeklong retreat at an all-inclusive spa for me and my best friend. It wasn't just any old spa; it was the mack daddy of all spas . . . Golden Door Spa Resort in Palm Springs, California. I mean, this place is to relaxation and tranquility what Liberace was to glittery capes and feather boas. The resort is a restorative body-and-mind experience in an enchanting little desert oasis, and I was elated to try it out. Especially since it wasn't costing me a dime, aside from the fuel I had to put in my car to get there.

Now I'm not entirely sure how this fitness guru woman convinced the resort to extend such a generous offer to a couple of rambunctious teenagers, but she must have worked some major hocus-pocus, black magic voodoo on those people. Or who knows—maybe she slept with someone. I'll refrain from judging, since I got a seriously high-end vacation out of the deal. Sort of.

My best friend and I prepared for our road trip like we were moving across the country. We spent hours packing our suitcases full of important items. You know, things like high heels, short skirts, and oodles of sparkly eye shadow—all the essentials for a week of intensive meditation and exercise. I think I may have tossed in a pair of sneakers and some yoga pants at the tail end, right before we jumped into my convertible and sped down the Los Angeles freeway like we were on the lam.

We were ready for a week of serenity, self-reflection, and spiritual rejuvenation. Now all we had left to do was recharge our cell phones, hit up a Starbucks, and blast the mixed tape we'd made for the road trip. Which, I imagine, consisted of tunes from cerebral, top-notch artists like Milli Vanilli and Ace of Base. Hey, it was 1994. Cut us a little slack.

A few hours later, we arrived at the most peaceful place I've ever seen. Even the parking lot was at one with nature, and that's saying a lot for a slab of concrete. We checked in and made our way to the rooms. They were luxurious despite their lack of a television, which elicited frantic questions like "How are we going to survive?" and "What will happen to us if we miss an episode of *Melrose Place*?" Thankfully, there was a full schedule of activities. (Plus, we called someone to tape *Melrose Place* for us.) We were in for a week of yoga classes, outdoor hikes, Pilates, massages, Jacuzzi-soaking, meditation in the Japanese gardens, and fine dining. Who could ask for anything more? Except maybe a few cute boys to flirt with, but that wasn't in the cards.

Apparently the potato chips and beef jerky we'd shoved down our throats on the car ride over weren't enough to satiate our appetites, so we headed to the dining area. We'd heard rave reviews about the food, which is organic and grown on the property. The meals are all prepared according to body weight and fitness goals, so we eagerly awaited our heaping plate of something delicious. What arrived was rabbit food. And I would venture to say most rabbits would have been bummed. Apparently my fitness goal for the week was to become a starving, gaunt, bitchy adolescent.

I glanced at my friend. "This is just the first course, right?" No such luck. I stared at the salad in front of me like it was a plate of swarming bees, as my stomach made a noise that I could swear sounded like, "Where's the nearest Taco Bell?" We survived two days of that healthy madness before we hightailed it out of there to the nearest Italian joint, gorged on heaping mounds of spaghetti and meatballs, and then checked out of the resort early.

Now, some of you might think all this sounds ungrateful. You might think it was rude of us to complain, ruder of us to sneak away to pig out on pasta, and even ruder still to walk out (peel out like the Dukes of Hazard) from such a lavish gift. And you'd be right. But don't worry—karma has come back to take a big old chunk out of my ass. Because these days I could seriously go for a few well-balanced meals prepared by someone other than me, and the only meditating I've done lately is over whether or not my kids will go to bed before I pass out from exhaustion.

CUT TO . . .

Twenty years later, I would do damn near anything to have a week in that magical place. Do you hear me, Golden Door? I would give an arm, a leg, and possibly my wine supply for a week at your resort. Okay, that's crazy talk. I would never be demented enough to give up my wine supply. I do have kids, after all.

My cradle chronicles

The scholars got it wrong. It doesn't take a village; it takes a Xanax. I'm not insinuating that you should take uppers, downers, or whatever is in between, but I *am* suggesting you find a *healthy* form of stress-reduction. I'm a huge proponent of me-time, even though it's tough to come by. Sometimes the thought of setting a moment aside to indulge in my own relaxation seems impossible, but it's imperative. In the long run, I get more done when I allow myself a little break! Being burned-out does not make for better parenting.

I admit I'm not the best at heeding my own advice on this subject. Scheduling me-time seems to be a ridiculous notion when I can barely get out of the weeds long enough to take a pee break. Making quality time for myself is an ever-changing, constantly evolving process. Priorities shift, work schedules fluctuate, and personal needs change. As your baby moves through different phases of growth, falls into a different nap pattern (such as suddenly refusing to take one at all), or decides she doesn't appreciate having babysitters as much as you do, you'll find your me-time will readjust to fit the circumstances.

The secret is to vow to carve out that time, no matter what. I can't tell you how many moms I've met who have responded to that idea with "Well, that's easy for you to say, but you're not in my shoes. You have nannies and housekeepers and all that jazz." Well, I hate to bust the stereotypical image of an actress wide open, but . . . no, I don't. Far from it, in fact. My husband and I handle everything on our own. Sometimes that means I wind up sacrificing whatever brief chunk of time I've set aside for myself, but I've found that trying to squeeze the time in is half the battle! It reminds me that my own needs don't always have to come in last place.

Precious "Mom"ents

Here are the ideas I try to keep in mind so I don't forget the importance of my me-time.

Finding time for yourself doesn't directly translate to ignoring your kids.

It always bugs me when people automatically jump to the conclusion that me-time involves leaving one's children to fend for themselves while Mommy locks herself in the bedroom with earplugs and the latest issue of *Vanity Fair*. No one is insinuating that making time to relax should compromise your parenting! The idea is to find a way to take a breather while still upholding responsibilities . . . especially responsibilities of the living, breathing, diaper-wearing kind. Sometimes that means putting your baby in her swing for five minutes so you can scarf down a piece of pizza, and sometimes it means enlisting your husband or a babysitter to stay with her while you get pampered. Or read a book. Or *write* a book, for that matter. As much as the guilt might mentally harass you, it's okay to have someone else watch your kids so you can spend two hours nurturing your sanity and your spirit. You aren't failing your children by taking care of yourself.

Don't say you can't find the time.
In your new, baby-focused, solitude-free world, full of constant physical and emotional commitment, "I just can't find a moment for myself" should be considered blasphemy. You can, and you should.

Sometimes it just takes a little creativity and a modification of your expectation of what me-time is. I used to think it meant heading out for a mani/pedi and a glass of champagne. Now my me-time is taking ten minutes to paint my own nails, while chugging a cup of cold coffee left over from breakfast. Sometimes I get crazy and sneak in a little piece of chocolate when my girls aren't looking. Then I *really* feel like I've gotten away with something!

Stretch your mommy me-time bounds.
Me-time isn't necessarily defined by trips to the gym, massage therapy, or perusing the *Huffington Post*. My me-time often involves my kids! I know that sounds counterproductive and like I'm directly contradicting the point of me-time altogether, but it's the truth. Me-time is what you make of it. It's all about doing something for yourself. It's about treating yourself to something that makes you feel good, and that doesn't mean your kids can't be a part of it. Sometimes sitting down to cuddle with my girls is exactly what I need to ground me.

Take it where you can get it.

Everyone needs to recharge their emotional batteries, but not everyone's path to relaxation looks the same. Sometimes your daily dose will revolve around whether or not your kids let you go to the bathroom by yourself (yeah, right!). And trust me, it's pretty pitiful when the only rest you get is sitting on the toilet. I would know. Still, try to recognize the opportunity for what it is and embrace it. If you're feeling really ambitious and someone else is around to keep an eye on the kids, hide a magazine under the bathroom sink and sneak in a few pages while you can! There's nothing like reading about the newest Hollywood breakup to make you feel saner.

Know your own boundaries.

Some things are simply nonnegotiable. For example, if I don't eat, I'm a disaster. It's no joke; I become an ogre. Hence, I have to make time for lunch—for everyone else's sake, if not for mine. This sounds simple enough, but I can't tell you just how often I ignore my grumbling stomach anyway. Taking the time to make a sandwich when there are a million other things to get done often seems like a waste. Of course, my attitude when I'm hungry says otherwise.

We all have needs we ignore because our parenting and busy schedules take precedence. You might require a certain amount of sleep each night to feel like you can function properly, or a chance to be outside in the sun for a few minutes each day so you don't get depressed. You might even put off showering because it just isn't convenient to stop what you're doing. Whatever your neglected needs might be, know your limitations and don't be afraid to interrupt your schedule for them. When I make the conscious decision to nurture my own basic needs, I find I have more patience in the face of adversity. Which is a good thing, because sometimes that adversity is called *I have a whiny three-year-old!*

Time your me-time appropriately.

If you notice you start turning into Grouchy McFussypants every day around 2:00 p.m., that's probably an obvious slot to set aside for yourself. My witching hour is around 5:00 p.m. That's when I'm trying to wrap up work for the day, my girls are begging for my attention, the dogs start getting restless for their kibble, I'm trying to assemble our family dinner, and I'm eagerly anticipating my husband's arrival home from work. That's when I'm fatigued from a full day's worth of errands, entertaining my kids, and busting my ass to complete everything on that floor-length to-do list. Although this is the most hectic time to try and reserve for myself, I sometimes turn some music on, light my candles, and indulge in some cooking therapy. It's one of the ways I've found I can combine an activity that absolutely must get done with one that gives me a chance to decompress.

Learn how to say no.

I've discovered this is a major step on my path to maturity (which is an endless work in progress). I knew I was officially on my way to adulthood when I learned not to accept every invitation that came along. I will always go out of my way to attend my girls' activities and school functions, or momentous occasions for friends and family, but sometimes I have to draw the line whether I want to or not. When I've spent two weeks scarfing down meals at the kitchen counter, volunteering to host a dinner party isn't on the agenda.

Create a zone that's reserved for you and you alone.
My happy place is my closet. I know that sounds stupid, but it's the only spot in my house where I can close myself off and have a time-out. Sometimes mommies need those too! Am I getting killer advice from my tank tops and warm hugs from my winter sweaters? Far from it. But simply existing in my own space for five minutes can sometimes be more beneficial than a day at the spa . . . which I *might* have time for by the year 2032.

Respect that caring for yourself means caring for your family.
You aren't being selfish by taking time to refuel. In fact, you are being selfless! No one wants to become resentful or so worn down that they face-plant into the Friday night meatloaf. Being the best parent you can be means you have the energy and levelheadedness to handle whatever comes your way. I've discovered it's tougher to tame temper tantrums when I'm ready to throw one of my own!

You're not alone.
It's important to recognize your husband's desire for solitude too. I've found it's really easy to get caught up in the daily

grind and forget my hubby needs his own version of down-time. Is he looking to luxuriate in a bubble bath, take a yoga class, or enjoy some shopping therapy like I am? Not likely. In fact, some of my husband's free-time needs baffle me. Still, I realize the importance of encouraging him to take a break too . . . even if it involves rigging a makeshift beer chute while simultaneously watching *2001: A Space Odyssey* and blowing leaves off the driveway. Which, apparently, isn't as inconceivable as one might think.

Create a routine.
The more you work me-time into your schedule, the more natural it will feel. With any luck, it will eventually become an automatic part of your itinerary. You have to start somewhere! None of us can reach the goal of everyday me-time without starting at day one. So commit to it!

THE MORAL OF MY STORY

Sometimes mommy me-time seems like it's as magical, mystical, and elusive as a unicorn. But that doesn't mean I'm going to stop searching for it, and you shouldn't either! (The me-time. Not the stupid unicorn.) Regardless of how you choose to spend your mommy me-time, I hope you'll approach it whole-heartedly and encourage your fellow moms to do the same. I mean, who doesn't love an excuse to relax over cocktails with the girls?

Doing my best to pull off some preflight entertainment. And failing miserably.
Photo courtesy of Jenna von Oy.

CHAPTER 21

Sisterhood of the Traveling Motherhood

A SCENIC VIEW OF MY PAST

I spent much of my childhood traveling to New York City for auditions. I did so by way of the Metro-North commuter train. Connecticut is really just a hop, skip, and jump to Manhattan, but it's a bigger hop, skip, and jump than a kid should be making on her own. Initially, my first manager used to accompany me on these trips, but she started bowing out for reasons unknown . . . well, unknown until we discovered she was stealing some of the hard-earned money I'd made from commercials. Nice gal. One would think it was in her best interest to keep schlepping me to auditions, since that would have given her more funds to embezzle, but nobody's saying she was an insightful crook. Or even a mildly intelligent one, for that matter. Consequently, the onus of getting me to work and auditions fell on my parents, who had other kids to worry about too.

One afternoon in 1984, when I was seven, my dad was called in to work early and my mom got stuck taking me to New York for a callback. A callback is the next step up from a basic audition, when the casting agents have begun narrowing the field, so it wasn't to be missed. My sister, Alyssa, was two at the time, and my brother, Peter, was five. For whatever reason, Pete and I were both out of school that day and Alyssa was still too young to attend. This meant my daring mother had to haul three lively (a polite way of saying *rambunctious*) kids on some frenetic, cockamamie excursion to the city during, as one might expect, rush hour.

My mom endured forty-five minutes of car ride to the Fairfield train station hearing, "Are we there yet?" and the ever-popular "Mommy, I need to go to the bathroom," only to be followed by ten minutes of trying to keep us from plunging off the train station platform onto the electrically charged tracks below. Desperate for any help she could get, my mom promised us a Coca-Cola if we were on our best behavior. Since soda was the Holy Grail for us, we were quick to dispose of our horns and don our halos.

The cars were jam-packed with professionals looking spiffy in their suits, poring over the Dow Jones Industrial Average, and eating their bagels. And there we were—harried, disheveled, and looking like we were headed to amateur hour at Coney Island. There were no seats to be had, so my brother and I clutched my mother's jacket tightly as she herded us from cable car to cable car. Pete was terrified to jump from one to the next, so my mom was juggling her purse, an umbrella stroller, a diaper bag, a two-year-old, and a traumatized five-year-old. Commuting to Manhattan was old hat to me by then, so I was a little less of a handful. Unless you count the fact that I never shut up. Which probably didn't help my mother's mental state.

We finally found a single seat at the front of the train, across from a woman in a trench coat. The gentleman next to her was observant enough to recognize my mother's struggle (undoubtedly a dad), so he gave up his spot for us. At least this meant two of us could sit down. My mom helped me and Peter get situated, then scrambled to find a place to stow the bags and stroller. That's when things really began to go awry.

As my mom reached up to put the stroller on the overhead rack, the clasp came unhinged and bonked Poor Trench Coat Woman on the head. My mom was mortified and immediately began apologizing. Poor Trench Coat Woman smiled, assured my mom she was fine, and went back to reading her novel.

That's when I decided to take my mom up on her earlier promise. "Can we have our soda now?" I've always had impeccable timing. My mom desperately glanced toward the bar car, which was all the way at the back of the train. In other words, back through all the cars we'd just traipsed through. If I'd known what *defeated* meant at the age of seven, I might have recognized it on my mother's face. She looked over at Poor Trench Coat Woman, who'd just been clobbered with the baby stroller, and asked, "Would you mind watching our bags while I take the kids to get a soda from the bar car?" The woman nodded with sympathy. I imagine she also had visions of my mother sneaking in some consolatory kamikaze shooters while retrieving our refreshments, though, to my knowledge, that didn't happen.

And so my mom and her kiddie caravan headed to the rear of the train, to the grimy, smoke-filled bar car. With no regard for my mother's current juggling act, the bartender handed her two paper cups of soda. Perfect. Because it's *super* easy to carry a toddler on your hip and keep two cups of liquid from sloshing everywhere while walking the length of a moving train. We finally made it back to our seats, with Traumatized Peter crying, Blabbermouth Jenna chattering away, and Jostled Baby Alyssa nearly slipping out of my mother's grasp. At least the soda was still intact.

But it was too good to be true. My mother went to put my sister on my lap, and that soda flew into the air and landed on . . . wait for it . . . Poor Trench Coat Woman. Who, I suppose, we should now refer to as Poor, Sticky, Soda-Soaked Trench Coat Woman. The karma gods were not smiling down on us that day. Or maybe they were getting their revenge. Once again, my mom started apologizing profusely and grabbed some cloth diapers to begin cleaning the woman off. "I hope you have kids and understand what I'm going through," my mother told her humbly.

Which is when Poor, Sticky, Soda-Soaked Trench Coat Woman opened her coat to reveal a baby bump. After a much-needed moment of silence, the guy across the aisle said, "Bet you wish you'd met this lady *before* you decided to get pregnant, huh?"

Cut to . . .

We moms are nothing if not brave. Just when we've sacrificed a good portion of our sanity to battles with teething and sleep deprivation, we make the brilliant decision to drag our kids on a vacation somewhere. Misery may love company, but so does motherhood. Especially when you're trying to survive a road trip or wrangle a baby at thirty thousand feet.

My cradle chronicles

Traveling with kids requires three parts insanity, two parts desperation for a vacation, and one part hope that the kids will have such a good time (or get so worn out) you'll forget how horrific it was to get there in the first place. I realize not all travel is based on heading to a vacation destination, but no one in their right mind makes a habit of dragging babies on interminable car rides and plane flights unless there's a light at the end of the tunnel. It's the road less traveled for a reason. And sometimes visiting family results in travel plans . . . All I can say about that is there's a lot we'll put up with in the name of love. Regardless of the journey's end, you might have to go through nine levels of hell to get there, and your mental marbles may wind up being tossed out the window somewhere over the Great Lakes.

Traveler's assurance

Here are some general rules I've found helpful when traveling with small children.

Bring supplies.

Stuff your carry-on bag or suitcase with as much crap as you need to entertain your child for the duration of your trip. Because boredom is bad. Very, very bad. Pack snacks, a change of clothes in case of catastrophe (bring a set for you too, while you're at it), and toys. Preferably ones that don't have small pieces, won't wind up hitting the old lady five rows back in seat 27B on the nose, or make so much noise that folks can hear it over their in-flight movie. This includes things like LEGOs, plastic swords, and Tickle Me Elmo. Fortunately, your child will be too young to play with most of those items for a while, but you may want to file that away for future reference.

Flights require hours of forced amusement within a confined space, and you're the resident one-woman show. Sometimes you have to set your normal I'd-never-let-my-kid-play-with-that parameters aside and break out the iPad so your kid can watch *Sesame Street* episodes or play with the *Pat the Bunny* app. It's all in the name of self-preservation. Other times, you have to drag the whole arts-and-crafts station along. Again, that probably won't come into play until later on, but the point is to keep them busy with new and interesting activities that don't involve running down the aisles and sending flight attendants scattering like bowling pins.

The same is true for car trips (though thankfully there's no flight crew to piss off), so haul as much as you need to keep from banging your head against the window. Sometimes you have to drag along everything but the kitchen sink. And the DVR. And the liquor cabinet. (Actually, you may want to bring at least a small selection from that.) We've rolled up to hotel lobbies looking like the Beverly Hillbillies, complete with the child potty seat regally resting on top of our bellhop cart like a trashy backwoods mascot, so it could be worse . . . You could be us. Even if you're the most imaginative, recreation-improvising, distraction-inventing mom on the planet, traveling is a draining ordeal. Especially when you're spending hours in a flying sardine can.

If your child is still an infant, the only item you can pack that offers any entertainment value is your breasts. So prepare to provide nonstop in-flight or roadside service.

Don't forget diapers and wipes.

I think it's pretty obvious why you're screwed if you forget diapers, but forgetting wipes is equally detrimental. I once sprayed my breast milk all over an airplane window and had to use my jacket to clean it up. Thank God it didn't head the other direction and hit the sweet old grandpa snoozing to my left, or it would have been a whole different level of messy. Still, accessible wipes would've been nice.

Wipes are the gods of travel cleanup. They wash sticky hands, sop up the apple juice your kid dumps in your lap ten minutes into the flight, and sanitize after you stop at that less-than-tidy gas station bathroom. You also don't want to be stuck without wipes if your kid has a massive diaper blow-out. Five hours of existing in tight quarters with a diaper that smells like a stinky goat isn't a good way to start your trip. Now that I'm thinking about it, you may also want to pack the biggest bottle of hand sanitizer they'll let you board with. And plastic bags to dispose of said foul diaper.

Don't drag your kids to a weeklong food-and-wine festival.
Make sure you plan your vacation around child-friendly entertainment. Ditto for making sure the resort or hotel is kid-compatible. If you want to go live it up on a tropical island where men parade around in leopard-print thongs (God forbid), leave your kids with Grandma and Grandpa. Children don't get excited about a mud bath or a quiet picnic in the vineyards. They want good old-fashioned family fun. They want anthropomorphized mice who sign autographs, and colorful rides with catchy songs that give you earworms for the next two weeks. So basically, they want the antithesis of the vacation you want.

Don't be dumb enough to convince yourself your kid can forego naptime.
I know traveling alters the normal routine, but try to plan your trip around nap schedules, if at all possible. When flying with my girls during their infancy, I always tried to make sure they were ready to breastfeed during takeoff (this helps their little ears cope with the rapid air pressure changes) and then sleep, courtesy of the food coma, immediately thereafter. Because if your child is sleeping during the flight, do you know what that means? That means you and your husband are canoodling over quiet adult conversation. Better yet, it means you're having a plastic cup of crappy airline wine and cracking open a juicy romance novel. Need I say more?

Know how to change a diaper while your kid is standing up.
This technique is essential for all types of travel, whether

you're stuck in a scary roadside gas station stall or wedged in an airplane restroom. Changing a diaper while standing with your kid in a bathroom the size of a Matchbox car is no easy feat, so master it before you find yourself in that predicament. Because when your kid has a poopy diaper in hour one of a three-hour flight and you're hauling his red-faced, screaming butt past the entire cabin of economy-class passengers only to find that the bathroom has no changing table, it isn't an option to wait until the flight is over. You take what you can get and you improvise.

There's an art to changing a baby this way, so don't leave it for crunch time. If you have an infant who isn't to the standing stage yet, it's a totally different story. This is more appropriately termed "You're shit out of luck." Do not attempt to change said dirty diaper in your lap while seated in the main cabin. I repeat: do *not* attempt to change the diaper in your lap . . . unless you're trying to put a target on your back with all your fellow passengers and you plan on spending the rest of your day wearing Eau de Excrement.

Expect catastrophe.
Not that I want to be overly cynical, but wouldn't it be better to assume things will go wrong and then be pleasantly surprised when they don't? You might get a flat tire, the airline might lose your luggage, the theme park might suddenly be under two feet of snow, or the five-star hotel you booked online might look like Bates Motel up close. Your kid might start teething the day you get there, decide he's suddenly terrified

of going to bed in any sleeping vessel but the one you left at home, or boycott restaurant high chairs. Shit happens. It's all about rolling with the punches and praying those punches don't turn into a total technical knockout. Either way, it's probably best not to set your traveling expectations on a really high pedestal.

Find a way to ignore the jackasses.
When your infant starts shrieking at the top of her lungs because the cabin pressure is doing a number on her ears, or she's crabby because you've just suffered through a five-hour flight delay only to sit on the runway for forty-five minutes more before takeoff, don't expect understanding from the twenty-something dude with spiky hair and safety pins in his eyebrow. Or anyone else for that matter. Not everyone will be sympathetic, so all you can do is concentrate on your child. Everybody else can suck it.

I don't say this to be inconsiderate of the general public. I actually despise the thought that anyone might find me or my girls to be rude or ungracious, and I'm a huge believer in teaching my children to be polite, well-behaved, and well-mannered. But kids are kids. They all have their moments. (For that matter, so do I.) I'm very sensitive to this issue, and I go out of my way to try and be considerate of fellow passengers.

Still, despite my best efforts, I often overhear ignorant and insulting comments made . . . simply because I've endeavored to leave my house with two young children in tow. After all, if we're batshit crazy enough to become parents in the first place, doesn't that mean we've tacitly agreed to remain cooped up in our homes until we send them off to college? Well, the folks who abide by that line of thinking will just have to find a way to coexist with us loons. Until they start offering adult-only flights, specifically tailored to those who would prefer to remain a continent away from every child in existence, we're all bozos on the same bus. Anticipate eye rolls, looks of disdain, nasty comments under people's breath, and the occasional request to switch to a seat farther away from you. Let them go—it's their prerogative, and not everyone likes children. With that attitude, I promise you'd rather not have them next to you for an entire flight anyway.

Pretty-please don't fall for the whole bribing-people-on-flights thing. This is a new fad that drives me up a freaking wall. Or cargo door, as the case may be. It was a pretty cute and clever idea for the first mom who thought of it, because she came by it organically. Kudos to her! But now it has become a trend to butter up fellow passengers with candy, earplugs, love notes, or who knows what else, and I don't like the idea that people feel entitled to door prizes for putting up with my kid. It's not like I'm toting my baby to an R-rated film or asking random strangers to babysit her while I hit up the airport bar. And where does it all end? Pretty soon, we'll be expected to fork over hush money to the flight attendants. Parents will move from lollipops and gumdrops to entertainment like jugglers and sword-swallowers (though turbulence could cause some serious problems with that). You know the one thing I could get on board with? Magicians that astound the mile-high masses by making people's cell phones disappear during takeoff and landing. Talk about unbearable flight nuisances!

Own it.

Globe-trotting with kids is all about determination, endurance, and nerve. You have to bring your moxie and you can't use it sparingly. I'm not saying you should have a devil-may-care attitude if your kid pukes all over someone, incessantly kicks the seat ahead of him, or manages to commandeer a stranger's laptop and hurl it across the airport; I sincerely hope you'll take responsibility for the things that deserve an apology. I'm all for common courtesy and saying I'm sorry when something is my fault. But I feel like people too often expect us to apologize when our kids are just being kids. In general, society has managed to lose all of its tolerance for the process of growing up. Or maybe it just never had any tolerance to begin with. Either way, no one should expect an infant not to cry, and no one should fault the parents when he does. I mean, come on, do people really think we like hearing our child get upset? Or, for that matter, do they think we enjoy listening to him spend hours screeching within inches of our eardrums? And yet, for whatever reason, no one gets stared at with more venom than the parents of a screaming child. Even when that parent is doing everything in his or her power to remedy the situation.

You know what's worse than a crying baby? Being trapped on a flight next to the woman who opens up nail polish and begins giving herself a pedicure, the guy who hasn't seen a stick of deodorant in thirty-plus years (if ever), or the woman whose dog just shat all over its carrying case and she pretends it didn't happen for the remainder of the flight. (Yes, I've been in the air with *all* those people.) You know why it's worse? Because adults have a choice to be compassionate or considerate or civil. No baby gets on a flight and thinks, *Let me make everyone's life a living hell for the next four hours.*

At the end of the day, planes are public transportation, and not every member of the public possesses that little thing called tact. Which is why you have to own your situation. You don't need to feel guilt-ridden over the fact that someone nearby might need to turn his noise-canceling headset up a notch. Leave your humiliation in your luggage and wear your big-girl pants on board. Do your best to soothe your baby, and let everyone else order a stiff drink.

The sisterhood of the traveling motherhood.

This is one of those critical instances when we all need to stick together. And you know what? For as many insensitive people as you come up against out there, there are three times that many who will extend compassion and chivalry when you need it most. They'll hold a door open for you, help you with your luggage, or reassure you when you're at your wits' end. Those are the angels disguised as fellow passengers who put your diaper bag into the overhead compartment for you, forgive and forget when your baby spits her plums all over their white blazer, or distract her with funny faces so you can spend five minutes eating your overpriced, subpar airline snack.

The truth is that most of the population has children, so the majority of passengers have been in your shoes at one point or another . . . whether they choose to remember it or not. Every now and then you'll sit next to the grandma with seven grown kids of her own, and eleven grandchildren between them, who will pat you on the hand and gift you with the words "You are such a good mom." And for a moment, all will be right with the world.

The trick to finding these allies is learning how to read between the lines . . . or perhaps the gray hairs and sympathetic wrinkles left behind from years of raising kids. Take note of the woman who says, "Well, hello there!" to your baby as you pass by or the man who smiles and immediately checks his phone for the screenshot of his own little girl. Sometimes you'll notice the twinkle in someone's eye or the telltale burp cloth sticking out of their briefcase. No matter what the sign may be, keep that knowledge in your back pocket and know you aren't alone out there.

THE MORAL OF MY STORY
The journey of a thousand miles begins with earplugs and ends with exhaustion. And possibly bribery. I've discovered that home isn't just where my heart is; it's where my sanity is too.

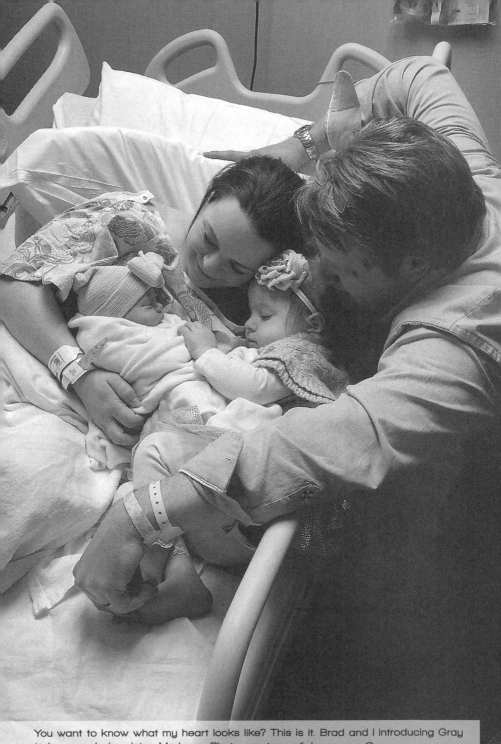

You want to know what my heart looks like? This is it. Brad and I introducing Gray to her new baby sister, Marlowe. *Photo courtesy of Jenna von Oy.*

CHAPTER 22

All You Need Is Love

A SCENIC VIEW OF MY PAST

I've obviously never been one of Tinseltown's more ravishing ingenues, but that doesn't mean I haven't met my fair share of leading men. I've coexisted on-screen with some of Hollywood's hottest sex symbols, fawned over others at charity events (which probably went over like an incontinent mule in the public swimming pool), and even dated a couple . . . not that I'm planning to kiss and tell, so you can stop salivating all over the book pages now. Would all those fine fellows remember meeting me? Hell no. Most of them wouldn't recall my name if I'd had it branded on their butts. Still, that doesn't change the fact that they made a lasting impression on me at one point or another. I'm going to milk those memories for all they're worth and embellish them like a bedazzled iPhone case when I'm crowding ninety-seven and can't see my feet past my sagging tits. Wouldn't you?

The truth? Most of the meetings I'm referring to, as exciting as they may sound in theory, were entirely innocuous. I sat next to Tom Cruise at a dinner once, exchanged a few phone conversations with Usher, signed autographs for Andy Garcia's children, and cohosted some random promos with Ben Affleck. I've hung out with Mario Lopez socially, worked alongside James Marsden and Will Smith, and had Mark Wahlberg ask for my phone number. (The poor guy clearly needed to get a decent pair of eyeglasses.) Michael Jordan even lowered his infamous shades and grinned at me while we were both guests at Prince's Minneapolis compound, Paisley Park, years ago. (Which is a story for another day.) Oh, and Gary Coleman dropped a bad pickup line on me by asking my astrological sign and complimenting me on my "pretty toes." That doesn't totally fit here, but it's an anecdote that's too amusing not to share. But my favorite of these instances involves the one and only, dapper and distinguished—not to mention ridiculously handsome—Mr. George Clooney.

In 1996, I was in San Antonio for the NBA All-Star game and Stay in School celebration, when a highly sought-after invitation was delivered to my hotel room. My presence was formally requested at the local Planet Hollywood opening. As one can imagine, this was a flashy, star-studded event that wasn't to be missed, so I donned whatever frightening '90s ensemble I'd chosen at Contempo Casuals and headed out to greet the press.

The basketball game had succeeded in amassing a collection of celebrities that could make every sports fan, film buff, band groupie, and television watcher twitch uncontrollably and wet their panties a few times over, so the size of the crowd was mind-boggling. Throw in the celebrity backers of the afore-mentioned famous restaurant chain, and that red carpet was hosting more stargazing than a planetarium. Hollywood had essentially swarmed San Antonio like the biblical plague of locusts, albeit with slightly more hedonism on display.

I nibbled on barbecue chicken pizza, boogied within five feet of the dirty dancer himself, Patrick Swayze, and listened to Bruce Willis rock out on his harmonica. I chatted with Charles Barkley, got too shy to introduce myself to Luke Perry, and mostly hung around with friends such as Alfonso Ribeiro. But the highlight of my evening came when I spotted George. Let me rephrase that. The highlight of my evening came when George spotted *me*.

Fully expecting such an esteemed VIP to avert his eyes from the giddy teenage girl with her jaw not-so-covertly flopping on the floor like a hooked bass, I was shocked when he beelined straight for me instead.

After grinning that roguish George grin, he called out, "Hey, Jenna!"

I looked around to see where the thief who'd stolen my name was. There was no one behind me. Suddenly, I was being hoisted off the ground and hugged like a long-lost friend. So *that's* what it means to be swept off of one's feet! Once I was back on solid ground, my mind started reeling. What was going on here? Was I dreaming? On *Candid Camera*, perhaps? One of the sexiest men in America had just hugged me, and I had no clue why. I was also hard-pressed to remember how to form words or stand up. Thankfully, the latter was solved by a nearby planter, which I was clutching for dear life. If I went down, I was taking a giant plastic palm tree with me.

My hands began sweating profusely, a dark blush eclipsed my face, and I stammered, "Um . . . Hello, Mr. Clooney."

George feigned surprise. "Mr. Clooney? You don't remember meeting me, do you?" The amusement danced across his face and lit up his eyes.

Remember him? What the heck was he talking about? Of course I remembered him. I'd seen *One Fine Day* multiple times. But meeting him? No way. How could anyone forget meeting the guy who graced every magazine cover this side of the equator? I was dumbfounded.

"We met at the NBC press tour a few years ago," he explained graciously. "I was on *Sisters* and, of course, you were on *Blossom*. It's okay if you don't remember. I guess I was just some old man to you." He smiled that thousand-watt smile.

In that moment, I may or may not have choked on a mini slider. Had George Clooney just referred to himself as "some old man"? As if! I tried to backpedal with an apology.

"That's okay," he told me. "I think I can manage to let you off the hook. Oh, but next time?"

I looked up at him expectantly.

"You'd better call me George." And with that, he walked away. That's one class act.

CUT TO . . .

I may not be nearly as stirring as George Clooney, but doling out unexpected hugs seems to leave a lasting impression on my kids too. My mommy mantra is "When in doubt or all else fails, love, love, and then love some more."

My cradle chronicles

I've spent the bulk of this book offering you brash, sometimes crass commentary regarding all things motherhood. But underneath the jokes and jest, I'm a sentimental hopeless romantic who couldn't be more smitten by her husband and children. Motherhood is by far the best thing I've ever endeavored to do. Yes, it can be challenging, baffling, patience-testing, terrifying, exacting, and crazy-making at times. But it is also astounding, exhilarating, motivating, magical, wonderful, glorious stuff. Moreover, it manifests a limitless, inexhaustible, and immeasurable love within you that manages to continue growing. I'm awe-inspired by it every day.

For all the challenges that come with the new-mommy learning curve, the beguiling moments far outweigh the strenuous ones. You just have to pause long enough to recognize them for what they are. Don't be afraid to take a break every once in a while, simply to appreciate the miracles around you. Some of the most breathtaking parts of parenting can be found in the smallest of details! The novelty of a toe wiggle, a smirk, a coo, a peaceful nap, a giggle, the first time your baby turns toward the sound of your voice—it's all inordinately captivating. Sometimes we just need a reminder to stand still, absorb the moment, and silently be grateful for the little glimpse of heaven we've been granted.

At the end of the day, the most important parenting creed

is to love. This seems like obvious advice, but it bears repeating. There will be occasions when frustration is the first passionate response that surfaces, so it never hurts to have the reminder. When you're so tired you can't pry your eyelids open with a crowbar, give love. When you're so frustrated you're afraid you might spontaneously combust, give love. When you feel overworked, underappreciated, and at your wits' end—you guessed it—give love. There's a reason the majority of songs and films are devoted to the subject. Endless, unconditional love is an incomparable thing!

Life will present its hard knocks daily—sometimes at your expense and sometimes at your child's. You'll long to impart every nugget of wisdom you've ever cultivated, heard, obeyed, observed, goofed up, followed, or failed at. And while it isn't realistic to think you can actually accomplish such a monstrous task, you'll make it your life's work anyway. Raising our children is the masterpiece that's never quite finished!

THE RAINY DAY ADVICE FUND

As you walk the parenting path, you may discover a few rugged roads and perilous potholes. You may also have to brave some inclement weather, so here are a few observations and suggestions to save for those rainy days.

Keep on smilin'.
It's a cure for the common scowl, and it's easily understood reassurance for your child, no matter how old they are!

Remember it's a passing phase.

When all the battles seem uphill, remind yourself it won't last forever. Eventually you'll look back and long for the days of sleepless nights and poopy diapers. It sounds crazy now, but you'll be ready to take a ride in your sentimental time machine before you know it! Wait until you have the second kid—it makes you realize just how much the first one has grown up . . . (Sigh. And sob.)

Do the write thing.

Even if you don't deem yourself a prolific writer, document whatever you can, however you can. Any creative outlet will do! I would probably draw the line at a papier-mâché diorama of your maternity experience, but to each her own.

If pregnancy has you on an abbreviated sleep schedule, use the time constructively by penning a journal for your little one to read someday. Don't feel guilty if you write in it only twice—she'll appreciate any effort you make! One day she'll ponder what the motherhood journey is like, and you'll have the opportunity to gift her with a special kind of insight. Not to mention, writing a journal will likely be cathartic for you, too. Also, during your pregnancy, it's always nicer to purge on paper rather than in the toilet. Not that I didn't do plenty of both.

Don't abstain from affection.

Some folks think "I love you" loses its meaning if it's uttered too often. I'm staunchly on the opposing team for this one. Of all the words in the English language, I find those to be the most effective. That sentence can't be said enough, especially to a child.

I can't picture any adult looking back on their youth and complaining, "I'm totally messed up in the head because my parents said 'I love you' too often!" I treasure the fact that my parents have always used that phrase unconditionally and unapologetically. Were there times I wished they wouldn't say it so openly? Sure. Like in front of my middle school friends. No teenager wants her folks to upend the supercool image that only exists in her head. But in retrospect, I can't recall if anyone actually made fun of me for it; I recall only how loved I felt by my parents. So do it anyway, as often as possible, and mean it every time it leaves your lips. Your child will infuse that way of thinking into his or her own marriage and parenting someday, and you'll have some remarkably awesome delayed gratification!

For now, your baby may not be able to say "I love you" in return, but you'll recognize the sentiment in his actions. Your child won't need to speak it aloud in order for your heart to hear it.

Reserve and conserve.
Love your child enough to save some of that love for yourself and your spouse too. Kids aren't the only ones who need to be nurtured and supported. The better your personal well-being, health, marriage, and emotional state are, the better your relationship with your child will be.

WORDS TO LOVE BY
My parents taught me by example that being a loving parent

goes far beyond bringing a child into this world and providing the necessary physical provisions. In my humble opinion, the following are words to live *and* love by:

Love comes from the heart, not the wallet.
Giving the gift of time, attention, affection, encouragement, and positive reinforcement will outweigh any material gifts you can ever offer. Showering a child with presents might provide some short-term fun, but love is the gift that keeps on giving. The latest, greatest toy can't tuck your child into bed at night, and the most expensive shoes can't say, "I'm proud of you!"

Love is boosting your child's confidence, no matter what.
Attend the dance recital, sit in the front row, cheer the loudest, and keep the encouragement going . . . even when your little girl falls on her butt, the tutu goes airborne, and she's a publicly humiliated puddle of tears. She may never share a stage with Baryshnikov, but she should know how satisfying it is to dance her heart out anyway.

Love is loving your child with all you have.
Someone once said, "Just because someone doesn't love you the way you want them to doesn't mean they don't love you with all they have." You may not love your child in a way that represents perfection to anyone else—or even to yourself, for that matter—but love your child with all you have. Make sure they know that fact is true above all else!

Love is knowing when to hold 'em and when to scold 'em.
It's not always clear-cut when to offer affection and when to engage in a little tough love. Sometimes there's a thin line between needing to give a time-out or a hug. You'll figure out how to finesse and properly balance that predicament on your own, but loving your child means you adore them while still setting age-appropriate boundaries! It also means extending advice and guidance when it's called for and allowing your child to grow and evolve by solving problems on his own sometimes too.

Love doesn't discriminate.
Make sure your child knows your love doesn't hinge on height, weight, looks, smarts, style, career path, friend and relationship choices, or accomplishments. Who cares if your kid wants to dance the hokeypokey or raise chinchillas to play the glockenspiel for a living, as long as he has passion?

Love teaches morals, honesty, and generosity.
It reminds us to write thank-you notes, open the door for strangers, tell the truth, extend common courtesies, protect those who can't protect themselves, and give back to those who are less fortunate. It finds beauty and wonder in the world around us, fosters creativity, and champions individuality. It practices humility and shines through faults, flaws, frustrations, and failures. It makes sure we teach our children those monumental life lessons too!

Love never gives up.
On the darkest day of the most merciless month of the most

ruthless year, when it seems like things can't possibly get any more turbulent, rise up and conquer . . . for your child's sake, as well as your own.

Growing up can be both a brutal and beautiful journey. Fortunately, you are the solid foundation your child will rely on. You won't save her from every scratch, scrape, burn, or scar, but you'll be her salve and saving grace. You'll help her up, wipe her tears, pick up the pieces, cry with her until she laughs, hold her hand, carry her, challenge and inspire her, believe in her, and love her for who she is. You'll forgive her when she won't forgive herself, dare her to dream big, show her how beautiful life is when you color outside the lines, and teach her to be her own unique version of "perfect." You'll never let her forget she was the answer to your prayers, and your heart will love her in ways you can never quite verbalize. (Even if you've made a valiant attempt to do so by writing a whole book about it!) Love, in any capacity, is not meant to read like a fairy tale; parental love is no exception. So nurture it, cherish it, embrace it, and let it lead you!

Love in the time of motherhood

Let's end this thing on a funny note, shall we? Here are some of the brilliant things you have to look forward to in your first year of motherhood!

You know you're the parent of an infant or toddler when . . .
1. You cheer like a 49ers superfan over your child's bowel movements.

2. Your desk paperweight is a baby monitor or a breast pump.

3. You find Cheerios floating in your coffee.

4. Your child sticks a kazoo in your belly button, and you don't find that to be at all strange.

5. You have products festooning your house that have alien-sounding names like Bumbo, mamaRoo, and WubbaNub. And you're exceedingly thankful for every one of them.

6. You don't remember the last time you were allowed to shower or go to the bathroom by yourself, and the thought has crossed your mind that if God were a woman, mothers would be equipped with a self-cleaning option and built-in colostomy bag.

7. You use lingo such as "meconium" and "NoseFrida" in your everyday vocabulary, but you think the folks who say "OMG" and "chillax" are creepy.

8. You're totally out of touch with pop culture, but you know every word to every episode of *Elmo's World*.

9. You've considered saying you're bilingual, since you can speak fluent Toddlerese.

10. You've forgotten what you look like in a dress and heels. Or a suit jacket. Or anything that has to be dry-cleaned.

11. Going on a bender means you drank three too many cups of coffee before 7:00 a.m. And that won't stop you from throwing back a couple more before noon. Also, you think decaf is for featherweights and fools.

12. Your DVR boasts more episodes of *Curious George* than *Scandal.*

13. You get overly sentimental about losing a pacifier or packing baby bloomers away in the attic.

14. Singing karaoke now consists of belting out "Pop Goes the Weasel" in the shower. Using your loofah as a microphone, of course.

15. You accept that sometimes what you wear to the grocery store is more about what isn't plagued by poop and spit-up than what matches. Since when do purple polka dots and red stripes clash?

16. You've learned to do everything one-handed, including but definitely not limited to making dinner, finishing e-mails, getting dressed, changing diapers, writing thank-you notes, breastfeeding, and perusing the latest blogs on *PEOPLE.com/*

babies. Also, the last of those examples is the only world news you've caught up on in weeks.

17. You can't keep your eyes open past 9:00 p.m. Ahem. Make that 8:30. (Yawn.)

18. You find some sort of sticky green substance on your clothes, and there's no chance in hell it's margarita spillage.

19. Baby wipes have become a more versatile tool than WD-40 or duct tape.

20. It suddenly dawns on you that you've been listening to Baby Mozart lullabies in the car for the last twenty minutes, even though your child isn't in there with you.

21. Your biggest accomplishment of the day is finding a way to get some unidentifiable hardened substance (likely baby cereal) out of your hair, without cutting a major chunk of your locks off.

22. You can't think of any place you'd rather be than with your kids. Even more than a spa day. Or a night out with the girls. Or taking part in an adult conversation. Or having a glass of wine . . . Okay, this last one might be debatable.

THE MORAL OF MY STORY

You're about to become a line cook, a housekeeper, a teacher, a translator, a nurse, a chauffeur, a professional wrestler, and a jungle gym. All at the same time and without a built-in pension plan or 401K. But you know what? Nothing will ever come close to making you feel as accomplished. I wouldn't trade the love of my children for riches, fame, expensive cars, a Malibu mansion, or a lifetime supply of coffee and chocolate. I mean, without my kids, to whom would I bequeath the important things like that ridiculous *Blossom* hat collection? The truth is that having my daughters has overshadowed every role I've ever played, every success I've ever known, and every glamorous Hollywood experience I've ever encountered. It's the greatest and most moving story I'll ever write.

You have some incredible and incredibly intense days to look forward to, so embrace each one with marvel and moxie. I wish you luck, love, and lots of comedy along the way. Now go forth and make some incomparable memories . . . and don't forget to laugh your way through them!

ACKNOWLEDGMENTS

Acknowledgments are notoriously boring, so let's see if we can sass this thing up a bit. I want to thank the following people for their help, expertise, love, support, encouragement, inspiration, and commiseration over wine. Extra-special thanks to those who let me make fun of them or throw them under the bus . . .

My husband, Brad: For being my partner in crime. Sherlock had Dr. Watson, Bonnie had Clyde, Sonny had Cher, and I have you. (Okay, maybe those were bad examples.) The point is that I can't imagine raising children with anyone else. There isn't enough room here to express my love, gratitude, and appreciation, but thankfully we'll always have our wedding vows. *All my kids—Gray, Marlowe, Bruiser, Bailey, Mia "Moose," Boo, and Ruby:* For giving me a reason to be called Mommy. You are profound blessings in my eyes, whether you have feet or paws. *Mom, Dad, Pete, Alyssa, Tyler:* For being the unknowing participants in a published book, simply because you got stuck with me as a family member. Oh, and Mom, sorry for all those gray hairs I've given you; I promise karma will find me. *My husband's family:* Most people are fortunate if they have one family to love and support them. I'm such a lucky gal that I was graced with two!

The Medallion team—my editor Emily Steele, Art Director Jim Tampa, Sales and Marketing Director Brigitte Shepard, and Senior Vice President Heather Musick: For championing my project and making the process of giving birth to a book one hell of a lot easier than giving birth to a baby. *My literary agent, Margaret O'Connor:* Thank you for believing in a sitcom actress–turned–author and for helping me to get this book sold before my daughters are old enough to have their own kids. *Carey Burch:* For introducing me to Margaret. I owe you *far* more than a celebratory dinner at City House, my friend! *Kelly Garner:* For being an all-around kick-ass manager. Thank you for your unparalleled loyalty in a town where loyalty is hard to come by. *The Imperium 7 crew, especially Tracy Mapes and Steven Neibert:* Thank you for being on my team! *My publicist, Tej Bhatia-Herring:* For diving into the deep end with me. *Sarah Michaud and Lesley Messer:* For suggesting I begin writing a mommy blog on *PEOPLE.com.* You ladies are the reason this book became a thought in my head in the first place! *My book cover photo shoot crew: Karan and Harry Simpson of Mimosa Arts Photography, Lorena Lopez, and Tianna Calcagno:* Thank you all for putting your artistic touch on the book cover, and for your extra efforts to make this undercaffeinated, overscheduled mom look beautiful! *Brooke Boling and Micah Schweinsberg*: For so graciously allowing me to include some of the beautiful photos you've taken. *Tammy and Pamela of PLH Bows:* For generously providing some of Gray's cover ensemble.

My Mommy Mafia, especially Lisa Dorian, Beth Jones, Katie Palmissano, Brittany Inman, Lila McCann, and Cindy Alexander: I was able to write a best friend's guide because I had best friends to guide me first. *My incredible inner circle, especially Barclay DeVeau, Justin Kopplin, JD Inman, Brad Harlan, Sarah Price, and Jenn Schott:* For supporting me, challenging me, proofreading chapters, laughing at my joke attempts, and being honest when those attempts failed miserably. *Kal, Dulé, Mayim, and all my other treasured friends who were unwittingly dragged into this via my personal anecdotes:* Thanks for giving me something to write about. *My third grade teacher, Mrs. Niedzielski:* For making me realize my love for writing and for letting me know it would eventually lead somewhere. We did it!

And finally, to every mom out there who embraces her imperfections wholeheartedly and knows she's a better parent because of them. You are damned good at what you do, and don't you forget it! Long live the parenting outcasts everywhere.

Coming soon:

SITUATION
MOMEDY

A Very Special Episode in Toddlerdom

JENNA VON OY

MEDALLION

February 2017